JOHN CALVIN
THE MAN AND HIS ETHICS

GEORGIA HARKNESS

JOHN CALVIN

*The Man
and His Ethics*

ABINGDON PRESS   NEW YORK • NASHVILLE

PRINTED AND BOUND BY THE PARTHENON PRESS
AT NASHVILLE, TENNESSEE, UNITED STATES
OF AMERICA

TO THE MEMORY OF

JOHN CALVIN

A MAN OF GREAT FAULTS

AND GREAT VIRTUES

PREFACE

It is now almost four centuries since Calvinism was born. John Calvin adopted the Protestant faith sometime between April 1532 and November 1533, and in 1536 he wrote the first edition of his epoch-making treatise, *The Institutes of the Christian Religion.* Today, adherents of Calvinistic churches number in their membership many thousands, and in churches indirectly influenced in form or doctrine by Calvin are many other thousands. Though his theology is in eclipse, it is far from obsolete.

The significance of Calvin's ethics has been neglected in the making of many books upon his theology. Yet even in his own day, the impression made by his moral ideas was probably as great as that made by his doctrine, and it has been more lasting. Through various channels—mainly French, Dutch, Scotch, and English—Calvinistic morality made its way to American shores, and the morality of the Protestant portion of the western world still bears its stamp. The Puritan conscience is in large measure the Calvinistic conscience, and in spite of tendencies to decry everything "puritanical," the Puritan conscience, or its effective heritage, persists.

To all but a few of those whose religious or moral ideas have been molded by him, Calvin is but a name. The name connotes usually a shadowy figure—often a sinister figure—one who believed in predestination and other strange ideas that nobody now accepts. Yet the thin, imperious theologian who taught predestination and ruled Geneva in the quarter century which spanned the middle of the sixteenth century was one of the strongest personalities of all time. Frail in body, gigantic in intellect, and iron-clad in soul, he laid the stamp of his personality on future Calvinists, and others. He was a man of great faults and great virtues; and these faults and virtues were crystallized into a moral code which after four centuries is still effective in our social order.

PREFACE

The influence of Calvinism upon one aspect of modern social ethics, the spirit of capitalism, has been recognized since the publication in 1904-1905 of Max Weber's treatise, *Die protestantische Ethik und der Geist des Kapitalismus*. This essay is of permanent significance and has called forth an extensive controversial literature. However, Weber drew most of his documentary evidence from the writings of the English Puritans of the latter part of the seventeenth century, and the Calvinism of that day was not that of its founder. His essay reveals no first-hand acquaintance with Calvin. Nor have any of Weber's critics, so far as I have been able to discover, made a textual study of Calvin's economic ethics. In fact, I have found no book in English which deals primarily with any phase of Calvin's moral theory. Yet Calvinism cannot be understood apart from Calvin. It is to fill in this hiatus in reference not only to Calvin's economic concepts but his moral philosophy in general that this study has been undertaken.

The first three chapters are biographical, for Calvin's moral ideas were inextricably bound up with his personality. Since the Calvinistic conscience was set firmly in a theological framework, it has also seemed necessary to restate the major outlines of Calvinistic doctrine. A summary is given in chapter IV. The two following chapters consider the ethical implications of certain religious convictions arising from the duty of glorifying God. The remainder of the book deals with problems of social ethics in the family, the economic order, and the state.

The purpose of the book is to examine as thoroughly as possible Calvin's moral ideas and their application. To do this, I have combed the fifty-nine volumes of the *Calvini Opera*, and have attempted, as far as the compass of the book would permit, to make available in English the most pertinent source material from Calvin's writings. While the *Institutes* deal mainly with theological rather than ethical questions, Calvin's sermons, commentaries, and letters abound in ethical material in Latin and French which has hitherto been largely overlooked. Though the limits of space have necessitated much sifting, I have either paraphrased or quoted

PREFACE

in translation the passages which are most characteristic of Calvin's point of view and which bear most directly on present day conditions.

I have also tried in some measure to show how Calvin's influence spread and what practical effects it had. In particular, I have suggested at intervals its connection with Puritan ethics, and through Puritanism its effect on present day morality. However, to trace adequately the processes by which Calvin's Calvinism grew into that of his followers in various countries through even one century, to say nothing of its transformations down to the present, would be a task requiring the writing of many volumes. If the book gives a faithful account of the original Puritan conscience as found in Calvin himself, it will have fulfilled its purpose.

The research necessary for the writing of the book was made possible through the generosity of the Sterling Foundation of Yale University. To the scholarly mind and friendly counsel of Professor Roland H. Bainton of the Department of Church History of the Yale Divinity School, I am much indebted for assistance both in directing the research and criticizing the manuscript. To Professor Reinhold Niebuhr of Union Theological Seminary and Professor George C. Cell of Boston University I owe my initial interest in the subject. My thanks are due also to other friends— to Professor Amy M. Gilbert and Professor Harry C. York of Elmira College for their critical judgment on some chapters, to Rev. Emmett W. Gould for helpful suggestions as to form and style, and to Miss Catherine Akerman for efficient clerical assistance.

Citations from the *Institutes* follow in general Allen's translation and those from the commentaries the rendering of the Calvin Translation Society. For other translations the author is responsible.

GEORGIA HARKNESS.

CONTENTS

CONTENTS

PART III. THE CALVINISTIC CONSCIENCE AND MAN'S DUTY TO MAN

CONTENTS

PART I
A STUDY IN CONFLICTS AND CONQUESTS

PART I

A STUDY IN CONTRACTS AND CONCERTS

CHAPTER I

FORMATIVE YEARS

"As it is easy for malevolence to calumniate his character, so the most exalted virtue will find it difficult to imitate his conduct."[1] So wrote John Calvin's biographer and successor in the Genevan church, Theodore Beza, eleven years after the great reformer's death. For almost four centuries, Calvin's memory has been honored and vilified. No man in the history of the church has been more admired and ridiculed, loved and hated, blessed and cursed. The sources of so varying a judgment become apparent from the story of his life.

1. EARLY LIFE

John Calvin was born at Noyon, Picardy, on July 10, 1509. The family name was Cauvin, but Calvin seems early to have adopted the spelling by which he was destined to be known. His father, Gérard Cauvin, was a lawyer and a person of considerable importance as secretary of the bishopric and attorney of the cathedral chapter at Noyon. Tradition says that Calvin's mother, Jeanne LeFranc, was a woman of exceptional beauty and piety. Little is known of her except that she died in Jean's childhood and the father remarried, and still less is recorded of the step-mother.[2] Three sons, Charles, Jean and Antoine, and two daughters grew to maturity. The Cauvins were loyal Catholics, and though not of great wealth they were people of social standing in Noyon.

Gérard Cauvin was apparently anxious to give his sons an edu-

---

[1] Theodore Beza, *The Life of John Calvin* (Sibson translation, Philadelphia, 1836), p. 98. Also *Opera*, xxi, 172.
    Calvin's works with other contemporary material relating to him occupy fifty-nine volumes of the *Corpus Reformatorum* under the title of *Joannis Calvini Opera Quæ Supersunt Omnia*. Beza's biography in the Latin original is in the *Opera*, vol. xxi, pp. 119-172.
[2] A. Lefranc, *La Jeunesse de Calvin* (Paris, 1866), pp. 5-7.

3

cation, and when Jean was twelve he secured for him a benefice in the church at Noyon and later a more lucrative one at Pont l'Évêque. The incomes were used to defray the expense of his schooling, the duties connected with the offices being performed by a priest who was paid a fraction of the stipend thus received. The conferring of such benefices upon non-participants was then a common practice looked upon much as a scholarship is today. At this time Calvin probably received the tonsure, the only sign of office he ever held under the Roman church.

Calvin was a very precocious child, and early displayed both the intellectual and personal qualities which were destined to lay their stamp upon his life work. Beza says of him, "Even in his tender years he was in a surprising manner devoted to religion, and a stern reprover of all the vices of his companions."[3] At the age of fourteen he entered the University of Paris[4] where he displayed unusual skill in Latin and dialectics, and acquired the foundations of his later ability to write a Latin that is almost unequalled in clarity and vigor. He seems already to have felt a mission to reform his associates, and a legendary story says he was so censorious that his fellow-students called him "the accusative case."[5]

Gérard Cauvin had originally intended the most talented of his sons for the priesthood, and the securing of the benefices was a step in this direction. But Cauvin *père* was not merely a religious man, he was still more an astute observer of men and things! Before Jean had finished the work of the Faculty of Arts at Paris, which he completed at nineteen, his father had decided that his profession should not be theology but law. Beza gives the reason in a sentence which speaks a volume, "for the father thought the law opened a surer road to riches and honors."[6] The change may also have been due in part to the fact that by this time his father had

---

[3] *Life*, p. 2; *Opera*, xxi, 121.
[4] In the Collège de la Marche. He was soon transferred to the Collège de la Montaigu, where he studied under the scholarly theologian, Noël Béda.
[5] Le Vasseur, *Annales de l'église cathédrale de Noyon* (Paris, 1633), p. 1158; Kampschulte, *Johann Calvin, seine Kirche und sein Staat in Genf* (Leipzig, 1869), i, 225.
[6] *Life*, p. 3; *Opera*, xxi, 121.

quarreled with the chapter at Nóyon and was out of favor ecclesiastically. In any case Jean, in spite of his strongly religious bent, acquiesced in his father's wishes and went to Orléans to study law.

During this period, if Beza's story may be trusted, Calvin imposed upon himself an intellectual discipline so rigorous that he undermined his health and laid the foundations of the dyspepsia which was to harass him through life. His custom was to take a frugal supper, "pursuing his lucubrations until midnight," and then in the morning before arising review and digest his studies.[7] However disturbing to his health this experience may have been, there can be no question that Calvin's iron spirit was encased in a frail body, and he did the almost herculean tasks of his later years in the face of serious physical handicaps. This may explain in part the note of irascibility in his temper. Preserved Smith says of him that the way Calvin ruled his sick body is a symbol of his rule of a sick world, with tyranny and an iron will.[8]

Calvin's legal studies were continued at the University of Bourges, where he studied under the famous Italian jurist Alciati.[9] His father died when he was twenty-two and he was under no further pressure to continue his law course, but he did so and was licensed to practice. Though Calvin's own interests were always in the field of religion rather than law and he never used his legal training professionally, this training was of incalculable value in his later work at Geneva. Nobody but a trained jurist could have carved out so successfully the ecclesiastical system which he there established, and both the theology and the organization of the Calvinistic church bear the stamp of a law-trained mind. The differences between Calvinism and Lutheranism can be accounted for in no small measure by the fact that Calvin began his career as a lawyer and Luther as a monk.[10]

[7] *Ibid.*, p. 4; *Opera*, xxi, 122.
[8] *The Age of the Reformation*, p. 181.
[9] Émile Doumergue, *Jean Calvin: les hommes et les choses de son temps*, i, 141. This work in seven volumes (Lausanne, 1899-1917; Neuilly-sur-Seine, 1926-27) is the most comprehensive biography of Calvin.
[10] Ernst Troeltsch, *Protestantism and Progress* (London and New York, 1912), p. 72.

After finishing his law course, Calvin went back to Paris for further study, his main interest being now in the field of humanistic culture. It was during this period, in 1532, that he published his first book, a commentary on Seneca's *Treatise on Clemency*. The book gives a keen critique of Stoicism, and shows great precocity for a youth of twenty-three. It gives evidence of his interest in ethics, but does not reveal any particular religious ferment. Up to this point Calvin had apparently seen no reason to break with the Catholic church.

However, it was during this second Paris period that the most important event of his life took place—his conversion to Protestant- ism. Comparatively little is known of the circumstances connected with this epoch-making event. Its external stimulus was probably his association with certain Protestant friends, particularly with Gérard Roussel, a disciple of Jacques LeFèvre, and with a kinsman Robert Olivétan. Other influences are probably to be found in the unrest which, proceeding mainly from the preaching of Luther and Zwingli, was pervading Europe; in an adverse reaction against the corrupt morals of the clergy which was inevitable to one of Calvin's "puritanical" moral code; in his study of the humanists, particularly Erasmus; and in a new interest in the study of the New Testament to which he was aroused by Olivétan. He speaks himself of his "sudden conversion" as coming direct from God,[11] and twice gives some account of it but only in the most general terms.[12] Its date cannot be located any more precisely than to say that it occurred sometime between the publication of his commentary on Seneca in April 1532, and November 1533.

The latter date marks the beginning of Calvin's outward conflict with Catholicism. His friend Nicolas Cop was to be inaugurated as rector at the University of Paris. Tradition says—though its authenticity cannot be verified—that Calvin wrote the address which Cop delivered. Part of a copy is extant in Calvin's hand, but may

[11] *Opera*, xxxi, 21.
[12] *Commentary on the Psalms, Opera*, xxxi, 21-24; *Reply to Sadoleto, Opera*, v, 412.

have been transcribed. In any case he had a hearty interest in it. The address contained too much of the doctrines of Erasmus and Luther to suit the conservative Catholics of the Sorbonne faculty, and both Cop and Calvin found themselves in uncomfortable quarters. Calvin was forced to flee from Paris.

His studies in Paris being thus abruptly disturbed, Calvin went to the home of a friend in Angoulême and later to Noyon. His home town afforded no quiet resting-place for its unhonored prophet, and imprisoned him "for uproar made in the church." [13] Whether he made his "uproar" himself, or whether he suffered from reflected obloquy from the heresy of his brother Charles who by this time was in considerable disrepute at Noyon, is a moot question.

His imprisonment was apparently of short duration, and we find him next living in seclusion at Basle where in 1536 he published the first edition of his great work, *The Institutes of the Christian Religion*. This theological classic went through five editions in Calvin's life-time, being successively revised and enlarged until it grew from six to eighty chapters. The preface of the first edition is a letter to Francis I of France protesting against his persecution of the Protestants, and is a masterpiece of apologetic literature. It is courteous, logical, and to the point—and Beza pathetically remarks that if Francis had only read it, it could not have failed to win him from the error of his course.[14]

After the publication of the *Institutes* Calvin went to Italy and then back to Paris and Noyon to settle some matters connected with his father's estate. At this juncture occurred one of those minor accidents which change the course of history. Calvin intended to go to Strassburg, but the direct route through Lorraine being blocked by war, he went by way of Geneva instead. Stopping there overnight he met William Farel, who was then in the throes of a vigorous but unorganized attempt to establish the new Genevan Protestant church. The chaos of the situation needed the touch of a master-hand, and Farel was quick to detect in Calvin the helper he

13 Lefranc, *La Jeunesse de Calvin*, p. 201.
14 *Life*, p. 10; *Opera*, xxi, 125.

needed. Calvin was reluctant to give up the prospect of a quiet life of study which awaited him at Strassburg, for this master-organizer was by nature retiring and studious, even somewhat shy. But Farel adduced one argument that was unanswerable. In an adjuration that was almost an imprecation Farel declared, "I denounce unto you, in the name of Almighty God, that if, under the pretext of prosecuting your studies, you refuse to labor with us in this work of the Lord, the Lord will curse you, as seeking yourself rather than Christ." [15]

Calvin yielded. In August 1536 he began his ministry at Geneva, and Calvinism was born.

2. THE FIRST GENEVAN PERIOD

The Geneva to which Calvin came was a vigorous, liberty-loving, cosmopolitan city of about thirteen thousand inhabitants.[16] It held high rank both as a commercial and ecclesiastical center, and its location at the crossroads of the great trade routes gave it strategic importance. The fires of political independence were burning strong from the recent successful fruition of an attempt stretching through twenty years to throw off the power of the bishop and the House of Savoy, and establish a self-governing state. Under Farel's leadership the city had the year before become nominally Protestant, the Mass having been abolished in August 1535. Its churches had been seized for Protestantism and its four monasteries and a nunnery closed. The Council[17] in charge of political affairs had already taken drastic measures to regulate private morals and to compel attendance at sermon. Yet the city was far from being Protestant in spirit. Its leaders were in the main actuated by considerations of political expediency rather than religious conviction, and the greater part of the action taken had been negative. "The Genevan church

---

[15] Beza, *Life*, p. 12; *Opera*, xxi, 125; xxxi, 26.

[16] H. D. Foster, "Geneva before Calvin," *American Historical Review*, viii, 2 (1903), gives the best account in English of the situation to which Calvin came. This has been reprinted in Foster's *Collected Papers*, pp. 1-29. Cf. also Doumergue, ii, 97-149, and Kampschulte, i, 3-218.

[17] *Infra*, p. 10.

as an organism cannot be said to have existed before Calvin. It had neither formal creed nor system of religious training. It had no rights of either property, discipline, revision of membership, or choice or dismission of pastors." [18]

Geneva at this time was not a very moral city. The influence of its priests and monks had not been morally wholesome. It had even been found necessary to set a special watch against the visits of "the religious" to its red light district.[19] In the Madeleine quarter every third house was a tavern.[20] Jollification which passed often into debauchery was common. Along with the sturdy virtues of an aggressive, self-governing city, it had all the vices characteristic of a wealthy, pleasure-loving, medieval town.[21]

In this situation Farel was struggling, with more vehemence and sincerity than tact, to clean up the city and establish Protestantism upon a firm basis. He was a preacher of fiery eloquence, but he lacked organizing ability. Geneva needed a disciplinarian and an executive, and in Calvin she found both.

Calvin set to work at once along the two lines that were to dominate his whole future activity, the establishment of purity of doctrine and purity of living. Articles of church government were drawn up, submitted to the Council, and accepted with minor modifications.[22] This is significant as a start in the direction of ecclesiastical organization, and in providing for lay inspectors to help the clergy keep guard over the morals of the people, the Articles laid the foundation for the Consistory which was later to play so important a part in the Genevan theocracy. Calvin's next step was to prepare a catechism for Christian instruction. This was based

[18] Foster, *Collected Papers*, p. 27.

[19] Hugh Y. Reyburn, *John Calvin* (London, 1914), p. 337. Reyburn's is the best one-volume biography of Calvin in English.

[20] Reyburn, p. 123, cites Galiffe as authority for this statement.

[21] On the moral laxity of the city at this period there is substantial agreement between Catholic and Protestant writers. Contemporary accounts are numerous, among the most interesting being the chronicle of an exiled nun, Jeanne de Jussie, published ca. 1640 as *Le Levain du Calvinism*, and the Protestant reformer Fromment's *Les Actes et Gestes Merveilleux de la Cité de Genève*, 1532-1536.

[22] *Opera*, xa, 5-14. The tenth volume of the *Opera* is in two parts, which will be referred to as xa and xb.

largely on the *Institutes* and was too long and elaborate for the use of children, but indicates Calvin's characteristic esteem both for doctrinal precision and the proper training of the young. A third move was to prepare a Confession of Faith which he expected all loyal Protestants to accept, thus drawing a clear line of demarcation and putting an end to the uncertainty as to who were Protestants.[23] It was thought that most of the citizens would accept it, and that those who were unwilling to do so would leave the city. But trouble was brewing which Calvin did not foresee.

The political affairs of the Genevan state were in the hands of a general assembly of the people and three councils.[24] These councils, to which we shall have occasion frequently to refer, were a Little Council of twenty-five members, a Council of Sixty, and a Council of Two Hundred. The government was practically a closed corporation consisting of the Little Council and the Council of Two Hundred, for the former elected the latter, who in turn elected sixteen members of the Little Council. The general assembly elected annually four syndics (chief magistrates) and a treasurer, and these with the four syndics of the preceding year made up the rest of the Little Council. Most of the business was in the hands of the Little Council, and where "the Council" is referred to, the Little Council is meant unless otherwise indicated.

After the adoption of the Articles, the Council under Calvin's influence continued for a time quite peaceably to pass legislation designed to tone up the morals of the people and to stamp out papal practices.[25] The singing of frivolous songs was forbidden, and a gambler was pilloried with his cards hung about his neck as a dramatic example to evil-doers. It was decreed that all images in homes were to be destroyed, and that on Sundays all shops were to be closed during the time of sermon. Before Calvin's coming, absence from sermon had been made an offense punishable by fine,

---

[23] It is uncertain whether the Confession is from the pen of Calvin or Farel. Doumergue, ii, 237-239, sums up the evidence but suspends judgment.

[24] Cf. Williston Walker, *John Calvin* (Putnam's, 1906), pp. 160, 166, 178 n.; Foster, p. 21.

[25] *Opera*, xxi, 207.

and to reinforce this edict the Council ordered proclamation to be made by trumpet that all inhabitants must go to church regularly and listen to the sermon devoutly.[26] The effect upon devoutness is not recorded.

In April 1537 the Council ordered fifteen hundred copies of the Confession of Faith to be distributed for the information of the people. In July the superintendents of districts were ordered to march their people to St. Peter's to accept it and swear an oath of fidelity to the city. At first no great difficulty was anticipated, but it soon became evident that there were breakers ahead. Large numbers of the city had never at heart been converted to Protestantism, and besides Catholic sympathizers there were many "Libertines"—freethinkers and free-livers—who found the Protestant system irksome and were not disposed to make any concessions to it. Still others objected on principle to anything which looked like encroachment of the church upon the power of the state.[27] By September, so many had refused to accept the Confession that the Council ordered that they be given another opportunity and then be expelled if they still remained obdurate. In November the decree was repeated. By this time there was great popular resentment, and it became evident that neither clergy nor Council could enforce the decree.

While these events were going on, Calvin was having other difficulties. Peter Caroli, semi-Protestant pastor at Lausanne, charged Calvin and Farel with being unorthodox on the question of the Trinity,[28] and demanded that they sign the Apostle's, Nicene, and Athanasian creeds. Calvin, orthodox Trinitarian though he was, was in no mood to be dictated to. To try to force a creed upon the Genevans was one thing; to have one forced upon him was quite another! He lost his temper so completely that his anger made him

---

[26] Reyburn, p. 71.

[27] The opposition of these "cæsaropapists" is well described by Eugène Choisy, *La Théocratie à Genève au Temps de Calvin* (Geneva, 1897), pp. 9-35, and by Frédéric Tissot, *Les Relations entre l'Église et l'État à Genève au Temps de Calvin* (Lausanne, 1875), pp. 18-26.

[28] Calvin gives his side of the story in his *Pro G. Farello et collegis ejus adversus Petri Caroli calumnias defensio, Opera*, vii, 289-339. Cf. also Doumergue, ii, 252-268 and Kampschulte, i, 295-298.

ill, and he refused point-blank to sign the creeds. This was a diplomatic error, for it brought upon him the suspicion of actual heresy. A meeting of the synod of the Swiss churches was called, Calvin was vindicated, and Caroli (whose morals were not above reproach) was removed from the ministry. But while Calvin won, the incident aroused much ill-feeling and caused still further opposition to the acceptance of the Confession.

Toward the end of the year, a quarrel arose which brought to a focus the question as to whether the Genevan church should rule itself or be ruled by the state. Should the ministers have the power to debar evil-livers from the Lord's table, or should the Council? Each body thought that excommunication lay within its own jurisdiction. Many of the Libertines were, in the eyes of Farel and Calvin, unfit to partake of the Lord's Supper, and they felt that it should be within the authority of the church to debar them. The Council, on the other hand, had some of these Libertines among its membership, and resented this assumption of power by the clergy whom they regarded as the employed servants of the state. This marks the beginning of a struggle which was to last almost twenty years, for the Genevan theocracy was not born without many pains. On January 4, 1538, the Council of Two Hundred offered a direct affront to Calvin and Farel by voting "that the Supper be refused to no one." [29]

With the elections of February 1538, more trouble arose. As the result of a political overturn, the majority of the Council and all of the magistrates were now of the party of the opposition. Consequently, there was no longer any possibility of enforcing discipline, and Calvin and Farel came in for a good deal of opposition and unchecked ridicule. [30] They were treated to nocturnal serenades of scurrilous songs, and became the butt of many vile jokes in the taverns. On complaint of Farel, orders were issued that no song was to be sung in which an inhabitant of Geneva was named, and no one was to go out after nine o'clock without a lantern on pain

[29] *Registres du Conseil*, xxxi, 146; *Opera*, xxi, 220.
[30] Reyburn, p. 74.

of imprisonment on bread and water for three days. But the storm clouds were too thick to be swept away by edict.

A further incident added to the friction. At this time overtures were made by some French officials looking toward the seizure of Geneva, and Michael Sept, a friend of Farel and Calvin, was charged with treason. Believing that an injustice was being done, the preachers promptly defended him.[31] The Council as promptly responded by enjoining the ministers to stick to their texts and not mix in politics! Calvin could look upon this only as a curtailment of his just liberty, and it was evident that a rupture was imminent.

The Lord's Supper, symbol of Christian unity, has more than once been the issue that has rent Christian bodies asunder. So it proved in this case, for the final break came over the manner in which the sacraments were to be administered. The Council voted that they were to live "under the Word of God under the ordinances of Berne."[32] Berne was politically anxious to control Geneva, and as a step to this end had asked the Genevan authorities to enforce conformity in the matter of the sacraments. This meant the use of unleavened bread in the Lord's Supper, the retention of the baptismal font at the church door, and the observance of Christmas, Easter, Ascension, and Pentecost as church festivals; for Berne had moved away from Rome less rapidly than had Geneva. The issue became concrete over the question of whether the bread to be used in the coming communion service was to be unleavened, as directed by the Council, or leavened, as preferred by the ministers.[33] The ministers were ordered point-blank to use unleavened bread, according to the Bernese custom, or refrain from preaching. Obviously more was at stake than the question of bread; it was a test case as to whether Council or clergy were to dominate church policy.

The excitement, already at white heat, was fanned at this juncture by the fact that Courault, the blind colleague of Farel and Calvin, was forbidden by the Council to preach; yet he did so in defiance of

[31] *Registres du Conseil*, xxxii, 33.
[32] Choisy, p. 32 f.; Walker, p. 208.
[33] The details of the controversy are recorded in the *Registres du Conseil*, xxxii, 31-36 and *Opera*, xxi, 223-226.

their order, using no very gracious words about the government. Farel and Calvin thought it their duty to defend him, even at the cost of further personal unpopularity.

As April 21, the day set for the Communion service, approached, the atmosphere was tense. No proclamation was needed to get the people out to church. Calvin was equal to the occasion in spirit, if not in political diplomacy. With dignity and sanity he declined to administer the sacrament, explaining that the people were in no mood to receive it and that to do so under such conditions would be to desecrate the Supper of our Lord.

On the following day, April 22, 1538, the Council met and ordered Calvin, Farel, and Courault to leave the city within three days. The next day the general assembly by majority vote corroborated this verdict. Calvin's comment upon learning of the decree reveals his mettle, "Well, indeed! If we had served men, we should have been ill-rewarded, but we serve a Great Master who will recompense us!" [34]

So Calvin left Geneva, thrust out, as many a minister since, by a church quarrel and the failure to see eye to eye with his parishioners. Both churches and clergy could learn lessons of coöperation from this experience—but we refrain from pointing morals. In this clash of Church and State, the State won, and in winning lost for a time its greatest statesman.

3. EXILE

Exiled from Geneva, Calvin on the invitation of Martin Bucer [35] journeyed to Strassburg and accepted a position there as preacher and professor of theology. It was with some reluctance that he again took up the responsibilities of public life, for he still yearned for a life of studious retirement. However, he threw himself vigorously into the duties of his new position, and Bucer found

[34] *Registres du Conseil*, xxxii, 36; *Opera*, xxi, 226.

[35] Calvin was acquainted with Bucer before coming to Geneva, and had been considerably influenced by his theology. The *Institutes* show the impress of Bucer's *Evangelienkommentar* published in 1527.

in him a very able colleague. He revised the service of public worship and gave the liturgy the form which, in major outlines, has been retained to the present in Calvinistic churches. Recognizing the value of congregational singing, he secured suitable music for the compilation of a Psalm Book, and even translated some of the psalms into verse himself for this purpose. He was always strongly opposed to instrumental music as savoring too much of Catholic practice,[36] and allowed no organ to be used either in Strassburg or Geneva during the period of his ministry. The organ of St. Peter's in Geneva stood unused until 1562, when its pipes were melted down and turned into flagons for holding the communion wine.

Calvin introduced into the Strassburg service not only congregational singing but the practice of extempore prayer—both of which were innovations in that day, and as at Geneva he laid great stress upon the sermon. He insisted that the expounding of the Word of God be the central part of the service. This marks the beginning of the Calvinistic emphasis on the sermon, in contrast to the Roman and Anglican emphasis upon the ritual. Calvin's own sermons were masterpieces of eloquence, and of intellectual as well as spiritual power. He had a wealth of apt illustrations and he knew how to speak the language of the common man without crudity. Under his preaching, compulsory church attendance was not the hardship it might now seem.

During the early part of Calvin's stay at Strassburg he was desperately poor. He was promised a salary of fifty dollars[37] a year, but it was six months before he received any of it. In this interval he suffered keenly of cold and hunger, and was forced to sell some of his books to buy food. A friend who learned of his poverty offered to supply him with money on condition that he

---

[36] Doumergue, ii, 521, quoting Calvin's statement in the *Opera*, xxx, 259, suggests also that he objected to it because it took the thought of the congregation away from the words of the hymn.

[37] Fifty-two florins. The florin was worth about a dollar, though it is impossible to state an exact equivalent.

would refrain from stating publicly his Reformed doctrines, but Calvin was not to be bribed into silence.

After a time his financial straits became somewhat less acute, and he began to contemplate a new venture. Calvin was now thirty years old, but he had never married and had never had much interest in women. He was far more concerned with the glory of God than with feminine charms. Celibacy would have been no hardship to him, but his religious convictions so drove him away from monasticism that he thought he ought to marry. Besides, he was far from well, and he thought he needed someone to look after his health. In an undated letter to a pastor whom Calvin thought too much opposed to the marriage of the clergy he remarks:

I whom you see so opposed to celibacy am not yet married. Whether I shall ever marry I do not know. In any case, if I take a wife it will be in order that, freed from many cares, I can consecrate myself to the Lord.[38]

Calvin apparently saw no impropriety in such a prudential motive. In a letter to Farel he states succinctly his idea of the fair sex:

I am not of that passionate race of lovers who when once captivated with the external form embrace also the moral defects it may cover. The only beauty which can please me must be that of a woman who is chaste, agreeable, modest, frugal, patient, and affords me some hope that she will be solicitous for my personal health and prosperity.[39]

Thus impelled, he began to cast about him a somewhat calculating eye. Two or three possibilities came to his notice, well recommended by friends. In one case the date of the wedding was fixed, but Calvin heard such disquieting reports about the lady's conduct that he interrupted the proceedings. He then took the task of selecting a wife into his own hands, and like most of the things he did himself, he carried it through with energy and success. In

---

[38] *Opera*, xa, 228.
[39] May 19, 1539. Herminjard, *Correspondance des Reformateurs dans les Pays de Langue Française* (Geneva and Paris, 1866-1897) v, 314.

August 1540 he married Idelette de Bure, a widow of his Strassburg congregation with whom he was well acquainted. She fulfilled all of his exacting requirements, and in spite of the somewhat unromantic and utilitarian nature of his courtship, he came to be very much attached to her. In 1542 their only child died at birth, and his wife, always an invalid after that, died in 1549. Calvin seems to have grieved deeply and sincerely at her death, and if one is inclined to censure him for going out to keep an appointment on the evening when she was dying,[40] one must remember that to Calvin public duty came before all private joys or sorrows. After she died he paid her the highest compliment possible in one of his temperament, that she had never in any way interfered with his work.[41]

Toward the church he had left behind him at Geneva, Calvin displayed the combination of magnanimity and pettiness which makes his character so difficult to evaluate. He seems in all sincerity to have tried to induce his friends to heal the breach. He wrote to the Genevan church urging cordial support of their ministers.[42] When Cardinal Sadoleto, taking advantage of Calvin's expulsion, tried to win back Geneva to Catholicism, Calvin was appealed to and he wrote for the Genevans a reply which is a courteous, dignified, and brilliant defense of the Protestant position.[43] Yet in a letter to Bullinger [44] he expresses a very poor opinion of the ministers who succeeded him and Farel, remarking that they are extremely ignorant and "never open their mouths without driveling."

. . . .

Matters were moving on at Geneva during the period of Calvin's absence. The Council secured Antoine Marcourt from Neufchâtel

[40] Letter to Farel describing her death, Opera, xiii, 229. He says he was "called away from home" but does not indicate the reason.
[41] Letter to Viret, Opera, xiii, 230.
[42] Letter to the Genevan church, June 25, 1539. Herminjard, v, 336-341.
[43] August 1539. Opera, v, 385-416. This letter became a classic statement of the Protestant position and elicited from Luther a word of greeting and approval. Luther and Calvin never met personally.
[44] Opera, xb, 208.

and Jean Morand from Cully to occupy the places left vacant, and set to work with renewed vigor to stamp out Catholicism and reform the morals of the city. The priests who remained in the district were told that they must go to sermon regularly or leave, and citizens suspected of having Catholic tendencies were interrogated as to their opinion of the Mass. The extent to which the attempt was made to enforce uniformity of religious belief is well illustrated by the treatment accorded a patriotic and honored Catholic, Jean Balard.[45] He had been a syndic and member of the Little Council for many years before Geneva became Protestant. Then he staunchly refused to go to sermon, and found himself in trouble. Asked by Farel before Calvin's arrival in 1536 why he refused to hear the Word of God, he had replied that he was willing to listen to the Word of God, but not to those preachers! The Council ordered him to leave the city within ten days if he would not go to sermon, and three weeks later voted that he be imprisoned and conducted to sermon daily if he would not go voluntarily. Apparently he yielded temporarily. Now in 1539 the Council again ordered him to leave the city with his family unless he would say that the Mass was a bad thing. His reply reveals his troubled spirit: "I am unable to judge, but since the Little Council and the Great Council say the Mass is a bad thing, I say it is a bad thing, and I am the worse to judge boldly of that of which I am ignorant and I cry to God for mercy and renounce Satan and all his works." One might think this would have satisfied the Council, but not so! Insisting on a definite affirmation, they wrung from him the statement "The Mass is bad," and he was allowed to stay and hold office. This incident, neither part of which occurred during Calvin's régime, clearly indicates that religious intolerance at Geneva was not of Calvin's creating.

[45] Balard is the author of a valuable piece of contemporary source material, *Journal ou Relation des Événements qui se sont passés à Genève de 1525 à 1531.* His story is told by Foster, pp. 18-20.

4. RECALL

With the departure of Farel and Calvin, the political contest had become keen between the "Guillermins," who were the followers of Guillaume Farel and Calvin, and the "Artichauds" or "Articulants," so-called from the articles of a treaty with Berne which members of this party negotiated. The hostile feeling which drove out Farel and Calvin underwent a reaction when popular feeling had cooled sufficiently to show the people their loss, and in the elections of February 1539 the Guillermins came into power. The independent spirit of the Genevese also asserted itself in full force in a political turn of fortune which brought the Artichauds into disfavor, for three members of this party who were commissioned to settle a dispute with Berne about the jurisdiction over some outlying territory surrendered to Berne in a manner which aroused a flame of popular indignation. The three negotiators were condemned to death in their absence; and in a street riot which followed, two deaths occurred. The leader of the Artichauds, Jean Philippe, was charged with homicide, and was executed in June 1540. These events effectively broke the political power of the opposition.

Religiously, the church was without a head. Marcourt and Morand were good men, but incapable of coping with the situation. In spite of his own slighting remarks about them, Calvin had urged that they be given the support and respect due the ministers of God. This request had some effect; but since they owed their positions to the Artichauds, they lost ground with the discomfiture of their party. In the fall of 1540, both resigned in discouragement and left the city.

On September 21, 1540, the Council voted to try to find means of bringing Calvin back to Geneva.[46] This was followed by further overtures, and in May 1541 Calvin reluctantly gave his consent. It was no mere desire to be coaxed that led to this long delay. Calvin was doubtless pleased to be asked; no one of his

[46] *Registres du Conseil*, xxxiv, 452; *Opera*, xxi, 265.

temperament could fail to be pleased to be invited to return to a post from which he had been driven in defeat. But he genuinely dreaded going back and taking up again the life of turmoil that he knew lay before him. He said he would sooner a hundred times die than shut himself up again in this hell of torment,[47] and there is no reason to doubt the sincerity of his reluctance.

Yet Calvin believed that the will of God must be done. No personal reluctance, in his judgment, could stand in the way of public duty or the call of God. He finally consented in order not to be of "those who have more care for their own ease and profit than for the edification of the church." [48] On September 13, 1541, three years and four months after his expulsion, he quietly reëntered Geneva and resumed his ministry.

[47] Tissot, p. 29.
[48] Ibid., quoting the Institutes, IV, iii, 11.

CHAPTER II

THE BIRTH OF THE GENEVAN THEOCRACY

1. GENEVA AS *CIVITAS DEI*

Upon Calvin's return from exile he settled down to the task which was to be his life work, the remoulding of Geneva into a "City of God." Accepting always the Scriptures as the ultimate authority, he sought to make *"la parole de Dieu"* effective in political and ecclesiastical as well as personal life, and he left no stone unturned for the accomplishment of this end.

To understand the fightings and fears and final victory of Calvin in Geneva, it is necessary to remember what he was aiming at. He was not attempting, as is often suggested, to make himself the personal dictator of the city. Nor was he trying to unite Church and State in an ecclesiastical absolutism. What he was trying to do was to make Geneva a city in which the Word of God should be the ultimate authority in matters of morals as of belief. This meant, of course, a rigid discipline, and a discipline in which the Church must play a very important part, but not a régime in which either Church or State could lose its identity or allow its functions to be swallowed up.

Calvin's political theory closely approximates that of Hildebrand, with the authority of the Bible replacing the power of the papacy.[1] He conceived of Church and State as two separate and distinct institutions, but he placed the Church above the State. The superiority of the Church lay not in its political power as such; rather, in its guardianship of the Word of God. It was the duty of the State, Calvin thought, to use its power—if need be, its sword-bearing arm—to enforce moral living and sound doctrine. But

---

[1] J. W. Allen, *Political Thought in the Sixteenth Century* (New York, 1928), p. 61 f.

it was to do this always according to the direction of the Word of God, and it was the prerogative of the Church to interpret the Word and will of God. The Genevan theocracy may more properly be called a *bibliocracy*,[2] for it was upon the Scriptures (and by implication upon Calvin's interpretation of the Scriptures) that the whole structure rested.

It should, however, be clearly understood that Calvin never made any pretence that the Church should rule the State in temporal matters. Its jurisdiction in civil affairs could only be advisory, and Calvin strictly enjoined obedience to the civil magistrates as a religious duty.[3] It was, of course, inevitable that clashes should arise, for in a régime where the State is the punitive instrument to enforce the Church-determined edicts of God, no knife-edge line of demarcation can be drawn between civil and ecclesiastical jurisdiction. Furthermore, there were many citizens of Geneva—some of them in high places—who were a long way from accepting Calvin's theory of the Church's right to manage even its own affairs, to say nothing of controlling affairs of State. There is evidence both of the strength of Calvin's personality and the power of his single-eyed devotion to what he thought the will of God in the fact that we find him, at the end of the long struggle, complete master of the situation.

Before his death Calvin became virtually the civil as well as the ecclesiastical dictator of Geneva. Nominally the Councils remained to the end the guardians of political authority, and Calvin would not have wished this to be otherwise. But in the later years we find the Church, in the person of Calvin, not only directing its own internal policy, but actually dominating the State as well. He ruled Geneva with a power unflinching in its sternness toward vice and heresy, yet tempered with a selfless devotion to the glory of God and the good of the people as he saw it, and with an

---

[2] Choisy, pp. 53, 277. Cf. Roget, *Histoire du peuple de Genève* (Geneva, 1870), ii, 18. Roget holds that it is incorrect to apply the term *theocracy* to the Genevan state because, in spite of Calvin's personal domination, the final jurisdiction always rested nominally in the Council.

[3] Chapter XI will discuss further this phase of Calvin's political theory.

authority that few desired to question. This power was not attained without many a battle.

The period of Calvin's second Genevan ministry extends from 1541, when he returned from Strassburg, to his death in 1564. This twenty-three year period falls into two parts; a period of struggle and turmoil from 1541 to the fall of the Libertines in 1555, and a period of victory and widening influence from that time till his death. Calvin spent many more years fighting for his ideals than he was privileged to spend enjoying the fruits of victory.

To grasp the relations of Calvin's ethical, political, and religious concepts to the times in which he lived, one must know something of the conflicts, defeats or near-defeats, compromised, and victories which finally came to fruition in the establishment of the Calvinistic state. We must accordingly narrate as briefly as possible a series of crucial incidents.

2. THE *ORDONNANCES*

When Calvin returned, he came with certain decided convictions. As suggested above, it did not lie within his purview, either then or later, to establish a régime in which the Church should have jurisdiction in civil matters. But he saw very clearly that if difficulties such as the dispute of 1538 over the Lord's Supper were to be avoided in the future, and if the Word of God was to be made effective in Geneva, there must be some organization which would give the Church more authority in spiritual fields. His first act, therefore, was to set in motion the machinery for an organization which would separate the civil jurisdiction of the State from the spiritual jurisdiction of the Church, and make the Church independent of civil control in spiritual matters.[4] This was no easy task, for no sharp line could be drawn between Church and State, and whatever reforms were enacted must be put through by the aid of the civil power.

---

[4] On the day of his arrival he asked the Council to choose a committee to prepare a written constitution for the Genevan church. *Registres du Conseil*, xxxv, 324; *Opera*, xxi, 282.

It was through the inauguration of a new ecclesiastical constitution, destined to be known as the *Ordonnances,* that Calvin hoped
to accomplish this end. The *Ordonnances* were a set of articles,
based on the Articles of 1537, but far in advance of these in stating
the outlines of an ecclesiastical executive and judicial system.
Calvin secured without much difficulty the sanction of the Council for the drawing up of such a set of *Ordonnances,* and a committee was appointed to compile them for submission to the Council. Calvin apparently had a poor opinion of the other men appointed, and with characteristic independence he did most of the
work himself. The Council was not at all inclined to let Calvin
have free rein in the matter, and his compilation was submitted
successively to the Little Council, the Council of Two Hundred,
and the general assembly for ratification. The jealousy with which
the government clung to its prerogatives is evidenced by the fact
that the Little Council refused to let Calvin see the changes they
made in his original draft.[5] However, after much discussion and
some modifications, the *Ordonnances* were officially adopted on
November 20, 1541, and were essentially, though not wholly, as
Calvin desired to have them.

The *Ordonnances* had two main objects: to define more precisely than before the duties of church officials and the relations
of their powers to those of the civil rulers; and to establish a new
ecclesiastical body, the Consistory, to represent the church explictly
in its guardianship of faith and morals. Calvin hoped thus to give
the church a workable executive organization and avoid further
dispute over jurisdiction.

The *Ordonnances* recognized four ranks of church officials;
pastors, teachers, elders, and deacons. The pastors of Geneva and
its dependent villages, forming a body known as the Venerable
Company, were to meet once a week to discuss the Scriptures, and
once in three months to point out each other's shortcomings. New
ministers were to be chosen by their fellow-ministers, but the Coun-

---

[5] *Registres du Conseil,* xxxv, 384; *Opera,* xxi, 286. The text of the first draft is
given in *Opera,* xa, 15-30.

cil in all cases was to pass on the appointment. The ministers were to preach, admonish, reprove in public and private, administer the sacraments, and in conjunction with the elders make "fraternal corrections." The teachers were to have a care for the instruction of the young, and the deacons to see to the relief of the poor. It is in connection with the third class, the elders, that the most striking innovation appears.

By the terms of the *Ordonnances,* the elders were organized into a disciplinary body of twelve laymen to be known as the Consistory. The duties of the office were "to watch over the life of each individual, to admonish affectionately those who are seen to err and to lead a disorderly life, and where there shall be need, to make report to the body which shall be appointed to make fraternal corrections." [6] The jurisdiction of the Consistory was advisory rather than executive. It could admonish and reprove; it could report offenders to the Council with recommendations for punishment by the civil arm; but its own severest penalty was to debar the offender from the Lord's Supper. Nor was this power of excommunication established without a protest. Calvin succeeded in having it conferred upon the Consistory by the terms of the *Ordonnances* in 1541, but in 1543 the Council withdrew it. It remained a disputed point until 1555, when it was at last firmly lodged in the Consistory's jurisdiction. [7]

Calvin wished the Consistory to be distinctly a church organization, and he would have preferred to have its members chosen by the Church with no interference by the Council. But the wary guardians of the State decreed otherwise, and provided that the Little Council should choose the elders in consultation with the ministers, two of the twelve members being chosen from the Little Council, four from the Council of Sixty, and six from the Two Hundred. [8] Furthermore, the presiding officer was always to be a syndic, thus ensuring at least the nominal dependence of the body

[6] *Opera,* xa, 22.
[7] *Infra,* p. 46.
[8] Calvin called them simply elders. The Council added the further designation "commissioned or deputed by the *seigneurie* to the consistory." Walker, p. 271.

upon the civil magistracy. But though thus hedged about, the Consistory succeeded in representing with considerable power the interests of the Church, for Calvin himself though not its president was always its dominating spirit. Its actual authority varied considerably from time to time according to the pro-Calvin or anti-Calvin composition of the Council.

The main tasks of the Consistory were to compel church attendance and to police the morals of the church members. In many cases it recommended the punishment of offenders; and admonition, reproof and public exposure, with fear of excommunication, were often sufficient incentives to righteousness without the need of calling upon the Council for coercive action. So successful were Calvin and his colleagues in instilling in the Genevans "the fear of the Lord," that the fear of rebelling against God's Word, in conjunction with fear of public censure by an ever-vigilant Consistory, went a long way toward setting people on the path of at least external rectitude.

3. TEMPERANCE AND PUBLIC MORALS

With the Consistory to aid him, Calvin now set himself to the task of toning up the morals of the city. Spying in private affairs was freely engaged in, for it was assumed that no good person would be doing anything he would hesitate to reveal to the public eye! Through the coöperation of the Council, the existing sumptuary legislation [9] designed to regulate private conduct was enforced more rigidly than before, and new edicts passed. During this period it was decreed that those who stayed away from church might have their houses entered and searched during the hour of worship, and the offender if found could be hailed away to prison. Foreigners in the city were to be expelled if any refused to go to church after three warnings. Three men were imprisoned for laughing during the sermon, and another severely reprimanded

[9] Sumptuary legislation had been common since the medieval period. It is a mistake to suppose Calvin originated it. Cf. Kent Roberts Greenfield, *Sumptuary Law in Nürnberg*, Baltimore, 1918.

for criticising the sermon and saying he liked the former preachers better.

The records of those times show a motley array of offenses for which the Consistory admonished and the Council punished.[10] Penalties were meted out, without respect of persons, for dancing; for playing cards on Sunday; for spending time in taverns; for cursing and swearing; for trying to commit suicide; for possessing a copy of the "Golden Legend"; for saying *requiescat in pace* over a husband's grave; for betrothing one's daughter to a Catholic; for having one's fortune told by gypsies; for eating fish on Good Friday; for shaving the tonsure on a priest's head; for saying there is no devil or hell; for arranging a marriage between a woman of seventy and a man of twenty-five; for arguing against putting men to death for religious opinions; for criticising the doctrine of election; for saying the Pope was a good man; for singing a song defamatory to Calvin. Action was of course taken against numerous other offenses, such as theft and adultery, which would have received punishment even in a less meticulous age.

Calvin's famous attempt at temperance legislation is also worthy of mention. Calvin was not a total abstainer. He says in the *Institutes,* "We are nowhere forbidden to laugh, or to be satisfied with food, or to annex new possessions to those already enjoyed by ourselves or our ancestors, or to be delighted with music, or to drink wine."[11]   On one occasion the Council presented him with a barrel of wine as a token of their esteem; and a friendly tiff between himself and Farel is on record, arising from Farel's insistence on paying the whole bill when they drank together in a wine-shop "for a consommation."[12]   In this acceptance of the legitimacy of wine-drinking he was the child of his age. But he went far beyond his age in his denunciation of drunkenness. To drink might be legitimate; to drink to excess was an offense against God, and a bestial practice. "If a man knows that he has a weak head

[10] From the *Registres du Consistoire, Opera,* xxi, 292 f., 422 f., 466 f., 653 f., 700 f.
[11] III, xix, 9.
[12] Reyburn, p. 329.

and that he cannot carry three glasses of wine without being over-come, and then drinks indiscreetly, is he not a hog?"[13] Calvin exclaims. And apparently Geneva abounded in such.

Taverns were numerous in the city, and were sinks of iniquity. Calvin was justified in thinking something must be done about them if drunkenness, lasciviousness, gambling, and idleness were to be checked. Accordingly, at Calvin's instigation the Council on April 29, 1546, passed an edict ordering the taverns closed and five "abbayes" substituted.[14] These abbayes were to be under the charge of respectable persons and were to sell bread and wine at cost. The regulations imposed were designed to make them quite model places! No swearing, back-biting or slander was to be permitted; no dancing or indecency; no singing of obscene songs. Card-playing was to be permitted if done quietly and not for longer than one hour at a time. The Bible was to be displayed in a prominent place, and religious conversation encouraged. One must say grace over his food and drink before partaking, and return thanks afterward. The abbayes were to close at nine o'clock. One was expected then to go home and go to bed in a sober, decent, and godly frame of mind.

But alas for Calvin's virtuous intentions! Even in an age more godly than the present, tipplers did not take kindly to engaging in religious conversation with their drinks, saying grace before partaking and returning thanks afterward. After three months, the abbayes were closed for lack of patronage, and the taverns were reopened. This was probably the most serious strategic error in Calvin's attempt to cleanse the morals of the city. However, the effort was not a total failure, for the agitation thus stirred up drove the worst of the taverns out of existence, and Geneva was a cleaner city for this short-lived experiment in prohibition.

. . . .

Another incident which illustrates the current propensity to meddle in private affairs, also the esteem in which Calvin was

[13] *Opera*, xxvi, 510.
[14] *Opera*, xxi, 380; Roget, ii, 232-234; Doumergue, iii, 70-73.

held as general adviser on all subjects, is the passage of regulations with regard to baptismal names. A citizen of Geneva, Ami Chappuis, presented his son for baptism with the request that he be named Claude. This innocent-sounding cognomen did not suit the minister [15] at all. It seemed to him to savor too much of papistry, as suggesting an idolatrous reverence for a saint who had formerly been highly esteemed in Genevan territory. So the minister said he would baptize the child Abraham. The father staunchly objected, and proceedings were brought against him.[16] Meanwhile the child went unbaptized. Such an agitation was created that the Council asked Calvin to prepare a list of objectionable baptismal names. He drew up the list and its prohibitions were enacted into law on November 22, 1546.[17] We can share his objection to the giving of such names as Angel, Baptist, Evangelist, Sunday, Sepulchre, Easter, Pentecost and Jesus; but tastes might differ as to the impropriety of using "double and ill-sounding names," and "corrupt" names (nicknames) such as Tyvet for Stephen or Monet for Simon. Many of the Genevans regarded the list as an irritating restriction, and it helped to breed discontent.

.   .   .   .

Sterner events were going on in Geneva during these years. Calvin did not add to the severity with which such offenses as adultery, treason, and heresy were punished. It was a stern age in which he lived, and he stood rather for mitigation of cruelty in the manner of inflicting punishment. But what he did do, through Consistory and Council, was to cause many more offenders to be brought to justice—or at least to punishment; for he demanded the full and stringent execution of the laws. From the modern standpoint, many of the penalties imposed, particularly those for heresy and witchcraft, were hideously unjust. As everywhere in those days, the death penalty was freely used; and it is estimated that between 1542 and 1546 fifty-eight persons in Geneva were

[15] Not Calvin, but one of his colleagues.
[16] Cited in the archives of Geneva among the criminal proceedings, *Opera*, xxi, 387.
[17] *Opera*, xa, 49; xxi, 386, 391.

condemned to death and seventy-six to banishment.[18] This number was abnormally swelled by the fact that a panic in 1545, with a general belief that the plague of 1543 had been spread by witchcraft and a conspiracy to place contagion on the door-knobs,[19] led to thirty-four of these executions. Keen thinker though he was, Calvin seems to have accepted without question the possibility of the commerce of witches with evil spirits;[20] and medical science was not yet sufficiently advanced to tell the Genevans that it was not witchcraft or conspiracy, but the filthiness of their streets and their own lack of sanitation that had spread the plague.[21]

4. RESTRAINTS

All these disciplinary measures betoken much power on the part of Calvin. But this does not mean that Calvin had his own way in everything. On numerous occasions the Council took pains to let him know that he was still the hired servant of the state. We have noted that the Council in 1541 refused to let him see their revised version of his *Ordonnances*. In 1542 they forbade him to initiate anything in regard to the Lord's Supper before a coming synod of Swiss churches. In 1543, in spite of Calvin's protests, the right of excommunication was taken away from the Consistory. In 1546, the Council refused to allow Calvin to modify the baptismal ceremony. In March 1548, Calvin was called on the carpet before the magistrates for certain "vivacities" of language. In November of the same year the Council—much to Calvin's disgust—insisted on examining one of his books before consenting to its publication. On various other occasions Calvin failed to secure the backing of the Council. Tissot exclaims, "Truly, here is curious omnipotence and a dictator much restricted in his movements! His propositions rejected, his words submitted to inquiry, his writings

---

[18] Smith, *The Age of the Reformation*, p. 171. Kampschulte, i, 422-428.
[19] *Registres du Conseil*, xl, 42, 60.
[20] *Opera*, xii, 55; xxi, 349. *Infra*, Ch. VI.
[21] An instance of the extent to which religion ruled in Geneva is the fact that when a certain doctor presented to the magistrates a remedy for the plague, they decided to have it examined by the "preachers, surgeons, barbers and physicians" of the city.

examined!"[22] While the Council and the Genevan people were quite willing to seek his advice on many subjects, they were not willing to place their ancient liberties in the hands of any dictator.

Calvin had many friends in Geneva, likewise many enemies; and the years from 1541 to 1555 are filled with conflicts. Most of the Catholics by this time had been exiled, or had managed to accommodate their consciences to the Protestant régime.[23] But the Libertines were still present in full force, and the rigidity of legislation in matters of private morals had swelled their ranks. The term Libertine, applied originally to free-thinking in matters of belief, had come also to connote loose living; and it was natural that those who wanted to drink, dance, dice, and follow the path of nature without the trammelings of a Calvinistic conscience should find Calvin's restrictions irksome and irritating.

Another source of friction was the fact that Geneva was becoming increasingly a place of refuge for persecuted Protestants. These refugees, attracted there by Calvin's preaching—many of them his country-men—were looked upon with favor by him, while the jealousy of the native Genevans was aroused by this influx of foreigners. Frequently the Libertine and anti-foreign opposition was united in the same persons, and the antipathy was thus heightened. Other opponents, few in numbers but strong in influence, contested Calvin's theology, or more often presented views which Calvin felt constrained to contest. In such a ferment of political, religious, and personal disaffection, clash and strife were inevitable.

5. MODERNIST HERESY

One of the earliest of these controversies was with Sebastian Castellio, destined to become famous later as the defender of Servetus and religious tolerance in opposition to Calvin's heresy-exterminating spirit.[24] Shortly before Calvin's return he had be-

---

[22] Tissot, p. 76.
[23] As in the case of Jean Balard, *supra*, p. 18.
[24] Author of two classics on religious tolerance, *De Hæreticis* and *Contra Libellum Calvini*. See F. Buisson, *Sébastien Castellion, sa vie et son œuvre* (Paris, 1892), for an excellent account of Castellio's life.

come a teacher in the Genevan school and in April 1542 was appointed its rector. During the plague of 1542 and 1543, when a minister was needed to go to those who were dying in the hospital, Castellio courageously offered his services, which the magistrates rejected because he was needed at the school, and was not an ordained minister. His conduct compares favorably on this occasion with that of Calvin, who accepted without protest the government's decree that he should not endanger his life which was "necessary for the Church." It compares still more favorably with that of the other Genevan ministers, who declared that they would rather go to the devil or Champel (place of execution) than to the hospital.[25]

In 1543 Castellio desired to change his teaching position for the active ministry, and applied to the Venerable Company[26] and Council for appointment. The Council favored the plan, but Calvin was obdurate in his opposition.[27] In Castellio's examination before the ministers he had questioned the inspiration of the Song of Solomon and the current Genevan interpretation of the clause, "He descended into hell." To Calvin, the rejection of an accepted book of the Old Testament was tantamount to saying that the Bible might not be true. If the inspiration of one book were questioned, the door was opened, Calvin thought, to any amount of theological and moral anarchy—and what would become then of *"la parole de Dieu"*? No such Modernist could be a preacher in Geneva!

Calvin prevailed. Castellio left Geneva in bitterness, and for the rest of his life he remained an opponent of Calvin and a champion of religious tolerance. One remark sums up his opinion both of Calvin and his theology—he wondered what Calvin's Christ had left for the devil to do![28]

---

[25] *Registres du Conseil,* May 1, 1543; *Opera,* xxi, 312. Buisson, p. 186.

[26] The ministerial body.

[27] *Opera,* xxi, 326-329.

[28] *De Hæreticis,* p. 27. He exclaims with reference to the burning of Servetus, "Dost Thou, Christ, command and approve these things? . . . Art Thou present at this butchery and dost Thou eat human flesh? If Thou Christ dost these things, or commandest them to be done, what is left for the devil?"

6. LIBERTY AND THE LIBERTINES

While these doctrinal difficulties were going on, Calvin was also
having plenty of trouble with the Libertines and those opposed to
the coming of the French refugees. In 1546 an affair arose which
brought all these forms of opposition into the open at the same
time. Pierre Ameaux, a member of the Council, drank too much
at a dinner party and became over-talkative. In his cups he made
remarks to the effect that Calvin was a bad man, that he was preaching false doctrine, that the magistrates could never decide anything
without first asking his advice, that he was getting to be more
powerful than a bishop, that if Geneva did not look out, these
Frenchmen would soon be masters of the city.[29]

Gossip had as many wings in those days as now, and it was not
long before Calvin heard of it. He was furious. Whether he
was the more incensed at the accusations directed at his person or
at his system it is hard to say—probably he was too angry over
both to make a distinction. In his judgment Ameaux had attacked
the authority of God and the authority of the Church, and severe
measures must be adopted. Ameaux was arrested and imprisoned.
By this time he was sober and scared, and willing to take back
his words. Some of the Council thought a simple retraction sufficient; others demanded that he be publicly humiliated. The party
favoring moderation at first prevailed. Then Calvin appeared before all three councils, declared Ameaux to be guilty of blasphemy,
and announced that he would not mount his pulpit again until
Ameaux had made adequate reparation for blaspheming the name
of God. The Consistory and the Venerable Company supported
Calvin, and the Council, thus challenged, did not dare to let such
an affront to God's honor go unpunished. In spite of considerable agitation in the city, Ameaux was declared guilty of having
spoken maliciously against God, the magistrates, and M. Calvin.
He was forced to make a tour of the city, clad in his shirt, bare-

[29] Choisy, p. 77.

headed, torch in hand, and on his knees beg mercy of God and the government.

Calvin thus won a signal victory, though at the cost of a rising discontent. It is easy to see in his action a petty sensitiveness. Yet one does not understand Calvin who does not see in his anger something deeper than mere personal pique. In all sincerity he believed himself to be God's representative, and his doctrine to be God's doctrine. To have let such charges go unchallenged would have been to be unfaithful to a divine trust. Above all else, God's glory must be upheld.

. . . .

Among the Guillermins who had been influential in bringing Calvin back to Geneva was Ami Perrin.[30] From being one of Calvin's warm supporters, his attitude shifted until he became the leader of the Libertines. This change of front was caused both by a deep-seated opposition to Calvin's regulation of morals and by Calvin's connection with the French refugees. It was brought to a head by another disciplinary incident.

Perrin's father-in-law, François Favre, was a person of wealth, and therefore of influence, in Geneva. Favre and his son Gaspard were people of no great moral compunctions, and the daughter, Madame Perrin, had been raised in the same household. They had a poor opinion of the Consistory and its discipline. Relying on their social standing as one of the first families of Geneva, they did not hesitate to say so.

In March 1546, a scandal occurred. Not only Perrin and his wife, but also Amblard Corne, then president of the Consistory, committed the indiscretion of dancing at a betrothal party! The dancers were imprisoned, and after serving a brief sentence were ordered before the Consistory for admonition. Corne readily submitted, but Perrin and his wife took a defiant attitude.[31] Shortly after this, Gaspard Favre was disciplined for bowling in a garden

[30] Perrin had been commissioned by the Council to try to induce Calvin to return. *Registres du Conseil*, Sept. 21, 1540; *Opera*, xxi, 265.

[31] *Opera*, xxi, 376 f.

during service, and Francois Favre was punished for offenses against the seventh commandment. The whole Favre-Perrin family was now ranged against Calvin and the Consistory. They contended that punishment by the civil authorities was enough, without the double indignity of being called before the Consistory for reproof after having served the sentence meted out by the Council.

There was doubtless justice in their contention, but the arrogance with which they made it was very irritating. Furthermore, the question was at stake as to whether those in high places could escape penalties imposed as a matter of course on plebeian offenders. Calvin was not inclined to make any concessions to rich reprobates. Moreover, the strength of his ecclesiastical system seemed to him to hinge upon the maintenance of the power of the Consistory.[32] He demanded vigorously the full execution of the penalty. The matter was settled temporarily by a vote of the Council that rebellious culprits should be sent to the Consistory after serving their civil sentence, while repentant offenders might be excused. It was thus a half-victory for Calvin.

But his troubles with Perrin were not ended. The next controversy came over a matter of costume. Slashed breeches were much in favor with the young men of Geneva, but had been forbidden by the Consistory as savoring too much of frivolity and luxury. Perrin, as chief military officer of the city, had asked permission of the Council for the holding of a target festival, and it had been granted. Seeing now a chance to set the Consistory against the Council and discomfit Calvin, he asked that the prohibition against this mode of attire be removed for the occasion. Again the air was tense, for the Council must choose between offending the Libertines and large numbers of the populace, or offending the ministers and Consistory by refusing to uphold their authority. The matter was referred to the Council of Two Hundred, where the Scriptures were searched and nothing discovered about slashed breeches. But Calvin with his usual persuasive skill appealed to Scripture for condemnations of vanity and pride, and

---

[32] Cf. letter to Viret, March 27, 1547. *Opera*, xii, 505.

urged that while the costume itself might be inconsequential, to fail to uphold the action of the Consistory would open the door to excesses and lead to contempt of God and the government.[33] He won, and Perrin suddenly discovered he had business to transact in Berne which necessitated his absence from the city.

. . . .

Perrin and his wife were destined to make trouble for Calvin for some years to come. The next episode in the drama brings into the lime-light another of the Libertines, Jacques Gruet. During one of Perrin's absences from the city, his wife was again guilty of dancing and of insolently defying the Consistory. Her imprisonment being ordered, she fled. But she left behind her a champion in the dissolute Gruet, who affixed a placard to the pulpit of St. Peter's with the inscription, "When you irritate us too much we explode. . . . When too much has been endured, revenge is taken. . . . We no longer wish to have so many masters." [34]

Gruet was arrested, and a search of his house revealed incriminating documents showing contempt for Calvin and his authority. Still worse, he charged Moses with saying a great deal and proving nothing, and on a scrap of paper were found the words, "All laws, human and divine, are made by the caprice of man." To cap the climax, on the margin of a passage in one of Calvin's books arguing for the immortality of the soul, Gruet had scribbled the words, "All nonsense." Gruet was tortured, found guilty of treason and blasphemy, and beheaded on July 26, 1547.[35]

From the modern standpoint, the execution of Gruet, like that of Servetus a few years later, was a gross miscarriage of justice. No outward act of treason could be charged against him except the posting of the placard, and the documents exposing him to the charge of blasphemy were private papers. But to understand the age of Calvin, it is needful to remember that to attack the Bible or its doctrines was to attack God, and to attack God was to com-

---

[33] *Opera,* xii, 561; Choisy, p. 90.
[34] Choisy, p. 92.
[35] *Opera,* xii, 563-568; xxi, 409.

mit the worst offense of which any individual could be guilty. To
have spared Gruet, in the opinion of Calvin and most of his contemporaries, would have been to be party to a heinous sacrilege.

. . . .

Calvin rejoiced openly at the execution of Gruet, and this event
and the defeat of Perrin in the breeches episode strengthened his
position. But the Perrinists were strong; there were rumblings and
undercurrents. The Libertines nicknamed Calvin Cain, named
their dogs for him, sung songs ridiculing him, and subjected him
to many petty annoyances. Such offenses were punished when
detected, but they were sufficient to make his life very uncomfortable and keep the fires of discontent always smouldering.

The figure of Perrin was ever in the offing like an evil genius,
and often in the foreground. Being chosen as ambassador to the
French court, he made negotiations for the bringing of a French
military force to Geneva, ostensibly as a defense against Germany
but actually to strengthen his own position. The plan being revealed through a French refugee and friend of Calvin, Laurent
Maigret, both Perrin and Maigret were placed on trial. Factional
feeling ran high, almost to the point of violence. In the midst
of a near-riot, Calvin with splendid courage went to the meeting-
place of the Two Hundred and by the power of his personality
and persuasive skill, calmed the populace and restored order.[36]
Both Perrin and Maigret were freed, but matters hung in delicate
balance.

[36] *Opera*, xii, 632; xxi, 418. His courage is praised even by those whose estimate
of Calvin is generally hostile. Audin, in his *Histoire de la vie, des ouvrages et des
doctrines de Calvin*, i, 394, describes the incident dramatically:
"The Council assembled. Never was it more tumultuous. The parties, wearied
of speaking, cried, 'To arms!' The people heard the cry. Calvin arrived alone.
He was received at the end of the hall with threats of death. He crossed his arms
and gazed fixedly on the agitators. No one dared to strike him. Then advancing
into the midst with his breast bare he said, 'If you wish blood, strike here.' Not
an arm moved. Calvin then slowly ascended the staircase. The hall was about to
be filled with blood. Swords glittered, but at the sight of the reformer the weap-
ons were lowered and some words sufficed to allay the excitement. Calvin, taking
one of the councillors by the arm, came down from the staircase and cried to the
people that he wished to speak to them. He spoke with such force and emotion
that the tears ran down his cheeks and the crowd retired in silence. . . . From
that point it was easy to predict that victory would rest with the reformers." Quoted
by Reyburn, p. 142.

7. THE INVIOLABILITY OF PREDESTINATION

Calvin authority was in very unstable equilibrium from 1548 to 1551. At this juncture, doctrinal difficulties reappeared. Jerome Bolsec, a "reformed" Carmelite monk, appeared in Geneva and ventured publicily to attack the doctrine of predestination. As he was speaking from the pulpit, Calvin entered unobserved, listened, and then proceeded to refute him in a manner that Beza says left Bolsec little standing-ground.[87] But this was only the beginning of a long controversy. To attack predestination was not merely to attack a doctrine; it was to attack Calvin's own standing as a religious teacher.[88] He had the matter laid before the civil authorities, and Bolsec was arrested and imprisoned. Upon being challenged to recant, Bolsec defended himself skillfully, refused to take back his words, and persuaded the Council to write to the other Swiss churches to ask their opinion on predestination. This was obviously an affront to Calvin, implying that there might be some question about the matter; and with characteristic energy Calvin hastened to get letters off denouncing Bolsec in strong terms a week before the official letter was dispatched. But even this strategy was not wholly effective, and when the replies came in they were so luke-warm and even evasive with regard to predestination that Calvin was very much disappointed.[89] Berne went so far as to say that Bolsec was "not a very bad man," and that predestination was a question of such difficulty for many excellent men that it would be well to exercise moderation.

The prospect looked bright for a Bolsec victory. But Calvin was not to be beaten without playing his best card. In an appeal to the congregation, he so eloquently set forth the importance of right views on predestination that the Council was obliged to yield to popular opinion. On December 23, 1551, Bolsec was banished for "false opinions, contrary to the Holy Scriptures, and pure

---

[87] *Life*, p. 52; *Opera*, xxi, 144.

[88] Calvin believed the real author of the criticism to be Satan, with Bolsec as his instrument. *Opera*, viii, 254.

[89] *Opera*, xiv, 213, 218.

Evangelical religion." [40]   He eventually returned to the Roman faith, and twenty-six years later took his revenge by publishing a scurrilous and grossly derogatory biography of Calvin. [41]

.   .   .   .

Another fuss over predestination, likewise stirred up by a former monk, came the following year in a controversy with Jean Trolliet. Trolliet had desired to join the Geneva ministerial staff, and Calvin had said he was unfit. This aroused the opposition both of Trolliet and of many friends who wanted him as pastor, and Trolliet now attacked the *Institutes* as heretical, on the ground that predestination would make God the author of sin. [42]   Calvin complained to the Council that Trolliet was slandering him, and said that if Trolliet were upheld he would resign his ministry and leave the city. The Council were in a ticklish position, for they had no desire to alienate Trolliet or his friends, and there was not a little feeling afloat that perhaps Trolliet might be right. But they were still more loath to lose Calvin, and they knew that when he said he would leave the city, he meant it. After considerable altercation the matter was settled by a vote of the Council that the *Institutes* present "the holy doctrine of God," and that in the future no one should speak against that book or its doctrine. [43]   But another vote took the edge off Calvin's victory, for the Council refused to punish Trolliet and a few days later declared him to be "a good man and a good citizen." This was as much as they could do at straddling the fence.

8. SERVETUS

The most serious, and the most famous, of all Calvin's doctrinal controversies was with the Spanish physician, Michael Servetus. It has left a blot on Calvin's name for which a partial palliation may be found in an understanding of his theological position and

[40] *Opera*, viii, 247.
[41] Bolsec's biography ascribes to Calvin certain sexual excesses, of which—whatever his other faults—Calvin certainly cannot be held guilty.
[42] *Opera*, xiv, 335 f.
[43] *Registres du Conseil*, November 9, 1552; *Opera*, xxi, 525.

the temper of the times, but for which no complete exoneration is possible.

Servetus was a man of much ability as a physician and scholar, and discovered the pulmonary circulation of the blood in 1546, three quarters of a century before William Harvey.[44] In 1531, at the age of twenty, he displayed not only a keen critical insight but a fearless defiance of orthodox thought in the publication of a book entitled *De Trinitatis Erroribus*.[45] This called for such opposition that he was compelled to conceal his identity, and he assumed the name of Villeneuve. In 1535 he edited an edition of Ptolemy's geography. This volume, apparently innocuously non-theological, was later to cause him much trouble, for he included in it a statement that Palestine was not a land flowing with milk and honey.[46] In 1540 he settled as a physician in Vienne, France, and set to work on a second theological volume, *The Restitution of Christianity*. This aimed to refute the Nicene conception of the Trinity, which he called "a sort of three-headed Cerberus," and to substitute an essentially pantheistic conception of God, with a denial of the preëxistence of Jesus. He also rejected predestination, denied the efficacy of infant baptism, and was in advance of his times in the principles of Biblical criticism in that he interpreted Old Testament prophecies as referring primarily to contemporary events. Such doctrine was obviously dangerous heresy, and he planned to publish the *Restitution* secretly.

While working on this volume, Servetus in 1545 entered into correspondence with Calvin. With more temerity than judgment, he lent a copy of his manuscript to Calvin. Calvin, with more evangelical zeal than courtesy, refused to return it! Calvin gave as excuse the fact that he had lent it to his friend Viret, who

[44] His peculiar union of medical with theological interest is evidenced by the fact that he first announced this important discovery as a casual illustration in a theological tract. *Christianismi Restitutio*, 1553, Liber v, p. 169.

[45] His position might now be termed Unitarian, though he did not deny that Jesus, from the time of the incarnation, was the Son of God. He rejected preëxistence and the current Trinitarian conception.

[46] Servetus borrowed the statement about Palestine from Pirckheimer who in turn took it from Leonard Frisius. Servetus omitted it in the edition of 1541.

failed to return it to him; but it does not redound to Calvin's credit that the manuscript was produced eight years later as incriminatory evidence in Servetus' trial. Servetus had to set to work and rewrite his manuscript, and it is probable that his esteem for Calvin was not thereby increased. During the correspondence Calvin sent Servetus a printed copy of the *Institutes,* which Servetus marked up with uncomplimentary annotations and returned. The correspondence soon lagged, leaving a legacy of bad feeling on both sides. Calvin's personal irritation against Servetus was mixed with and over-shadowed by his horror of what seemed to him the most damnable sort of heresy, and in a letter to Farel [47] he declared that if Servetus should ever come to Geneva, he would not leave the city alive if he could help it.

In 1553, Servetus had a thousand copies of his manuscript secretly printed at Vienne, one of which fell into the hands of a friend of Calvin's at Geneva, Guillaume Trie. It happened that Trie was just at that time in correspondence with a Catholic cousin of his at Lyons, Antoine Arneys, who was trying to win him back to the Roman faith. Being twitted of the laxity of faith prevailing in Geneva, Trie replied to Arneys that it was in Catholic France rather than Geneva that heresies were permitted, and he cited Servetus and his *Restitution* as example. A few pages of the *Restitution* were sent by Trie to Arneys as proof of Servetus' guilt. Arneys at once laid the case before the ecclesiastical authorities at Lyons, and induced Trie to secure from Calvin further evidences of Servetus' heresy. Accordingly, the annotated copy of the *Institutes* and several of Servetus' letters to Calvin were turned over to the Catholic authorities. These documents were all the evidence needed to incriminate him.

There has been much question as to the willingness with which Calvin supplied this evidence. Trie himself says Calvin gave it very unwillingly, and Calvin later denied having had any communication with the Inquisition officials.[48] While it is probably

---

[47] February 13, 1546. *Opera,* xii, 283.
[48] *Opera,* viii, 479.

true that he had no *direct* communication, and may have had compunctions at making such use of private correspondence, the fact remains that it was through evidence supplied by Calvin that Servetus was arrested, imprisoned, and condemned by the French Inquisition to death by slow fire. Whatever the degree of responsibility, the fact cannot be dodged that Calvin delivered Servetus to the Inquisition, and then tried either by a lie or a subterfuge to cover his part in the matter.[49]

Servetus, however, was destined to have further adventures. Through clever management and the help of friends, he escaped over the walls of his prison on the morning of April 7, 1553, and slipped out of the hands of the Inquisition. He started for Italy, but the problem of how to get there was not an easy one. The Spanish Inquisition had sent his own brother to France to catch him.[50] His baffled persecutors at Lyons were not likely to deal kindly with him if he were taken. Popular sentiment was kindled to such a pitch that the death sentence was executed in effigy [51] upon his picture, first by hanging and then by burning. Such danger in France explains in a measure his apparently foolhardy act in going to Italy by way of Geneva.

Upon arriving at Geneva on August 13, 1553, he was detected almost immediately. He went to church on Sunday afternoon [52] —it would have been dangerous for anyone in Geneva *not* to go to church—and while listening to one of Calvin's sermons he was recognized. Through Calvin's instigation he was arrested and put in prison. Calvin apparently felt that the Lord had delivered him into his hands, and he frankly hoped for his execution. Any more charitable interpretation is invalidated by his own statement in a letter to Farel written August 20, "I hope the judgment will be

---

[49] Walker's judgment is probably correct, that Calvin did not institute the proceedings, but from the time of Trie's second letter to Arneys was the chief, though indirect, agent in the matter.

[50] Marcel Bataillon, *Honneur et Inquisition*. Bull. Hisp. xxvii, No. 1, Jan.-Mar. 1925, Bordeaux.

[51] *Opera*, viii, 784-787.

[52] The date proves that it was Sunday. Castellio is the only authority for saying that he was caught in church.

capital in any event, but I desire cruelty of punishment withheld." [53]
We shall not attempt to enumerate all the details of the trial.
The unreturned copy of the *Restitution* manuscript was now produced. The statement in the Ptolemaic geography about the non-
fertility of Palestine was cited as evidence that Servetus was defying
the authority of the words of Moses, and therefore blaspheming
the Holy Spirit by whose inspiration Moses spoke. At the presen-
tation of this charge, "the villainous cur," says Calvin, "only wiped
his muzzle and said there was nothing bad about this." [54] Further
charges were brought against Servetus' statement that some of the
Old Testament prophecies might be taken as descriptions of local
situations instead of prophecies of future events. [55] The copy of
the *Institutes* containing Servetus' notes was again produced, every
page, Calvin said, being "defiled with vomit." Servetus was pushed
to a public affirmation of his pantheism, and according to Calvin's
account, [56] made his statement in a defiant fashion that could
scarcely fail to antagonize the court. While attempts were made
to bring charges against his moral character, these had to be
dropped for lack of evidence, and the condemnation centered about
his denial of the doctrine of the Trinity and rejection of infant
baptism.

Though Servetus had no doctrinal supporters in Geneva, some
of Calvin's enemies, particularly Perrin and Berthelier (of whom
more later) would gladly have seen him released in order to discomfit Calvin, and they endeavored to assist him. The trial dragged
along for two months and a half, during which time a contest
between Berthelier and Calvin over the right of excommunication
threatened to overthrow Calvin's power. But at no time during
the trial did Servetus have a fighting chance of acquittal. He was
refused an advocate, being told with grim humor that he could
lie well enough without one! When both Servetus and Calvin were

---

[53] *Opera*, xiv, 590.
[54] *Opera*, viii, 497.
[55] In particular, that Isaiah 53 referred to Cyrus and not to Christ. Choisy, p. 133.
[56] *Opera*, viii, 496. However. the public records say nothing of the incident
which Calvin describes.

asked to prepare statements of their cases in Latin, Servetus included abusive statements that were bound to be prejudicial. The general sentiment against heresy which prevailed, combined with Servetus' own belligerence and tactlessness, settled the question. He was looked upon not only by Calvin but by people in general as a dangerous citizen who was spreading the worst kind of contagion, and was therefore to be exterminated like the plague. The Council, however, took the precaution to write to the principal Swiss churches to get their judgment on the question.[57] The replies which came back were unanimously hostile to Servetus.[58]

On October 26, the Council ordered that he be burned alive on the following day. In spite of an effort by Calvin to secure for him a more merciful death, the sentence was executed. He met his death with steadfastness and prayer, calling upon the Son of the eternal God to grant him mercy.[59]

It is impossible to assess with accuracy Calvin's part in this judicial murder. That he desired Servetus' death and thought the welfare of the church required it, is clear. It is equally clear that he would have preferred a milder form of execution. He took the initiative in causing Servetus' arrest and bringing him to trial, but beyond that point he had comparatively little to do with the manner in which it was conducted, or with the final imposition of the sentence. The responsibility rests heavily enough upon Calvin, and it rests still more heavily upon the intolerant spirit of the age.

9. THE LORD'S TABLE AND CHRISTIAN UNITY

We must pass over the toleration controversy between Calvin and Castellio which grew out of the burning of Servetus,[60] and return to the story of Calvin's difficulties with the Libertines. At

[57] *Registres du Conseil*, August 21, 1553; *Opera*, xxi, 549. This was done in opposition to Calvin's wishes.

[58] *Opera*, viii, 555-558, 808-823.

[59] Walker, p. 342, suggests that the whole doctrinal controversy is epitomized in the distinction between the "eternal Son of God" and the "Son of the eternal God."

[60] So much criticism was stirred up outside of Geneva that Calvin published in February 1554 a defense of the action in both Latin and French under the title *Defensio orthodoxæ fidei de Sacra Trinitate contra prodigiosos errores Michaelis*

the outbreak of the Servetus affair Calvin's authority in Geneva was in precarious status; at the end it was strengthened. In the middle of it occurred an incident, already alluded to, which threatened to bring Calvin's ministry to an abrupt close.

It will be recalled that the terms of the *Ordonnances* had originally placed the power of excommunication in the hands of the Consistory, and that the Council had voted the withdrawal of this power in 1543. From that time on, the matter had been in an unsettled state, the Council claiming the power and Calvin as staunchly maintaining that no civil body could have jurisdiction over the Lord's table. As no test case arose, the question remained unsettled. But in 1548 Philibert Berthelier, libertine in life and in political affiliation, had begun to defy the right of the Consistory to excommunicate. The matter was raised again in 1551 and came to a sharp issue in September 1553 in the midst of the Servetus trial.

Because of the general shadiness of Berthelier's character and his activities in defense of Servetus, the Consistory at Calvin's instigation voted at this time that he could not be admitted to the Lord's table. Berthelier promptly appeared before the Council and demanded that it supersede this ban of excommunication and admit him to the communion service which was to be celebrated on September 3. Against Calvin's urgent protest, the Council acceded to Berthelier's request.[61]

Calvin was apparently defeated. But it was not his habit to accept defeat without vigorous resistance. He secured a meeting of the Council for the Saturday preceding the communion Sunday, and used all his argumentative skill to try to induce the Council to rescind their action. Seeing that strong measures were necessary, he told them point-blank that he would sooner die than give Berthelier the communion, and warned them that if Berthelier

Serveti Hispani. Castellio in the next month published a reply (already probably in preparation), *De Hæreticis an sint persequendi.* In September Calvin's statement was reinforced by another *De Hæreticis* written by Beza. This led to the writing of Castellio's *Contra Libellum Calvini*, though he was unable to get the latter published.

[61] *Opera*, xiv, 605, 654; xxi, 551.

presented himself he would be forced to refuse it to him. As in the Trolliet case, the Council knew that Calvin meant what he said, and that he was ready to give up his ministry rather than obey their order. But the order was not rescinded.

Apparently Calvin had failed again. It looked at if, after all his years of struggle, the events of 1538 were about to be repeated. Calvin prepared to accept defeat.

The next day, before a crowded congregation, Calvin again affirmed his position and forbade anyone under ban of the Consistory to present himself for the Lord's Supper. He preached what was virtually a farewell sermon, and prepared the table.

Then he waited for Berthelier to appear. It was a tense moment. If he presented himself in defiance of Calvin's statement, Calvin could only abide by his word, and terminate his ministry.

Berthelier did not appear. A good deal of water had gone over the dam since 1538, and in spite of Calvin's precarious authority the Council saw in him too valuable a leader to let go. Saving its face outwardly, the Council had secretly advised Berthelier not to present himself.

So the crisis was averted. The matter was not settled, for the Council's public action remained unrescinded. But morally it was a victory for Calvin. He had preached what he fully expected would be his last sermon; yet he was still a minister in good standing, the head of the Genevan church.

The communion matter—symbol of so much besides the body and blood of Christ—dragged along. In November Berthelier renewed the struggle. The other Swiss churches were appealed to for their opinion, with varying replies. In October 1554, a commission was appointed to consider the question, and in January 1555 Calvin had the satisfaction of seeing the power of excommunication, by vote of all three Councils, permanently lodged in the Consistory.[62] By the fall of the Libertine party in that same

---

[62] This was done by a *de facto* recognition of the Consistory's power rather than by an overt rescinding of the Council's former action. Had the Libertines remained in power, the question might have arisen again. Cf. Choisy, p. 166.

year, any further danger of a recurrence of the controversy was averted.

10. A VICTORY WITH CONSEQUENCES

The year 1555 marks a turning-point in Calvin's fortunes. Never again was his authority in Geneva to be seriously jeopardized, though he still found himself embroiled in external controversies over such matters as predestination and the right to punish heretics. The excommunication victory was soon to be followed by the complete discomfiture of the party of the opposition. Political and social, rather than religious, factors were mainly responsible for their defeat.

During all the years of Calvin's ministry, Protestant refugees had been pouring into Geneva. They were a superior group who had had the energy and initiative to leave their homes for conscientious reasons.[63]   The majority came from France, but there were others from England, Scotland and Italy who found in Geneva a haven of refuge and in Calvin a protector.

The presence of such refugees, though they might be persons of most estimable character and ability, could scarcely fail to stir up jealousy and resentment among large numbers of the native Genevese. The party of the opposition was led by Perrin, with Philibert Berthelier and his brother Francois, Pierre Vandel, and others as warm supporters of an anti-foreign movement.

The matter was brought into the foreground by the granting of a number of admissions to citizenship by the Council against the wishes of Perrin and Vandel. On the evening of May 16, 1555, the aroused Perrinists held supper parties of protest in two of the taverns, and after Perrin and Vandel had gone home, the main body of the banqueters joined forces and paraded through the streets in a menacing manner. A street riot ensued. A stone thrown by one of the anti-foreign group, Comparet, hit a Calvinist member of the Council, though without doing him serious

[63] Kampschulte remarks, "There was perhaps in the Protestant world no other community that could show so many noble, distinguished and aristocratic names," ii, 247.

injury, and the syndic Aubret tried to arrest Comparet. Resistance and hot words followed. Cries of "kill, kill," "beat down the French," added to the turmoil. Perrin arrived on the scene and tried to snatch the baton of office from Aubret and from another syndic, Pierre Bonna. The riot was soon dispersed, Comparet and his brother were arrested, and the matter was apparently ended.

But not so. Rumors spread, on the one hand, to the effect that the refugees were collecting arms and threatening to seize the city, and on the other, that the riot was part of a premeditated plot against the refugees. Both rumors were apparently without foundation. To Calvin and his friends, however, the affair assumed the appearance of a serious attack, not only upon the rights of the refugees and the order of the city, but upon the authority of the government.[64] The majority of the Council at this time were Calvin's supporters, and it was not difficult for them to believe the Perrinists guilty of high treason.

Arrests were made and drastic action followed. Perrin perceived his danger and fled. Seizure of the syndic's staff was a grave offense, and he was sentenced to have his hand cut off and then to be beheaded. The Comparet brothers, with Calvin's approval, were tortured in an attempt to elicit information regarding a conspiracy. Under the rack they said the riot had been premeditated, but denied this again before their execution. A number, including Francois Berthelier, were beheaded, and a similar sentence was decreed against Philibert Berthelier, Vandel and some others who had fled. Several others were banished, and the wives of the condemned were likewise driven from the city. Any effort to aid the fugitives to return was forbidden under pain of death.

By such strong measures was the Libertine party crushed. As a political force its power was ended. It is easy here, as in the Servetus case, to say that Calvin was inhumanly bloodthirsty. In fact, he received a good deal of contemporary criticism from the other Swiss churches for his part in the affair. It is again difficult

[64] *Opera*, xv, 675 f. Letter to Bullinger, June 15, 1555.

to assess the responsibility accurately and dispassionately. Officially, Calvin's share in the condemnations was slight, for the Council took the initiative in the arrests and meted out the penalties. Unofficially, he was certainly responsible in no slight measure, for he approved the action of the Council and felt that the authorities had been, if anything, too lenient toward the offenders. He was doubtless impelled by a mixture of motives, in which his feeling that Providence was meting out a just punishment upon the wicked was linked with a sense of relief at the removal of a group of men who for years had been the chief movers in the thwarting of his plans. Any judgment will do him less than justice which forgets that Calvin believed, with all the strength of an iron-clad soul, that these plans for which he labored were not merely his plans but *God's* plans. If stern measures were necessary to uphold God's glory, then stern measures must be taken.

After these years of turmoil, Calvin was to enjoy a few declining years of calm. With the fall of the Libertines the long struggle was ended, and the Genevan theocracy was born.

CHAPTER III

FRUITION

The last nine years of Calvin's life were fruitful but comparatively uneventful. Each year saw a broadening of his influence and a strengthening of the church, but there is less of specific happening to record. We shall pass over them much more hastily than the years of turmoil surveyed in the preceding chapter.

1. MORE PUBLIC MORALS

With the removal of opposition from the Libertines, Calvin set to work still more vigorously to tone up the morals of the city. New sumptuary legislation was passed, some of it calculated to protect the physical as well as moral safety of the city, such as regulations against leaving sewage and garbage in the streets and lighting fires in improper fire-places and unswept chimneys.[1] Calvin's practical mind would doubtless have given much more attention to such matters, had not preoccupation with political and theological questions crowded these into the periphery.

Ecclesiastical discipline was also tightened. Calvin proposed that all who stayed away from the Lord's table for a year without permission should be punished.[2] Later he recommended a public profession of repentance by those who had been excommunicated,[3] and suggested that leaden tokens be given for the sake of convenience and accuracy to all who were entitled to receive the sacrament.[4] As laxity about attendance on the Wednesday morning service had crept in, the police were instructed to go through the

[1] Reyburn, p. 207.
[2] Opera, xxi, 667.
[3] Ibid., 727.
[4] The use of "communion counters" has been kept up in some of the Scotch churches to the present.

50

shops on Wednesdays and see who might be loitering there during
the hour of service.

This period marks the institution of the Grabeau, a curious
practice which would have slight chance of success in the twentieth
century. It will be recalled that by the terms of the *Ordonnances,*
the ministers of the Venerable Company were expected at stated
intervals to point out each other's faults for mutual edification.
This practice was now extended also to members of the Council.
They were to meet once in three months "in love and charity" for
criticism and censure of one another, and everybody was expected
to profit by these frank statements of the brutal truth. Strangely,
there is no record of any serious quarrels arising from the practice.
This is probably not to be set down so much to the equanimity of
the Council members, as to reluctance to speak the whole truth
and nothing but the truth. But even though the members may
have defeated the purpose of the Grabeau by speaking smooth
words to each other, the inauguration of such a practice gives
evidence of Calvin's disciplinary thoroughness.

The records of these years show an interesting array of repri-
mands administered and punishments imposed.[5] One man, charged
with sleeping in church and making a great noise when awakened,
defended himself by saying his legs were stiff, and no offense
intended. Another was put on bread and water for three days for
criticizing Calvin's sermon and saying he did not stick to his text.
Another was called to account for saying Calvin instead of Mr.
Calvin. Another was expelled for three months for saying prayers
to the Virgin, and a family was expelled for having a child bap-
tised by a priest. Many were dealt with for drinking from a spring
near St. Cergues which was thought to have supernatural medicinal
properties, and was therefore branded as a "fountain of idolatry."

In the midst of these efforts to improve Geneva's morals,
Calvin was forced to the dregs of bitterness by scandal in his own
family. In 1557 the wife of his brother Antoine, who lived with
Calvin, was caught in the act of adultery with Calvin's hunch-back

5 *Opera,* xxi, 661 ff.

servant, Pierre Daguet. The Council banished the wife and gave a divorce to Antoine, who remarried.[6] While Calvin was not responsible and felt deeply chagrined over the whole affair, the scandal, the divorce and the remarriage were all eagerly seized upon by his enemies. He was doomed to suffer similarly again, for in 1562 his step-daughter Judith was found guilty of the same offense. This blow was almost too much for Calvin, and he retired to the country for a time while the tongues of the scandal-mongers buzzed.[7]

2. THE FOUNDING OF THE UNIVERSITY

The most important event of Calvin's closing years was the establishment of the University of Geneva.[8] There had long been a school at Geneva, provision for free compulsory education having been made by Farel in May 1536 before Calvin arrived. We have noted that Castellio was at one time its head-master. The school continued after the breach with Castellio, but was so inefficient that parents often felt obliged to send their children to other cities for instruction.[9] Calvin saw that the time had come to strengthen the facilities both for general education and for religious instruction, and in 1558 induced the Council to provide for enlarging the school and raising it to collegiate rank. A set of buildings was put up, most of which still stand, and Calvin undertook the task of enlisting a competent faculty. Owing to a shake-up in the school at Lausanne, he was fortunately able to secure the services of Theodore Beza, who was henceforth to be Calvin's right-hand man and for many years his successor in the leadership of the Genevan church. Beza came with the intention of being professor of Greek, but was installed as rector. Other able teachers were secured, and on June 5, 1559, the inaugural ceremony took place by which the University (then called the Academy) was formally opened.

---

[6] Protestantism had not yet moved far enough from Roman practice to sanction divorce readily. Antoine Calvin's remarriage created much adverse comment.

[7] Letter to Bullinger, *Opera,* xix, 327.

[8] Cf. Charles Borgeaud, *Jubilé de 1909—Schola Genevensis, 1559—Pages d'histoire universitaire réunies à l'occasion du jubilé,* Geneva, 1908.

[9] *Opera,* xa, 66.

The discipline of the new college, as might be expected where Calvin had a hand, was quite different from that of today. Students had to be very circumspect. They were forbidden to dance, to dice, to play cards, to attend banquets or go to taverns, to promenade the streets, to take part in masquerades or "mummeries," to sing indecent songs.[10] The usual penalty for infraction of these prohibitions was a fine of sixty sous and imprisonment on bread and water for three days, and corporal punishment was not unusual. Life was rigorous and earnest. Activities began at 6:00 A.M. in the summer and at seven in the winter, introduced by an hour of attendance upon sermon. Debates about compulsory chapel had not yet emerged!

The establishment of the Academy was Calvin's crowning achievement in the building of a Christian state. It provided free instruction of all grades from primary work through a college course, and made special provision for the teaching of religion. It drew students from all over western Europe, though the majority of its non-resident students were from France, and the Calvinistic teaching was thus spread over a very wide area. The doctrinal instruction given was so thorough that "a boy of Geneva could give a more rational account of his faith than a doctor of the Sorbonne."[11] Though the need of preparing men for the ministry was an important reason for the establishment of the university, Calvin was also actuated by a profound sense of the need of an educated Protestant laity. Broadly educated himself, he attracted learned scholars to the school and put it on a plane which gave it a high reputation and wide influence. Its honorable history still persists as a worthy memorial to its founder.

3. RECOGNITION

The year 1559 is noteworthy in Calvin's history for another reason; namely, the conferring of citizenship upon him by the Council.[12] Calvin had now lived in Geneva twenty years, and

[10] Reyburn, p. 286.
[11] Ibid., p. 289.
[12] Registres du Conseil, lv, 163; Opera, xxi, 725.

no native son could have served its interests more zealously. But until December 25, 1559, he was not a citizen. His indifference to personal prestige is evidenced by the fact that he had apparently never given the matter any concern, and was quite willing to be Geneva's foremost servant without being her foremost citizen. However, there can be no doubt that he was pleased at this evidence of official recognition by the civil authorities with whom, and against whom, he had so often struggled for the upbuilding of a Christian commonwealth.

Calvin's unconcern about the technicalities of citizenship is characteristic of his general lack of self-seeking. He was even less attracted by pecuniary reward than by civic honors. He lived, and died, a poor man. His house was scantily furnished, and he dressed plainly. He gave freely to those in need, but he spent little upon himself. The Council at one time gave him an overcoat as an expression of their esteem, and as a needed protection against the winter's cold. This he accepted gratefully, but on other occasions he refused proffered financial assistance and declined to accept anything in addition to his modest salary. During his last illness the Council wished to pay for the medicines used but Calvin declined the gift, saying that he felt scruples about receiving even his ordinary salary when he could not serve.[13] When he died, he left a spiritual inheritance of unestimated value and a material estate of from fifteen hundred to two thousand dollars.

It meant a great deal to Calvin that his office as a minister of God should receive due recognition, and he was willing to fight for it with all the passion of his soul. Yet from a personal standpoint he did not look upon himself, nor did most of the people of Geneva look upon him, as other than a humble servant of God who had been called to the leadership of the Genevan church.

4. IN LABORS ABUNDANT

Both the lightening of internal pressure and Calvin's growing reputation brought him in this period into a widening sphere of

[13] *Opera*, xxi, 813.

usefulness. People came from far and near to ask his advice, and
he developed a voluminous correspondence. Any point arising in
one of the Reformed churches, of which by this time there was a
considerable number, was almost certain to be laid before him for
settlement. He gave generously of his time for such matters,
though they made heavy inroads upon his failing strength. He
found time also to give advice to large numbers of the Genevans
who sought his counsel on all sorts of subjects, from the choice of
stoves to the choice of wives. He had to pay the penalty of increasing demands which comes with success, and he labored to
the limit of his powers for the good of the people and the glory
of God.

Those who see in Calvin only unfeeling sternness overlook the
almost feminine gentleness which he displayed in many of his
parish relationships. He grieved with his people in their sorrows
and rejoiced in their joys. Some of his letters to those who had
suffered domestic losses are masterpieces of tender sympathy.
When a wedding occurred or a baby came to grace a home, he
took a warm personal interest in the event. It was not unusual
for him to stop on the street in the midst of weighty matters to
give a school-boy a friendly pat and an encouraging word. He
was hospitable, and entertained often in a simple way. His
enemies might call him pope or king or caliph; his friends thought
of him only as their brother and beloved leader.

Beza cites a statement which should give courage to any present
day clergyman who finds his time for writing and study invaded by
the requirements of parish duties:

> When the messenger called for my book, I had twenty sheets to
> revise, to preach, to read to the congregation, to write four letters, to
> attend to some controversies, and to return answers to more than ten
> persons who interrupted me in the midst of my labors for advice.[14]

His other contemporary biographer, Colladon, gives a suggestive picture of the characteristic range of his activities.

[14] *Life*, p. 102.

He preached every day of each alternate week. He lectured three times each week on theology. He was at the Consistory on the appointed day, and spoke all the remonstrances. What he added at the conference on the Scriptures every Friday which we call the Congregation . . . was the equivalent of a lecture. He was not neglectful in the visitation of the sick, in special remonstrances, and in other innumerable concerns having to do with the ordinary exercise of his ministry. But besides these ordinary labors he bore much responsibility for the faithful in France, teaching, exhorting, counselling and consoling them by letters in their persecutions, interceding for them or procuring intercession when he thought he saw some means.[15]

Calvin worked with indefatigable industry, and neglected neither the priestly nor the prophetic duties of his office. Beza estimates that he preached two hundred and eighty-six times a year, and lectured about one hundred and eighty times. Preaching always to the same audience, he was obliged constantly to prepare fresh sermons, a large number of which have fortunately been preserved. In addition to the extensive correspondence which he carried on, he was engaged almost steadily in theological writing. During his ministry he revised and greatly enlarged the *Institutes* four times; wrote many tracts; and prepared expository commentaries on nearly every book of the Bible. His literary contributions fill the greater part of the fifty-nine quarto volumes of the *Calvini Opera.* He had the temperament of a man who can drive himself with tremendous energy to the accomplishment of a chosen end. And this end was, in Calvin's judgment, one which so far transcended all others that any personal consideration sank out of sight. One must work with untiring zeal when one labors for the glory of God.

5. CLOSING DAYS

Even a soul of triple bronze must be encased in a human body. From his student days, Calvin had been subject to severe attacks of indigestion. He frequently suffered from headaches, perhaps as a consequence of digestive disorders; and as already noted, the violent attacks of anger to which he sometimes gave

[15] *Opera,* xxi, 66.

way were doubtless both a cause and an effect of physical disturbances. As he advanced in years, he suffered great pain from anal ulcers and stones in the kidneys. Still more serious disorders appeared in pulmonary hemorrhages, and he began to show symptoms of tuberculosis. By the fall of 1563, it was evident that he had not long to live.

In the midst of such physical handicaps, Calvin kept up his work as long as he could. He continued to preach when he was unable to walk and had to be carried to the pulpit in a chair. When his infirmities became such that he was confined to his room, he still kept up an extensive correspondence and gave advice to many. Among the activities of this period was a valiant attempt to induce Henry of Navarre to remain faithful to the Reformed cause. He felt that he could not lay down his work while God gave him strength.

On February 2, 1564, he lectured for the last time at the Academy. Four days later he preached his last sermon. On March 27, he was carried to the City Hall in a chair and appeared before the Council to present his friend, Nicolas Colladon, as rector of the school. On April 2 he was carried to church and partook of the Lord's Supper. On April 27 he spoke to the Little Council in his room, expressing his gratitude for their friendship and—true to his convictions to the end—urging that they recognize their shortcomings and humble themselves before God. This address reveals, without ostentation, his own awareness of his powers and his limitations.

I thank you exceedingly for having conferred so many honors on one so plainly undeserving of them, and for having borne so patiently with my numerous infirmities . . . and though in the discharge of my duty I have had numerous battles to fight, and divers insults to endure, I know and acknowledge that none of these things has happened through any fault of yours.

I earnestly entreat that if in anything I have not done what I ought, you will attribute it to want of ability and not to want of will, for I can truly declare that I have sincerely studied the interests of the state. Though I have not discharged my duty fully, I have always tried to promote the public good; and if I did not acknowledge that the Lord has sometimes made my labors profitable, I should be guilty of dissimulation. . . .

I also acknowledge that in another matter I am greatly indebted to you; namely, for having borne patiently with my vehemence, which was sometimes carried to excess. My sins in this respect have, I trust, been pardoned also by God.[16]

On the following day he spoke his farewell to his colleagues of the Genevan ministry. His reminiscences on this occasion reveal much of Calvin's spirit, and express again in simple dignity his estimate of his achievements.

When I first came to this church it had well-nigh nothing. There was preaching and that is all. The idols had been sought out and burned, but there was no reformation. All was in confusion . . .

I have lived in marvelous combats here. I have been saluted in mockery of an evening by fifty or sixty gun-shots before my door. Fancy how that could shock a poor student, timid as I am and as I confess I have always been. After that, I was hunted from this city and betook myself to Strassburg. Having dwelt there for some time, I was recalled, but I had not less trouble than before in the discharge of my duty. They set dogs on me, and these gripped me by my coat and legs. They cried "scoundrel, scoundrel" after me. I went to the Council of the Two Hundred when they were fighting, keeping back the other ministers who wished to go. When I entered, they shouted, "Withdraw, withdraw. It is not you with whom we have to do." I replied, "I shall not. Go on, villains, kill me, and my blood will witness against you and these benches will require it at your hands." Yes, I have been in combats, and you will have more of them, not less but greater. . . .

Although I am nothing, I know that I have suppressed three thousand tumults in Geneva. Be strong and of good courage, for God will preserve this church and defend it. I assure you God will keep it.

I have had many faults which you have had to endure, and all that I have done is of little worth. The wicked will seize upon this admission, but again I say that all I have done is of little worth, and I am a poor creature. Nevertheless, if I may say so, I have intended well. My faults have always displeased me, and the root of the fear of God has been in my heart. . . .

As concerns my doctrine: I have taught faithfully, and God has given me grace to write. I have done it with the utmost fidelity, and

[16] *Opera*, ix, 887; xxi, 164 f. Reyburn, p. 314.

have not to my knowledge corrupted or twisted a single passage of the Scriptures; and when I could have drawn out a far-fetched meaning, if I had studied subtlety, I have put that temptation under foot and have always studied simplicity. I have written nothing through hatred against any one, but have always set before me faithfully what I have thought to be for the glory of God.[17]

On May 2, Calvin wrote his last letter, which appropriately was addressed to his life-long friend and most intimate correspondent, Farel. Soon after, Farel in spite of the infirmities of age made the trip from Neufchâtel to Geneva for a last visit. On May 19, the day when the ministers met for mutual criticism, Calvin had them assemble at his house. He spoke briefly with them, and tried to join in the common meal. It was his last effort. Mind and soul were still alert, but the body had run its course. On May 27, Calvin died.

The next day he was buried like any humble citizen, in a plain wooden coffin and without pomp or ceremony. It was his own wish that his burial be modest, and that no stone should mark his resting-place. Somewhere in the cemetery of Plain-palais he was buried. Here the visitor is shown a plain stone slab bearing the initials J. C., but "no man knoweth his sepulchre until this day."

. . . .

Calvin was only fifty-five when he died. It is easy to let one's imagination play with speculations as to what he might have left behind him, had his life been spared, as Wesley's was, for another thirty years of service. Yet it seems clear that his history-making and Kingdom-building work was done.

Before Calvin's death, the Genevan state was firmly established on the principles of the Word of God, as he saw it. Moral infractions there still were, but the drunkard, the harlot, the blasphemer, and the idler had been driven under cover so effectively that John Knox called Geneva "the most perfect school of Christ that ever was on earth since the days of the Apostles."[18] While

---

[17] *Opera*, ix, 891 ff.; xxi, 167. Walker, p. 436 f.
[18] Letter of December 9, 1556, to Mrs. Locke. Reyburn, p. 274.

such praise from Calvin's disciple and ardent admirer may be discounted, there is little doubt that by the time of Calvin's death, Geneva was morally the cleanest city of all Europe.

The ecclesiastical system instituted by Calvin in the *Ordonnances* and fought for through so many battles was now an established fact. It was destined to form the frame-work of Calvinistic—particularly Presbyterian—organization, and through this of not a little of state organization, in succeeding centuries.

Calvin's theological doctrine, too, was a rounded system. In fact, his theology changed scarcely at all in content from the first publication of the *Institutes* in 1536, when he was only twenty-seven, though subsequent editions show a growing elaboration of argument and precision of form.

The last edition of the *Institutes* was brought out in 1559, the same year in which the University was opened. From that year, Calvin made no striking or historic contribution. To few men is it given to round out the work of life so fully before the summons of death.

PART II

THE CALVINISTIC CONSCIENCE AND MAN'S DUTY
TO GOD

CHAPTER IV

THE THEOLOGY OF THE CALVINISTIC CONSCIENCE

1. MORALITY AS *LEX DEI*

Calvin did not have an ethical system in a philosophical sense. To the "frigid" theories of the philosophers he gave short shrift.[1] Like Jesus, he was concerned, not with ethical theory, but with the practical question of how to live in obedience to the will of God. Unlike Jesus, he conceived the will of God in terms of Biblical literalism and set up a legalistic moral code. Calvin had an ethic— a powerful, dominant, driving ethic—and it rested on his bed-rock conviction of the absolute and final authority of the Will and Word of God.

Calvin was not an ethical theorist; yet few men of any age have had a more clear-cut set of moral ideas. Seldom did he have the shadow of a doubt as to what was right and what was wrong. Never did he waver in his conviction that it was his duty to impose these moral convictions upon himself, and upon everybody within reach of his tongue or pen. Though it be at the cost of sweat and anguish and even blood, God's righteousness must be upheld. Had he been more of a theorist, Calvin might have been less certain that he knew God's will. But Calvin was a theologian and a jurist. He was sure he knew what God demanded, and he felt himself called to be God's prosecuting attorney in the celestial battle against unrighteousness.

Strong as was Calvin's emphasis on moral obligation, it seems not to have occurred to him that the moral mandates he imposed

---

[1] "It [the Gospel] ought to affect the whole man with a hundred times more energy than the frigid exhortations of the philosophers." *Institutes*, III, vi, 4.

References to the *Institutes* will hereafter be indicated without other designation, by giving the number of the book in large Roman, the chapter in small Roman, and the section in Arabic numerals.

on himself and the Genevans needed any justification other than the command of God and the Scriptures. The law of nature was to be obeyed, but only because it coincided with the law of Moses. He had, as we shall see, a good deal of regard for human welfare and spoke many words of sound common sense about the just treatment of one's neighbor, but the idea that the *summum bonum* could be the enrichment of personality—either in oneself or another—was foreign to this thinking. For the hedonistic outlook he had the utmost scorn, and many of his invectives against the Libertines are ablaze with denunciations of the pleasure-seeking attitude. We are not, to be sure, to make ourselves miserable in this life—it would be insulting God to refuse to use the gifts he offers—but we are ever to remember that this life is but a pilgrimage to the life beyond where lies our true felicity.[2]

In the Decalogue, Calvin says, are found all God's commands for moral living. The rest of the Levitical injunctions, in fact all the moral precepts of the Bible, are but interpretations of its meaning. Even Christ has added nothing; he has but restored to its pristine purity the moral law which had been glossed over and corrupted by the rabbis.[3] To Christ's teaching nothing can be added, for he "has spoken in such a manner as to leave nothing to be said by others after him."[4] It is a perverse error to suppose Christ a "second Moses" to supplement the limitations of the Mosaic law.[5] The doctrine put forth by the early fathers and by God's true ministers adds nothing to what is found in the Scriptures. The Reformed doctrine is not new, as some ignorantly claim; it is but a true interpretation of the old doctrine given by God to man for all time in the law of Moses. The law of the ten words is an infallible rule revealing with perfect justice the whole will of God, and all particular laws are compassed within it.[6]

---

[2] III, ix, 1-4; III, xviii, 3.
[3] *Opera*, vii, 81. *Contre les Anabaptistes.*
[4] IV, viii, 7.
[5] II, viii, 7.
[6] Calvin believed that the ceremonial requirements of the Mosaic law had been set aside by the coming of the Gospel, but not its moral injunctions. *Opera*, xxviii, 107. Ser. on Deut. 23: 12-17.

A homely example will make clear the way in which Calvin thus subsumed all moral precepts under the Decalogue. He was staunchly opposed to a practice then common in theatrical performances, that of men's putting on women's clothes to take the part of female characters. (Fortunately for Calvin's peace of mind, women did not yet wear male attire.) The Scriptural justification for this scruple he found in Deuteronomy 22:5, "The woman shall not wear that which pertaineth unto a man, neither shall a man put on a woman's garment; for all that do so are abomination unto the Lord thy God." He discourses at length upon this evil practice, then remarks that the Lord is not here giving an eleventh commandment, for the whole law is given in the ten. But which of the ten? The answer in Calvin's mind is clear. "When God forbade adultery he not only forbade the act . . . but he forbade as a whole all immodest actions, both in dress and conversation." [7] To dress up like a woman is to break the seventh commandment!

The sum of all morality, then, is to obey the Ten Commandments, and thus to obey God. Yet before the Ten Commandments can be obeyed they must be interpreted. Calvin saw this; and he had no idea of admitting the right of everybody to interpret the Decalogue at will. As the rest of the Bible was written to show the true meaning of God's law as revealed to Moses, so must later expositions make clear the application of these commands. But how? Calvin had a simple answer. He believed firmly that God had imparted to his elect servant, John Calvin, the wisdom to do this for the Genevan church and for all who sought his counsel. Through Calvin's lips, God spoke.

In Calvin's sermons, commentaries, tracts and letters he has much to say about how a follower of the true doctrine must live if he would obey God's law. From these statements and from the legislation he recommended it is possible to learn Calvin's view of almost every problem of practical morality. Whether or not this

---

[7] *Opera*, xxviii, 20. Ser. on Deut. 22:5-8.

view be also God's is another question—but a question Calvin did not see.

2. BIBLICAL INTERPRETATION

More consistently than any other Reformation leader, Calvin taught that the Bible was the sole authority in matters of faith and conduct. He drew at length upon the pronouncements of the early church fathers—so far as their views harmonized with his own. He drew upon the Schoolmen more extensively than one who was attacking their church so vigorously and scornfully was willing to admit. But above all else he drew upon the Bible (or upon his interpretation of the Bible) for his system of doctrine and system of morals.

There was nothing new in this. The other Reformation leaders claimed also to rest their doctrine upon an infallible Bible, and the only new element was the intensity and consistency with which Calvin adhered to the principle. Like all the rest, but again with more rigid consistency, he believed implicitly that *his interpretation* of the Bible was the true one. It seems not once to have crossed his mind that Castellio might be right in saying that the Song of Solomon was a Hebrew love-tale falling below the rest of the Bible in divine inspiration, or that Servetus might possibly not be defying Moses and blaspheming the Holy Spirit in questioning the fertility of Palestine. Calvin was not wholly a traditionalist, for in some instances—for example, in his declaration that the taking of interest was not forbidden by the Scriptures—he went beyond his times.[8] Nor was he wholly a literalist, for in regard to practices apparently sanctioned by the Bible which Calvin did not approve of—such as polygamy in the Old Testament and community of goods in the New, he put forth a good deal of ingenious logic to show that the Bible did not really mean what it seemed to say.[9] But he was a thorough-going Fundamentalist. The writers of Scripture seemed to Calvin the "sure and authentic amanuenses of the Holy Spirit."[10]

---

[8] *Opera*, xa, 245-249.
[9] *Ibid.*, xb, 258 f.
[10] IV, viii, 9.

Calvin was not oblivious to the problem raised by conflicting interpretations of the all-authoritative Word. In his judgment the Church—if one means the Roman Catholic Church—has no rightful authority to interpret Scripture. Many of his sharpest thrusts are against the misinterpretations, and what he often terms the gross ignorance, of the Papists.

However, if "the Church" means the Reformed Church, that is another matter. Calvin's own attitude toward ecclesiastical authority is semi-Catholic.[11] A true church of God, he says, is one in which "the Word is purely preached and heard, and the sacraments administered according to the institution of Christ.[12] There was no doubt in his mind that the Genevan church was a true church, pure in doctrine and sacraments, and that the Roman churches were impure in both. The Church, if it be a true church, is thus for Calvin "the mother of all those who have God for their Father,"[13] and is the custodian both of salvation and of sound doctrine.

But who, within the Church, is to decide what constitutes sound doctrine? The ministers are to interpret the Word, and to them is given the power of the keys in matters of doctrine and sacrament.[14] Yet the ministers are merely instruments in God's hands. The Scriptures show everywhere, Calvin says, that prophets, priests and ministers are called to speak in the name of the Lord, and not of themselves.[15] In the last analysis, the Bible is not to be interpreted according to the authority of church or minister or any other human agent, but of God alone. It is his Holy Spirit which gives the power to read the Scriptures aright.

Calvin seems here to be on the verge of substituting the authority of inner experience for that of external pronouncement. Had he

---

[11] "For the Roman imperialism Calvin simply substitutes a Scriptural imperialism. The Biblical church is the ultimate and final authority over the really regenerate man. . . . This is simply Roman Catholicism without the name Roman." T. C. Hall, *History of Ethics Within Organized Christianity* (Scribners, 1910), pp. 519, 520.

[12] IV, i, 9.

[13] IV, i, 1.

[14] IV, i, 22.

[15] IV, viii, 2.

gone on to make this substitution, Calvinism would have had a
very different history. But he stopped just short of it. True, the
Holy Spirit gives the power to read the Scriptures aright. But
this inner witness of the Spirit by no means gives authority to
pick and choose at will! "Our Lord," says Calvin, "cannot permit
such an injury to his Word that one should emulate the wiles
of Satan and say, 'Go to, now, I will choose what seems good
to me.' He will not let a man make himself judge and sit above
God's truth which the angels adore in all reverence." [16]   On the
contrary, "those who are inwardly taught by the Holy Spirit
acquiesce implicitly in Scripture." [17]   And only the elect are thus
inwardly taught.

Calvin thus rested his whole system on the conviction that the
Scriptures are verbally inspired, and that when read aright by the
elect they have an absolute and unique authority. As for who
are the elect, that lies with God. Calvin never doubted that he
himself was one. And he believed with equal assurance that if
anyone disagreed with his reading of the Scripture, that person
was being led astray either by the devil or by the perversity of his
own nature.

It is to misjudge Calvin to see mere egotism or obstinacy in this
tacit assumption of his own infallibility as the mouthpiece of
Jehovah. He sincerely believed himself to be the humble instrument of God, speaking with no human wisdom but only with the
light which came to him from on high. He was, as we have seen,
singularly free from personal conceit. But he was very certain
that the Holy Spirit had given him grace to see in the Scriptures
the truth of God. When he said that one must acquiesce implicitly
in Scripture, what he meant was that one must acquiesce implicitly in Scripture with John Calvin's interpretation on all disputed passages. He was not the first to make such an assumption
regarding one's own powers. Nor was he to be the last.

His opponents could see presumption in this almost naïve self-

---

[16] *Opera*, xxvii, 233. Ser. on Deut. 13: 1-3.
[17] I, vii, 5.

assurance. Castellio remarked that Calvin talked as if he had been in Paradise,[18] and spoke of him sharply as "this Jew who reads Moses with a veiled face." [19] But Calvin saw no presumption in such certainty. Few of the Genevans saw any. It will be recalled that in 1552 at the close of the Trolliet controversy, even during a Libertine régime, the Council voted that the *Institutes* contain "the holy doctrine of God," and forbade anyone to speak against that book or that doctrine.[20] It was assumed without question by Calvin and his people that God had granted to him through the Holy Spirit the wisdom to read the Word of God aright. To doubt this was presumption.

3. THEOLOGICAL DOCTRINES

We must look now at the doctrines that Calvin believed to be so firmly grounded upon the Scriptures. The ideas which not only dominated his theology but most directly affected his ethics were the absolute sovereignty of God, man's helplessness and total depravity, and the doctrines of predestination and election.

Calvin's conception of the sovereignty of God is essentially Augustinian, though with more consistency than Augustine's warmly human, mystical nature would permit. God is the triune and just Creator, the all-powerful Governor, by whose sovereign will all things are determined. Man may seem to labor for his daily bread, yet it is God who nourishes him. Man may seem to earn rewards by his good works or bring upon himself the deserved penalty for his sins, but it is God who metes out rewards and penalties with a just, though often inscrutable, wisdom. No impersonal mechanism, or arbitrary decree of "fate," settles human destinies; the world of men and things is completely under the direction of an all-just, all-powerful, all-wise God.[21]

With Duns Scotus, Calvin held that the will of God is wholly unconditioned. God does not act as he does because it is good

---

[18] *Contra Libellum Calvini*, p. 19. Calvinus 4.
[19] *Ibid.,* p. 129. Cal. 122.
[20] *Supra,* p. 39. *Registres du Conseil*, Nov. 9, 1552. *Opera*, xxi, 525.
[21] Walker, p. 409 f., summarizes admirably the implications of this doctrine.

to do so; but because he so acts, the act is good. Therefore it is foolish, as it is impious, to ask a reason for God's action. He acts because he wills to act, and that for the trusting believer is reason enough. Calvin puts the doctrine unequivocally:

The will of God is the supreme rule of righteousness, so that everything which He wills must be held to be righteous by the mere fact of His willing it. Therefore, when it is asked why the Lord did so, we must answer, Because He pleased. But if you proceed further to ask why He pleased, you ask for something greater and more sublime than the will of God, and nothing such can be found.[22]

Had Calvin been more of a metaphysician, he could not have been satisfied to pass by so easily the nest of difficulties which beset the philosopher on such a basis. But Calvin was not a metaphysician; he was a theologian. To him it seemed fitting that men should "lower their eyes" [23] and withhold all idle, sacrilegious speculation as to the why of things. God disposes as he wills—and that is enough.

. . . .

In a system with these premises, it is obvious that man is bound to have a minor place. Man's utter helplessness is the correlate of God's absolute sovereignty. In fact, man is worse than helpless; for he is under the curse of Adam's sin. Neither righteousness nor reward can come to him through his own power or merit.

Adam, to Calvin, was a very real person. Had an evolutionist arisen then to cast doubts upon Adam's existence, Calvin would have thrust him out as the messenger of Satan, and would, no doubt, have burned him at the stake. Fortunately Darwin did not appear till the world was more nearly ready for his message. Calvin had no doubt whatever that all man's woes are the result of the original act of disobedience in the garden. Marriage, for instance, before the fall was a pure and stainless institution; after Adam

[22] III, xxiii, 2.
[23] *Baisser les yeux.* One is tempted to translate this "close their eyes"—to obvious facts. But this would be to misread Calvin. The ugly facts of life were real enough to him, but he believed that they were to be humbly and patiently accepted as the dispensations of an all-wise God.

sinned it became a necessary remedy for incontinence.[24] Before the fall, man was made in the image of God; by Adam's sin he became defiled with drunkenness, avarice, and all manner of evil desires. In all the events of life, even in such apparently commonplace matters as putting on and taking off our clothes, we are enjoined to remember our father Adam's sin, and be warned.[25] The familiar couplet of the New England Primer,

> In Adam's fall,
> We sinned all,

had not yet been formulated. But Calvin implicitly believed this, and used a great many more than six words in saying so.

Calvin accepted the Pauline conception of the solidarity of the race, leaning heavily upon Romans for his doctrine of man's fall through Adam and redemption through Christ. With Augustine, he believed that man not only had been originally created in a state of goodness but endowed with free will. Adam's sin has tainted the whole human race and robbed man both of his goodness and his freedom. In this state man suffers from "an hereditary corruption and depravity of our nature" and is totally helpless to lift himself from his fallen state. "The soul, when plunged into that deadly abyss, not only labors under vice, but is altogether devoid of good."[26] God, to be sure, has given man the law as his guide. But man is unable to perform saving works by which to redeem his soul from bondage, and the law serves but to convince him still further of his hopeless state.

In this condition of deserved and helpless condemnation, God in his mercy sends the eternal Son to enter into sinful flesh and suffer in man's stead. Through his three-fold office of prophet, priest and king, Christ's atoning work is wrought. As prophet he reveals God. As priest he makes atonement by his obedient life and death for the sins of men, and appeases the Father's wrath.

---

[24] *Opera*, xlix, 401 f. Comm. on I Cor. 7: 1, 2.
[25] *Ibid.*, xxviii, 20. Ser. on Deut. 22: 5-8.
[26] II, iii, 2.

As king he becomes the head of the church of the elect whom he has thus redeemed.

The person and work of Christ occupies no small place in Calvin's thought. Through Christ we find salvation; in Christ we find an example of perfect holiness. Yet Calvin's system of doctrine is more Hebraic than Christian. It rests more upon the Old Testament than the New. His writings lack the note of warm, personal fellowship with Christ, and in his moral injunctions the Decalogue looms above the Sermon on the Mount. The place of Christ in Calvin's scheme of things is theological rather than personal and ethical.

.   .   .   .

It is through the Holy Spirit that Christ's atoning work is made available to man. But not to everybody. Only God's elect can find salvation. Calvin follows Luther in rejecting the possibility of finding salvation through good works or sacraments or priestly absolution, and accepts the Lutheran doctrine of justification by faith. Calvin maintains that this act of faith is not a free act on man's part; it is rather the free gift of God to those to whom he elects to give it. The divine self-sacrifice of God in Christ, prompted by God's love for an undeserving and sinful race, is efficacious only for those whom the Holy Spirit incites to faith. Such faith leads to repentance, and with repentance comes justification, i.e., the imputation of Christ's merit to the penitent. A new life of righteousness then begins, and this leads on to sanctification, a process of spiritual growth which is bound to continue in God's elect *because* they are God's elect, though complete perfection in this life is unattainable.

Here we come upon the significance of two characteristic Calvinist doctrines which had more meaning in an earlier day than in ours, irresistible grace and the perseverance of the saints. God chooses whom he will for salvation, and man is as powerless to resist as to initiate this action of divine grace. And being once chosen, the elect are predetermined to persevere in the path of holiness. These doctrines, so comforting to the elect, so discouraging to those outside the fold who might like to be of the elect, fall strangely on modern ears. But they are a clear-cut conclusion from the rest of Calvin's system. If God is the all-powerful Governor and man is totally helpless and unworthy, it follows that God must do all the choosing of whom to save. And having once chosen, he cannot be expected to change his mind and let his elect backslide.

If Calvin's premises be granted, the doctrines of predestination and election thus become sun-clear. If God is all-powerful, he determines every act. If he is all-wise, he foreknows and *pre*determines every detail of human destiny. To say that some achieve salvation through their own initiative is to place limits on the divine sovereignty, and such an inconsistency Calvin rejects with inexorable logic. The empirical facts are that some appear to be saved and some to be damned; the only explanation consistent with the absolute sovereignty of God is to say that God elects some for salvation and others for eternal punishment.

Predestination was no new doctrine. Augustine and Luther had maintained it. But both had shrunk from carrying it to its ultimate conclusions. Augustine had said, as Calvin now did, that salvation comes only through the free mercy of God and that God elects some to be saved. But Augustine was not quite equal to drawing the stern conclusion that God elects others to be damned. So he side-stepped the issue by saying that God leaves some to their own devices, and merely *permits* some to be lost without decreeing that they *must* be. Luther's position was essentially Augustinian. While he was willing enough to say that the faith by which man may be justified is a divine gift, he had too high a regard for the love of God to say flat-footedly that God voluntarily chooses to withhold this gift from some. Zwingli emphasized much more clearly than Luther the universal causality of the will of God, and came close to Calvin's position. But not until Calvin do we find a theologian who carried the premises to their drastic consequences.

Calvin believed, to be sure, in a God of love and mercy who is willing to extend his grace to sinful men and thus bridge the impassable gulf which man has fixed for himself. But he believed still more in a God of power and justice, and in a divine sovereignty which must be upheld whatever the cost. With Luther the concept of love is the center of his idea of God; with Calvin, that of majesty.[27] And because of the transcendent majesty of God, if God chooses to leave some men in their sins and allow them to suffer the deserved penalty for their guilt, it is not for human minds to question or complain. Still less is it permitted to charge God with injustice. The sun is not evil if its light, falling on putrid flesh, causes foul odors to arise.

Calvin's premises are from his theology, his conclusions from the logical precision of his mind and the stern inflexibility of his temperament. Had Calvin been a warm-hearted but inconsistent mystic like Augustine or Luther, the course of Calvinism, and of history, might have followed a different channel.

4. PREDESTINATION VERSUS FREE WILL

Calvin's critics have frequently pointed out an irreconcilable conflict between his doctrine of God's absolute sovereignty and man's responsibility. The author believes this criticism to be just. Man must be free in order to be responsible. If one cannot justly be blamed for what one cannot help, the predestination doctrine leaves little ground for blame. Yet Calvinism calls men to account for their sins more sharply than does any other form of theological belief. There is a conflict here which Calvin did not reconcile.

But Calvin fully believed that he had solved the conflict; and to understand Calvin, one must see the question through his eyes. His doctrine of Adam's sin is the crux of the matter. Everybody is guilty of sin because of Adam's fall, while the power to escape sin comes only as the free gift of God. Man's power to do wrong is part of his hereditary corruption: his power to do right is the gift of God to the undeserving. For example, the tendency to unchastity which leads man to flagrant offenses against the moral

---

[27] Cf. Troeltsch, *Die Soziallehren der christlichen Kirchen und Gruppen* (Tübingen, 1912), p. 616.

law is his own fault; the gift of continence, bestowed upon a few, is a special endowment of God.[28] Man must blame himself for his sin; he must thank God if he is able to escape sin.

Calvin is very vigorous in his denunciation of the idea that God is responsible for human sin. He is at his best when he can refute this idea in the thought of another. He speaks with utter scorn of the scholastic doctrine:

> That invention which the Schoolmen have introduced, about the absolute power of God, is shocking blasphemy. It is all one as if they said that God is a tyrant who resolves to do what he pleases, not by justice, but through caprice. Their schools are full of such blasphemies, and are not unlike the heathen, who said that God sports with human affairs.[29]

He is still more vehement in an attack upon the Spiritual Libertines, who, according to Calvin, were pantheists who denied to man any free will. It is interesting to find this arch-opponent of free will rising up to smite the doctrine of a sect which questioned man's freedom and moral responsibility.

> After having forged a single spirit, destroying the nature of the angels in heaven and the devils in hell, and likewise human souls, they say that it is this one spirit which does everything. Not meaning what the Scripture does, when it speaks of God, that all creatures live and move in Him, are subject to His providence and serve His will: but that everything which happens in the world is to be directly regarded as His work. In so doing they attribute to man no free will, any more than if he were a stone; and they remove all distinction between good and evil so that nothing can be done wrongly, in their opinion, since God is the author of it.[30]

Calvin then illustrates by an incident which one suspects of being apocryphal, since the records contain no reference to an event which would almost surely have created a public uproar, had it occurred. A Libertine leader, Quintin (Calvin calls him "that

---

[28] *Infra*, p. 133.
[29] *Opera*, xxxvi, 391. Comm. on Isaiah 23: 9.
[30] *Ibid.*, vii, 183. *Contre la Secte des Libertins*. Ensuing quotations are from the same passage.

great hog Quintin"—nothing else is known of him), is said to
have encountered one of the faithful on the street at the scene
where a man had been killed. The following conversation is
reported:

"Alas, who committed this terrible act?"
Forthwith he [Quintin] replied in his Picardy dialect, "Since you
want to know, I did it."
The other, much astonished, said to him, "How could you be such a
villain?"
To which he replied, "It isn't me; it's God."
"What?" said the other, "are crimes to be imputed to God which He
commands to be punished?"
Then the rotten thing disgorged some more venom and said, "Yes,
it's you; it's me; it's God. For what you or I do, God does; and what
God does, we do, since He is in us."

This point being granted, Calvin says, it is necessary either to
impute sin to God, or to declare that there is no sin in the world,
since God commits none. "Thus," he argues, "all distinction between good and evil disappears. Then it follows that nothing can
be blamed as bad, since everything is the work of God. Men
with free rein can do whatever comes in their way, for they will
be in no danger of sinning, and to restrain some desire would be
to restrain God." He applies this in particular to the ethics of
domestic relations:

Example: Some one has committed adultery? One cannot chide
him for it; for that would be to blaspheme God. A man covets his
neighbor's wife? Let him enjoy her if he can; for he would only be
doing the will of God, and even that would be a divine act. Whoever
can seize his neighbor's goods, whether by subtle means or violence, let
him do so boldly. For he will do nothing which God does not approve.

After further discussion and more examples, Calvin sums up
what he regards as the dire and blasphemous consequences of the
Libertine view that man has no free will:

Three dreadful consequences follow. The first is that there would
be no difference between God and the devil—indeed, the god they forge

for us is an idol worse than a devil in hell.[31] The second is, that men would no longer have any conscience to avoid evil, but like brutes would follow their sensual appetites without discretion. The third is, that everything would have to be adjudged good—whether adultery, murder or theft—and all the worst crimes imaginable would be regarded as praiseworthy acts.

Seldom have the logical consequences of the destruction of man's moral freedom received keener analysis! Calvin could see clearly what it meant, when he was talking about the Schoolmen or the Libertines, to rest everything in the absolute power of God. But to few of us is it given to see ourselves as we see others. This gift was not granted to Calvin.

5. MORAL CONSEQUENCES

The leaders of the Reformation did not deliberately set out to enact changes in ethical concepts. What they were interested in primarily was the establishment of sound doctrine. If any alteration in ethical outlook came as a consequence of a new religious emphasis, it was an indirect and unforeseen, sometimes unwished for, development. Consequently it is not surprising to find them, for the most part, adopting the accepted moral standards of the day and urging people to righteousness on the basis of the traditional religious concepts. There is, of course, sharp differentiation in matters relating to duties which pertain to religious observances. A binding moral obligation to attend Mass becomes, in Protestant hands, a sin to be censured and publicly punished. The movement from a celibate priesthood to a married clergy effected certain changes in the ethics of the family. The rise of the Anabaptists, with their scruples against war and leanings toward a socialistic state, created the furor which always comes when any innovation in moral practice is suggested. Yet there cannot be said to have arisen with the Reformation a distinctive Protestant ethic in the sense in which there arose a distinctive Protestant doctrine. Differ-

---

[31] One is reminded here of Castellio's remark that Calvin's Christ had left nothing for the devil.

ences in religious outlook and theory, with differences in the social milieu, eventually brought about a differentiation on some points; but such changes came slowly, and were the result of cultural influences among which religion was not the only factor.

Calvin's theology had an effect upon his ethics, and upon the ethics of his followers. The Puritan conscience has had no little influence in shaping the moral standards of the American commonwealth, and the Puritan conscience owes much to Calvin. But it would be a mistake to suppose that Calvin's theology had all the effects that might be expected on the basis of theoretical considerations alone. People have always lived by habit and emotional drives far more than by intellectual concepts.

An excellent example of this appears in the doctrine of predestination. The most obvious logical outcome of a doctrine which makes man the helpless recipient of God's grace or condemnation would be moral inactivity. It is easy to point out theoretically that if man has no power to shape his destinies or save himself from his sins, there is no need of his trying to do anything about it. For Calvin no such justification of moral idleness ensued. No man of his day had a keener sense of the imperative obligation to strain every nerve to banish sin. Nor did the doctrine lead to moral lethargy in many of his disciples, either contemporary or subsequent. Few people of any age have worked harder to chase the devil into hiding than have the Calvinists.

Various practical effects, however, did ensue from the predestination doctrine in conjunction with the idea of the absolute sovereignty of God. One of these is the enhancement of the sense of moral obligation just referred to. The supreme virtue, Calvin says, is holiness. This means that above all else, God's honor must be exalted and God's will obeyed. To break in any least detail one of God's commandments is to offend God. To defraud one's neighbor of his rightful due is to offend God. To give rein to one's natural impulses toward pride or avarice or lewdness is to offend God. Any deviation whatever from the strict path of moral rectitude is a direct affront to the Almighty. And because he is the Almighty, and in his inscrutable wisdom has elected some for salvation, it is all the more incumbent upon the elect to pursue the path in which he has set them by his grace. Out of the doctrine of election grows another moral incentive. Nobody can say with absolute certainty of another whether or not he is of the elect, for the invisible church of the elect does not coincide with the visible church. Yet one may be assured of his own election by an inner witness, and what is more, one may reveal it by the quality of his works. Good works can never save a man —Calvin never tires of making clear man's helplessness—but good works may be a sign that God has saved him.[32] Naturally, one who feels himself thus chosen wants to give external evidence of it. To disobey the laws of God and continue in sin would be the clearest possible evidence that God's saving grace had passed him by. Thus it came about that the Calvinist labored with untiring zeal to "make his calling and election sure."

Nor was this a matter of mere display. The Calvinist doubtless had a natural, and quite pardonable, desire to reveal his election to his neighbors. But the election doctrine had an inner incentive which appears most clearly in contrast with the Lutheran conception. Luther made the witness of the spirit the chief criterion by which to distinguish the saved from the unsaved; Calvin accepted this but added an emphasis on righteousness and moral activity as the evidence of salvation which does not appear in Lutheranism. Luther was a mystic; Calvin a man of action. Luther looked upon the saved man primarily as the vessel or receptacle of the Holy Spirit; Calvin regarded him as the instrument or tool by which God's will is wrought.[33] Luther could say, "Tears go before works and suffering surpasses doing." Not so Calvin. Man as the tool of God, the executor of his ordinances, must be forever active. Faith must be an effectual faith revealing

---

[32] *Infra*, p. 183.
[33] Max Weber, *Die protestantische Ethik und der Geist des Kapitalismus*, in *Gesammelte Aufsätze zur Religionssoziologie*, pp. 108, 125. Weber makes a good deal of the economic influence of this conception of good works as the sign of salvation. I think Weber overstrains the point, for when Calvin talks of one's vocation he means usually one's divine "calling," not his secular occupation.

itself in outward deeds. This doctrine will receive further analysis when we study Calvin's economic influence.[34]

.   .   .   .

But Calvinism was not devoid of mysticism, and its mystical note had also its moral effects. One profound emotional effect the predestination doctrine had which it is difficult to regain in the present day. This is summed up in the familiar Puritan phrase, "to be willing to be damned for the glory of God." To ridicule this phrase is to miss the spirit of Calvinism.

To the Calvinists of three centuries ago it connoted a very real and transcendent religious experience. It meant an affirmation of God's supremacy in the cosmos, and a bowing of man in utter humility before the moral demands of an all-wise Providence. It meant a deep-reaching conviction that ultimately all things are in God's hands, and that however feeble man's efforts, the all-powerful Governor can be trusted to order human destinies aright. In short, it meant such a selfless devotion to the glory of God that the fate of any individual seemed insignificant if only this Transcendent Majesty be exalted.

We have traveled so far from such a mystical experience that it is hard to make the glory of God as meaningful today as it was to the Calvinists. Perhaps our nearest analogy is in the experience that comes occasionally when one finds himself small and helpless before the forces of nature, and sees in the power of the tempest or the majestic fury of the sea the hand of an all-ordering God. In an emotional crisis the religious spirit feels, sometimes, that it matters little what happens to *me,* or to my petty affairs, provided the will and work of God be done. This is akin to what the Calvinist meant when he said he was willing to be damned for God's glory.

Such a view could not fail to have moral consequences. It gives the key to something else often ridiculed, Jonathan Edwards' famous sermon on "Sinners in the hands of an angry God." Sinners would not be in God's hands at all unless God were the supreme determiner of human destinies. And sinners would not be in the hands of an angry God unless God hated sin. A God supremely righteous demands righteousness in his servants. A God supremely just and supremely powerful will not tolerate sin. Sinners must turn from their evil ways, or suffer the deserved penalty for their sins at the hands of a God of moral justice. This is strong doctrine, but an age of cock-sureness and self-esteem might learn something from it!

. . . .

The Calvinist's obligation to glorify God gave a potent, yet restricted, incentive to social morality. Man was enjoined to serve his neighbor. Yet if ever there came a clash between service of God and service of neighbor, it was inevitable that service of God would be put first. Likewise, it was inevitable that any effort at righteousness apart from religion would be looked upon with distrust. Calvin is very clear in his conviction that mere righteousness avails nothing if God's glory be not honored:

> For what kind of righteousness will you pretend to, because you refrain from harassing men by acts of theft and rapine, if at the same time you atrociously and sacrilegiously defraud the majesty of God of the glory which is due Him? because you do not pollute your body with fornication, if you blasphemously profane the sacred name of God? because you murder no man, if you strive to destroy and extinguish all memory of God? It is in vain therefore to boast of righteousness without religion. . . . We therefore call the worship of God the principle and foundation of righteousness because if that be wanting, whatever equity, continence and temperance men may practice among themselves, it is all vain and frivolous in the sight of God.[35]

Such a doctrine was destined to have a salutary, and at the same time a fatal, consequence. On the one hand it established the moral discipline of Geneva firmly on a religious basis. It went far toward the shaping of the Puritan conscience, for without the powerful drive of religious duty, it is doubtful whether either Calvin or the Puritans could have brought human instincts so fully under

35 II, viii, 11.

control. The Calvinist's exaltation of God laid the foundations of the American commonwealth upon the solid sub-base of religion. On the other hand, it implicitly cast reflections upon any morality not religiously engendered, and thus was bound to breed a spirit of supercilious intolerance toward those outside the fold. It tended to exalt the worship of God above the requirements of simple human justice; and has been in no small degree responsible for the feeling that religion concerns itself with matters of personal piety, while "business is business" and not to be mixed up in any embarrassing way with religious scruples.

.   .   .   .

A similar effect grew out of Calvin's characteristic emphasis upon sound doctrine. Doctrinal requirements were exalted above moral requirements.[36] To be more exact, the morality of enforcing sound doctrine was placed above the morality of loving one's neighbor. Calvin insisted that doctrine must be of the life and not of the lips only.[37] But for one's doctrine to be of the life, one must, from Calvin's point of view, be willing to strain every nerve to make this doctrine prevail. The actual effect in a case of clash between sound doctrine and sound morals appears clearly in the Castellio controversy. Calvin was not at all impressed, apparently, by the fact that Castellio had been willing to risk his life to minister to those dying in the pest-house when all the regular clergy refused to go. Castellio might be a sincere, high-minded, self-sacrificing citizen—but when he proved unorthodox on the Song of Solomon and a phrase of the Apostle's Creed, that was enough in Calvin's eyes to debar him forever from the Christian ministry.[38]

When Calvin placed doctrinal above moral requirements, it was with no thought of decrying sacrificial living. His whole dis-

---

[36] Beza sets forth clearly the view that doctrine is more important than life in his reply to Castellio's *De Hæreticis*.

[37] III, vi, 4.

[38] The certificate of dismissal which the Genevan ministers gave Castellio when he left to go to Basel makes the issue very clear. "In that office (the headship of the school) he so bore himself that we judged him worthy of the sacred ministry. That he was not admitted was not on account of any faults of life, nor any impious dogma regarding the chief points of our faith, but this one reason prevented which we have set forth." Herminjard, ix, 159.

ciplinary system was calculated to exalt and enforce righteousness; and though it was righteousness of an inflexible sort, it was tempered with a recognition of the duty of love and charity toward one's neighbor. He even recommended a measure of Christian liberty in things unessential (the *adiaphora*).[39] But he was very careful to say that neither charity nor liberty should carry one into the engulfing waters of heresy! With a frankness that leaves no room for doubt, he ranks liberty, charity and purity of faith in an ascending scale: "As our liberty should be subject to charity, so charity itself ought to be subservient to the purity of faith. It becomes us, indeed, to have regard to charity; but we must not offend God for the love of our neighbor."[40]

In this exaltation of purity of doctrine, Calvin was entirely sincere and entirely consistent. If it is man's supreme task to glorify God, and if God has given a clear and indisputable revelation of the truth in the Holy Scriptures, and if God sends his Spirit to enlighten the elect to read the Scriptures aright and acquiesce implicitly, and finally, if Calvin himself is of the enlightened and elect, then no alternative is left save to regard the doctrine of the *Institutes* as absolute truth and the supreme moral criterion.

So Calvin punished heretics. And Calvinists after him punished heretics. It has often been remarked that the New England Puritans were inconsistent in displaying intolerance toward those of other religious convictions when they themselves had fled from Europe as victims of religious persecution. But there was not the least inconsistency about it. It was ingrained in their theology to repudiate the idea that religion could be a matter of private interpretation; it was ingrained in their moral code that it was the duty of the elect to enforce purity of faith in the community by any disciplinary measures that might prove necessary. If men

---

39 Both Luther and Calvin have this doctrine of the *adiaphora*, but there are many more *adiaphora* in Luther's system than in Calvin's. Cf. Troeltsch, *Protestantism and Progress*, p. 82.

40 III, xix, 13. Calvin is not unmindful that Paul ranked charity above faith. But he explains this by saying that what Paul meant was merely that charity is serviceable to more people, since only the few can be justified by faith. Cf. *Opera*, i, 798.

suffered in the process, that was regrettable—but charity must be subservient to purity of faith. "We must not offend God for the love of our neighbor."

.   .   .   .

This exaltation of purity of faith above human sympathy suggests a further consequence of Calvinistic doctrine. The idea of God's towering greatness carried with it as a corollary the concept of man's littleness. Out of this came two tendencies almost diametrically opposed, yet both inherently Calvinistic. One is the obvious tendency to depose man. If the whole scheme of things exists not for man's benefit but for God's glory, it follows that the way any individual treats himself or his neighbor will be of minor consequence in comparison with the way he honors God. If the chief end of man is to glorify God and enjoy him forever, the first of Christ's two great commandments will overshadow the second, and the Decalogue the Sermon on the Mount. It is not by accident that so large a part of the doctrine and practice of Calvinism is built upon the Old Testament, for the exaltation of human personality which permeates the message of Jesus is foreign to its spirit. Calvin draws upon Paul for his conception of the atonement, but even this accentuates still further the gulf between man and God. A sovereign God does everything; undeserving man does nothing. A familiar Calvinistic hymn puts this characteristically:

> Alas! and did my Saviour bleed,
>   And did my Sov'reign die,
> Would He devote that sacred head
>   For such a worm as I?

It is not so bad to consider oneself a "worm"; there is a good deal of chastening and wholesome humility about such a concept. The energy now expended by theologians in trying to save God was unnecessary in a day when it was believed implicitly that God saved men. But however wholesome the awareness of one's own impotence, it has disastrous consequences when extended too literally to other "worms." It obscures the value of human personality, and the central teaching of Jesus sinks into the background. Exactly this thing happened in Calvinism, and herein lies an explanation of the severity and unfeeling piety of the Puritan temper.

.   .   .   .

Yet with this tendency to think lightly of man went another strain, less obvious on the surface, which was eventually to result in the exaltation of the individual man. On it the foundations of the Puritan spirit of political independence and economic individualism were laid.

Calvin, we have seen, rejected any sacramental or priestly medium of salvation. Each individual must travel his own way alone, save only as God sees fit to vouchsafe his mercy and grant salvation.[41] And God is no respecter of persons. Good works will not avail to purchase salvation for any—nor will money, or rank, or prestige, or power. Far from securing salvation through any such shallow channel as the purchase of indulgences or the saying of Masses, man is powerless before the will of an all-ordering deity. Even his money is a gift of God acquired through no merit of his. "Whatever a man possesses has fallen to his lot not by a fortuitous contingency, but by the distribution of the supreme Lord of all." [42] Position also is God's gift, not man's achievement. It behooves princes and lords, like common folk, to humble themselves before God. In the eyes of God, no external trappings will avail.

So the Calvinistic doctrine became a great leveller. We have noticed that Calvin refused to let François Favre and his rich and self-esteeming, but reprobate, family escape the penalty meted out for their offenses by the city of Geneva. This is wholly in keeping with his spirit and doctrine. Calvin and the Calvinists hated sham and self-glorification, for they believed profoundly that God's favor was not to be bought by any of the things which men call greatness. Calvin was not ready to say that all men are created free and equal; but he believed that all men are created equally un-

<hr>

[41] Weber, p. 94.   [42] II, viii, 45.

free, and out of this principle came reinforcement for the spirit of liberty.

.   .   .   .

In similar fashion, the autocracy of the Genevan state tended to suppress individual initiative, yet Calvin's system had in it the seeds of democratic action. Calvin believed firmly that citizens must obey without question the duly constituted authorities, for these authorities get their power from God. Magistrates rule as God's lieutenants. It says plainly in God's Holy Writ, "Be ye subject unto the higher powers." These higher powers, both civil and ecclesiastical—in Council and Consistory—by exercise of their authority in Geneva produced a regimentation of private life which has seldom been surpassed in stringency.

Yet Calvinism gave rise also to the spirit of independence, and fomented revolutions. We shall trace in a later chapter the historical processes by which it became, in theory and practice, the spiritual undergirding of resistance to tyranny. Suffice it to say at this point that Calvin believed not only that subjects must obey the higher powers, but that all men, rulers as common people, must obey the Higher Power from whom all human authority derives. Magistrates who disobey God thereby forfeit their right to govern; and lower magistrates by processes of constitutional resistance must depose the higher. It was not a long step, among Calvin's followers, to the conclusion that the overthrow of tyranny, if need be by force of arms, is the direct command of God. When the conviction is reached that the common man may defend his God-given rights against a godless ruler, the foundations of democracy are laid.

.   .   .   .

Calvinistic theology left another legacy which is still a vital issue. The clash between Fundamentalism and Modernism cuts through almost every Protestant denomination, but it appears in fullest vigor in the church which is the most direct lineal descendant of

Calvinism. There is a reason. It would be an over-simplification to say that the controversy which ejected Dr. Fosdick from the First Presbyterian Church of New York City in 1925 can all be traced to the work of Calvin in Geneva almost four centuries ago—but there is an intimate connection.

Calvin was a Fundamentalist,[43] and present day Fundamentalists who want historical as well as doctrinal and Biblical authority on their side are fully justified in claiming him. One finds Protestant Fundamentalism in its genesis—clear, direct, consistent—in the doctrine and practice of John Calvin.

But Calvin was not only a Fundamentalist: he was a keen thinker, a highly educated man, a scholar of towering intellectual capacity. He believed in education, and he set before his followers the requirement of both an educated ministry and an educated laity. He founded a university for the better education of the people and the training of young men for the ministry. He insisted that children be given free, compulsory education. He set the example for the high regard for education which led the Puritans to establish Harvard College in 1636, almost as soon as their feet had touched New England soil. He was the patron saint of New England Congregationalism, which produced Cotton Mather, Jonathan Edwards, and a host of other intellectual giants. And New England Congregationalism is now predominantly liberal in its theological outlook.

In Calvin's day, there was no particular difficulty in being both a Biblical authoritarian and at the same time a keen thinker with a trained mind. The spirit of modern science had not yet risen to trouble the waters of religious thought in any general way, and the principles of historical and Biblical criticism were not yet accepted by any except a few erratically independent and much-frowned-upon thinkers like Castellio and Servetus.

---

[43] The term is used here in its popular sense. In the sixteenth century the *fundamenta* were a weapon of liberalism, for the fundamentals were made as few as possible by liberal thinkers in order to lessen strife. Castellio and Acontius developed this type of thinking. Cf. Walter Köhler, "Geistesahnen des Johannes Acontius" in *Festgabe für Karl Müller* (Tübingen, 1922), pp. 198 ff.

But times were destined to change. Scientific and historical thought was bound to make headway. And as the church moved on into a changing world, the growing organism of religious thought found its living tissues confined by the fetters of a rigid authoritarianism. The fetters were not tight enough, as in the Catholic faith, to force its leaders and laity into conformity. Nor were they pliable enough to make way for a painless growth. Calvin had injected into the church two principles, temporarily but not ultimately compatible, which were destined in the years ahead to come into conflict. An authoritarian theology will not permanently lie down in peace with an educated ministry.

Calvinism is not the only factor which has contributed to the Fundamentalist-Modernist controversy. But it is a very potent factor, and its influence has spread into other folds not originally Calvinistic. Its effect appears clearly in a contrast of Presbyterianism with the largest non-Calvinistic Protestant denomination, the Methodist. The Methodist church has pursued its way comparatively untouched by the storms that have rent other denominations, and the difference is due in no slight measure to temperamental differences in the founders. Calvin was a theologian, with a theological system that was exact, precise, authoritarian. Wesley was a practical mystic, with a great evangelistic zeal and a theological attitude of "think and let think." The Presbyterian church has set a high standard of educational requirements for its ministry; the Methodist has stressed religious experience more than education and has opened its pulpit to almost every religiously-minded man who felt himself called to preach. The result is that the Presbyterian church has an educated ministry and theological controversy; while the Methodist has evangelistic zeal, a relatively less educated ministry and theological peace. Obviously, there are advantages and limitations on both sides!

.   .   .   .

The moral effect of the Calvinistic theology was to give rise to a set of paradoxes. Intense practical activity was joined with mystical self-forgetfulness; shrewd concern for success in this life with absorption in the next; zealous service to neighbor with equally zealous persecution for doctrinal aberrations; man's abasement with his exaltation; autocracy with democracy; conservatism with progress.

These paradoxes root in a fundamental inconsistency—the attempt to deny, and at the same time to affirm, human freedom. Each one follows consistently from its premises. In its development, each took on the color of the social environment and was molded by human impulse, yet never wholly lost contact with its intellectual foundations. Calvinistic doctrine, plus the logic of events, was predestined to be more fruitful than Calvin could foreknow.

CHAPTER V

THE CHIEF END OF MAN

Q. 1. *What is the chief end of man?*
A. Man's chief end is to glorify God, and to enjoy him forever.
Q. 2. *What rule hath God given to direct us how we may glorify
and enjoy him?*
A. The Word of God, which is contained in the Scriptures of the
Old and New Testaments, is the only rule to direct us how we may
glorify and enjoy him.

So runs the beginning of the Westminster Shorter Catechism.
This statement, formulated a century after Calvin's day, is the mani-
festo of Scottish and English Puritanism after Calvinism had taken
root and grown to power. It reflects the spirit of Calvin so accurately that it might well have come from his own pen.

It is difficult today to reconstruct the state of mind of one who
could be a great thinker and Christian leader, and could cause another to be burned at the stake for heresy. In an age which has
achieved some measure of tolerance, it is hard to appreciate the
value Calvin placed on doctrinal conformity. There is much in the
Calvinist's application of the doctrine of the chief end of man that
is stern to the point of cruelty. But it is to misread Calvin, and his
followers also, to see in it only sternness and cruelty. Calvin and
the Calvinists believed that man's chief end is to glorify God and
enjoy him forever because they had a great God—a God so far
transcending all human creatures that man could best find his own
joy and glory in exalting him.

This chapter will deal mainly with certain unlovely outgrowths
of the Calvinist's ideal. When one believes with his whole heart
that it is the chief end of man to glorify God, and that the Scriptures contain the only rule for the right performance of this chief

duty, and that *his own interpretation* of the Scriptures is the only true interpretation, then that person will not be very tolerant. He will view heresy as poisonous venom, and the heretic as a snake in the grass. He will punish blasphemy as a direct affront to the Most High. He will look with suspicion on any form of worship that appears to contradict the express command of the Most High, "Thou shalt have no other gods before me; thou shalt not make unto thee a graven image." This is what happened in Calvinism. Calvin and the Calvinists believed the three cardinal offenses against God to be idolatry, blasphemy and heresy. Of these we shall treat in this chapter. If the chief end of man be considered here largely in negative terms, this may be charged to the negatives of Calvin's doctrine and in turn to the older "Thou shalt nots" on which he built his system.

1. THE SIN OF IDOLATRY

The sin of idolatry loomed the larger in Calvin's thought for the reason that he was somewhat of an innovator.[1] In a sense, he rediscovered the second commandment, which had practically been buried out of sight for several preceding centuries. The medieval church approved image worship. It had been able to gloss over the prohibition against making graven images by the use of a form of the decalogue which combined the proscription of images with the worship of one God, the full number of commandments being kept by the division of the tenth into two parts.[2] The second commandment could thus be easily covered up, or dropped out. Luther adopted this form, and Lutheranism to this day has a decalogue which places the proscription of images parenthetically under the first commandment and divides the tenth. As late as 1548, Cranmer approved for use in the English churches a decalogue from which the second commandment was omitted.[3]

---

[1] Calvin was not the first to attack image worship. Iconoclasm had been practiced by Carlstadt, Zwingli and other Protestants before his time, and the introduction of the Reformation into Geneva had been accompanied by iconoclastic riots.

[2] C. H. Moehlman, *The Story of the Ten Commandments*, pp. 109, 110.

[3] The full text of the second commandment was restored to the Anglican Catechism in 1552. In 1563, the Heidelberg Catechism incorporated Calvin's reading.

Calvin went straight to the Scriptures, and found there what the medieval church had been leaving out. As early as the first edition of the *Institutes* in 1536 we find him saying:

That the law is divided into ten precepts, is beyond all controversy, being frequently established by the authority of God himself. The question, therefore, is not concerning the number of the precepts, but concerning the manner of dividing them. Those who divide them so as to assign three precepts to the first table, and leave the remaining seven to the second, expunge from the number the precept concerning images, or at least conceal it under the first; whereas it is undoubtedly delivered by the Lord as a distinct commandment. But the tenth, against coveting the property of our neighbor, they improperly divide into two. . . . Such a method of division was unknown in purer ages.[4]

The first two, Calvin says, forbid the toleration of any attitude, word or act which would detract from the pure worship of God. "The first foundation of righteousness is certainly the worship of God; and if this be destroyed, all the other branches of righteousness, like the parts of a disjointed and falling edifice, are torn asunder and scattered."[5] This being the case, God at the outset had to lay down, as a preface to the whole law, a provision to keep it from being abrogated by contempt. To "have no other gods before him" means to give him the sole preëminence. To this end he enjoins men to avoid all creature-worship, impiety, or superstition by which the glory of his deity might be obscured.[6] The second commandment adds explicitness to the first, and forbids us to profane his legitimate worship with carnal observances or superstitious rites. God commands us to flee from the "external idolatry" of representing him in visible form or paying religious adoration to images; he forbids us also to play the adulterer in our affections by giving to any creature the first place in our hearts

In 1566, the Roman church included the second commandment in its decalogue, and since then has authorized catechisms which include and others which omit it. The Council of Trent in 1563 sanctioned the veneration of images but warned against superstition and avarice in their use. Cf. Moehlman, 111 f.

[4] II, viii, 12.
[5] *Ibid.*, 11.
[6] *Ibid.*, 16.

which should be God's.[7]   When God calls himself a "jealous God" this means that he will brook no rival.   He has justly declared that he will avenge his majesty and glory upon those who transfer it to creatures or graven images, punishing transgressors to the third and fourth generation even as he shows mercy and goodness to the posterity of those who keep his law.[8]

.   .   .   .

This in brief, is Calvin's statement in the *Institutes*—all in very general terms.   But if one wants concreteness, there is plenty in Calvin's sermons!   Here "idolatry" means Catholicism; "superstitious rites" the saying of Masses, the use of incense and the veneration of relics; "graven images" the images of the saints.[9]   Calvin was blunt, and none too gracious, in denouncing and ridiculing all Roman practices which seemed to him to desecrate the pure worship of God.

Calvin's sermons and commentaries abound in condemnations of idolatry.   As the god Dagon fell before the ark of the Lord, so all idols must fall when God reveals his majesty through the preaching of the (Reformed) Gospel.[10]   It is in vain, he says, for the Papists to try to cover their iniquity by calling the objects they worship *images* rather than idols, for as God condemned the Jews for making images of Sicuth and Chion, so he forbids today all making of graven images.[11]

By the institution of the priesthood, Christ is robbed of his priestly dignity.   God promised that Christ should never have a successor but they make a million of them—and such people!   If they were angels of Paradise they would still have to be regarded as devils, but the Papists choose all the vermin of the world, all the riff-raff and rascals, and call them successors of our Lord Jesus

---

[7] *Ibid.*, 17, 18.

[8] *Ibid.*, 18-21.

[9] Cf. John Knox, "By Idolatry we understand, the Mass, Invocation of Saints, Adoration of Images and the keeping and retaining of the same: and all honouring of God not contained in his holy Word." *Book of Discpline*, ed. Laing, II, p. 188.

[10] *Opera*, xxix, 446. Homily on I Sam. 5: 1-6.

[11] *Opera*, xliii, 100. Lect. on Amos 5: 26.

Christ.[12] They make idols of the Virgin, and by giving her the office of advocate they further rob Christ of what was given him by the Father.[13] We should despise all crosses and mitres, all the flourishes of this world and the horns of the Pope by which he seeks to exalt himself up to God; and should look upon them as abominations full of rottenness and infection through which Satan, our mortal enemy, seeks to poison us.[14]

The Mass is as bad as the priests who preside over it. The promise which gives Christ's body to believers, under the symbol of bread, no more belongs to Masses than to Bacchanalia or Turkish feasts.[15] To bend the knee before a bit of bread is an idolatry no less iniquitous than was bending it before the Serpent.[16] "It is plain that the god whom the gesticulating priest keeps exhibiting whenever he turns round his altar is not brought down from heaven, but is of the kind extracted from a cook-shop!"[17] Since in the Mass Christ's body is traduced, his death mocked, and an execrable idol substituted for God, it ought to be called the table of demons rather than the table of the Lord.[18]

Calvin deals sharply with a practice common in his day, that of trying to be a Protestant at heart while attending Mass to escape persecution. Calvin was not the man to tolerate sham in any field, least of all in so holy a thing as the worship of God. To say that it is permitted to go to Mass if God be served in the heart is to admit a double heart. They serve idols in trying to please the enemies of God, and they value their lives above God's honor. It is not permitted to stamp two coins on one piece of gold or put two contrary seals on one public document, much less to try to deceive God or man by such duplicity. It is a great shame to pretend to serve God when one does not, "and a still greater shame

[12] *Opera*, l, 577. Ser. on Gal. 4: 1-4.
[13] *Opera*, xxix, 213. Ser. on Deut. 34: 1-6.
[14] *Opera*, l, 326. Ser. on Gal. 1: 8-9.
[15] "On Shunning the Unlawful Rites of the Ungodly," in *Calvin's Tracts* (Calvin Translation Society, Edinburgh, 1851), III, 385.
[16] *Ibid.*, 391.
[17] *Ibid.*, 385.
[18] *Ibid.*, 387.

that a mere worm of the earth should wish to take precedence of his Creator." [19]

Some say the idolatries of the heathen are forbidden, but not those of the Papists. No such extinction exists, Calvin says. [20] It is a general rule that "all human inventions which are set up to corrupt the simple purity of the Word of God . . . are real acts of sacrilege, in which Christians cannot participate without blaspheming God." [21] If some call this doctrine too severe and Calvin too strait-laced, this does not alter the fact of the case. "Let our soft-hearted folks now go and complain of me as too rigid. Whether I speak out or hold my tongue, we all continue to be bound by this law which God lays upon us." [22]

Some mean well, and are sincerely troubled. But if in their confusion they come to Calvin for advice, he will merely refer them to the general rule to flee all idolatry. To ask for more explicit direction would be like asking the preacher to cut out their gowns or sew their shoes after he has exhorted them to dress plainly. [23] God's word is unequivocal.

. . . .

One wishes, however, that Calvin himself had been a little more explicit about what should be done with such offenders. He was outspoken in his belief that persistent heresy merited the death penalty; he was far more guarded about Catholicism. Citing the authority of the seventeenth chapter of Deuteronomy, he says, "We have seen previously [24] that if a man or woman is found who has enticed others to pervert the service of God, he ought to die. Now here the Law is still more rigorous; that is to say, *that if an idolater is found in the midst of the people, whether man or woman, that*

---

[19] *Opera*, viii, 382. *Homily on Fleeing External Idolatry.*

[20] He admits elsewhere that there is a difference between the superstitions of the heathen and the Papists, but says that this is immaterial. *Opera*, xxvii, 292. Ser. on Deut. 14: 21-23.

[21] *Opera*, viii, 383.

[22] *Ibid.*, 384.

[23] *Ibid.*, 390.

[24] In the thirteenth chapter of Deuteronomy, Calvin's main authority for the use of the death penalty upon heretics.

ought to be a mortal and capital crime." [25] If this seem harsh, Calvin says, one must remember that a mortal creature is not to be placed before the living God. If a traitor is not to be pardoned, neither is an idolater.

Idolaters merit the death penalty. Catholics are idolaters. The natural conclusion of these premises is that Catholics merit the death penalty. Yet Calvin seems to have been very reluctant to complete the syllogism.

Though Calvin in scores of passages heaps ridicule or denunciation upon the Papists, I have been able to find only one in which he says that they ought to be put to death. In a letter to the Duke of Somerset, Protector of England during Edward VI's minority, he urges the rooting out of Roman abuses in that country in these words:

> There are two kinds of rebels who have risen against the King and the Estates of the Kingdom. The one is a fanatical sort of people who, under color of the Gospel, would put everything into confusion. The others are persons who persist in the superstitions of the Roman Antichrist. Both alike deserve to be repressed by the sword which is committed to you, since they not only attack the King but strive with God, who has placed him upon a royal throne.[26]

There is an intimation here that Calvin regards both Protestant heretics and Roman Catholics as sufficiently dangerous characters to make the death penalty justifiable. Yet even in this letter he drops the suggestion without developing it. He has much to say about the need of extirpating papal abuses, but only this brief word about extirpating the Papists themselves. Had Calvin really meant seriously to recommend the use of the death penalty, it is unthinkable that he would have been content to make the recommendation in so casual a fashion.[27]

[25] *Opera*, xxvii, 433 f. Ser. on Deut. 17: 2-7. Italics Calvin's.
[26] October 22, 1548. Bonnet, French ed., I, 276; English, II, 173.
[27] Lord Acton's interpretation (*History of Freedom*, p. 178), that Calvin desired to kill the Catholics but feared to say so, lest it bring persecution on the Protestants, seems to me quite unwarranted. Calvin was too outspoken in matters of conviction to justify the imputation of this motive.

Still more manifest evidence of his reluctance is the fact that he did not, in practice, attempt to employ the death penalty upon any Catholic. Servetus has no Catholic counterpart. Catholics were banished from Geneva, but there is nothing unique in this, since it occurred before Calvin's arrival and was a common practice. Aside from his insistence that the company of true believers be not polluted by the presence of Papists, Calvin's venom found expression in words rather than overt acts.

In a nature which usually drew conclusions with inexorable logic, this reluctance to advocate the killing of Catholic idolaters is significant. It indicates that Calvin was not, by his own volition, a persecutor, and that considerations of human charity sometimes outweighed legalism. It indicates, too, that in Calvin's eyes apostasy was worse than papistry; the virus of Protestant heresy a more deadly poison than that of Roman error. Of this we shall say more later.

2. RELICS

Denunciation was not Calvin's only weapon against the "superstitions and idolatries" of his day. He knew how to use a laugh to good effect. In speaking of God, he says, we must be reverent, but when it is a matter of the superstitions and follies in which the world has been so long entangled, one can only roar.[28] Upon occasion, Calvin himself could roar with rage or with mirth. His *Inventory of Relics*[29] gives a list of objects which received the adoration of pious Catholics, with many sly digs at the credulity with which they were venerated.

The Papists, he says, have the blood of Christ in a hundred places, liquid, coagulated, or mixed with water. They not only have the vessels in which he turned water to wine, but the wine itself. This also is found in many places, and may be drunk each year, with no diminution of quantity, by those who bring an offering. They have the shoes of Christ, though the apostles never

---

[28] *Opera*, ix, 866.
[29] *Opera*, vi, 409-452. Its full title is, "An Admonition, showing the advantages which Christendom might derive from an Inventory of Relics."

heard of them; and the table of the Last Supper, though the Last Supper was in a hired room and the table was left behind. They have two linen towels with which Jesus washed the disciples' feet, one of them bearing the imprint of Judas' foot. They have the bread on which the five thousand were fed, also the piece of broiled fish which Peter offered Jesus after the resurrection. "It must have been wondrously well salted," Calvin observes, "if it has kept for such a long series of ages." They formerly had St. Peter's brain, but it turned out upon examination to be pumice-stone.

There are enough pieces of the true cross to make a ship-load. Every little town has one, though some confess that they did not get theirs from Palestine, for it was dropped by an angel. The crown of thorns must have been planted again to grow twigs for relics, and the seamless robe has been many times divided. The spear with which the soldier pierced Jesus' side is in four different places. Six cities have the napkin with which St. Veronica wiped Jesus' face, and many others have fragments, though there is no mention of St. Veronica in the Bible. One napkin must have produced as many others as a hen does chickens!

There are crucifixes which grow beards, and many which have spoken. Tears, both natural and miraculous, also flow from crucifixes. They could not retain Jesus' natural body, but they have his hair and teeth, and two præpuces. The impression of our Lord's body on the linen grave-clothes has been preserved, likewise his foot-prints after the resurrection. Even the mark left by his hips on a stone at Rheims when he turned mason to help build that church is shown to the credulous.

Though the body of the Virgin ascended to heaven, her hair has been preserved, and they have enough of her milk so that if she had been a cow she could not have given so much in her whole life. Had she been of the race of giants, she would not have had a shirt so long as the one they possess, while they have shoes belonging to St. Joseph which would fit only a boy or a dwarf. It is strange, Calvin observes parenthetically, that it never occurred to them to preserve the parings of her nails. To speak of relics of an angel would seem a jest, did they not have the dagger and shield of the Virgin's attendant, the archangel Michael, the dagger resembling a boy's toy and the shield the brass circles on a horse's harness.

As for John the Baptist, ancient history says that his body was burned except the head, yet different shrines claim so many parts of it that he must have been a monster, unless the Papists are impostors. His ashes, supposed to have been scattered by the winds, have been caught and preserved at various places, while six churches have the finger with which he pointed to Christ.

Every apostle must have had four bodies, if one may judge from the number of fragments. There are enough pieces of Lazarus to make three bodies, though Magdalene, being a woman and necessarily inferior, has only two. St. Anne has two bodies, three hands, and an extra arm. Stephen's body must have been dissected, for his bones are in more than two hundred places. As for the lesser saints, there are a hundred wagon loads, and more, of their bones scattered about Europe. These are so mixed that one who worships before them runs the risk of worshipping the bones of a thief, a dog, or an ass, while the Virgin's ring may be that of a strumpet.

These are but a few of the items Calvin cites. In an enumeration which fills forty-three pages of the *Opera,* he ridicules the idolatry and superstition of the Roman church, and warns the followers of the true faith to fall into no such error.

3. FOOD AND SEASONS

Along with the veneration of images and relics, Calvin placed the observance of special foods and special days as practices instituted by the wiles of Satan to draw men from the true faith. Christianity, he says, does not hinge upon the observance or nonobservance of a day, or upon the eating of pork or mutton. In such quibbles "Satan often finds little subtleties to alienate us from the Gospel without our knowing it." [30] Calvin is for Christian

30 *Opera,* l, 276. Ser. on Gal. 1: 1-5.

liberty, but for a liberty tempered with restraint. However, like most reformers, he was more zealous for the exercise of liberty in matters which concerned his opponents' observances than his own. He could denounce the Catholics for making an issue over eating meat on Friday or observing saints' days, but he stood rock-ribbed upon the necessity of making everybody in Geneva attend the Protestant church service.

His discussion of Christian liberty in the *Institutes* contains a passage which analyzes with remarkable keenness the psychological effect of quibbling over non-essentials as a matter of religious scruple. It is aimed, of course, at Catholicism. Yet it gives a true picture of what Calvinism itself fell into in the hands of his Puritan followers. For this reason it is worth quoting almost in full.

We are bound by no obligation before God respecting external things, which in themselves are indifferent. . . . And the knowledge of this liberty also is very necessary for us; for without it we shall have no tranquillity of conscience, nor will there be any end of superstitions. Many in the present age think it a folly to raise any dispute concerning the free use of meats, of days, and of habits, and similar subjects, considering these things as frivolous and nugatory; but they are of greater importance than is generally believed. For when the conscience has once fallen into the snare, it enters a long and inextricable labyrinth, from which it is afterwards difficult to escape.

If a man begin to doubt the lawfulness of using flax in sheets, shirts, handkerchiefs, napkins and table cloths, neither will he be certain respecting hemp, and at last he will doubt the lawfulness of using tow; for he will consider with himself whether he cannot eat without table cloths or napkins, whether he cannot do without handkerchiefs. If any one imagine delicate food to be unlawful, he will ere long have no tranquillity before God in eating brown bread and common viands, while he remembers that he might support his body with meat of a quality still inferior. If he hesitate respecting good wine, he will afterwards be unable with any peace of conscience to drink the most vapid. . . .

In short, he will come to think it criminal to step on a twig that lies across his path. For this is the commencement of no trivial controversy; but the dispute is whether the use of certain things be agreeable to God, whose will ought to guide all our resolutions and all our actions. The necessary consequence is, that some are hurried by despair into a vortex of confusion, from which they see no way of escape; and some, despising God, and casting off all fear of him, make a way of ruin for themselves.[31]

There is no asceticism here. Neither the rigidity of Puritan morals in "things indifferent," nor the comfort-denying austerity of the Puritan menage, were in the intention of the founder of Calvinism. A "vortex of confusion" might have been averted by following his advice. The trouble lay in the lack of a criterion by which to tell what constitutes the "things indifferent." Calvin simply assumed that his judgment was the only true judgment—and paved the way for the undoing of his teaching.

4. BLASPHEMY

Calvin says a great deal in general, and not very much in particular, about the sin of blasphemy. His treatment of the third commandment in the *Institutes* contains a straightforward, rather brief, statement of the scope of the injunction, then goes off into a refutation of the position of the Anabaptists in condemning all oaths. Three things, he says, are involved in the commandment: first, to show a fitting reverence in every thought and word that refers to God; second, to abstain from abusing the holy word and mysteries of God for avarice, ambition, or amusement; third, to refrain from injuring God's works by obloquy or detraction. To "sanctify" the name of God is to praise God for his wisdom, justice and goodness. It is forbidden to utter the holy name lightly or rashly—and still more to "make it subservient to the superstitions of necromancy, to horrible imprecations, to unlawful exorcisms, and to other impious incantations." [32] Taking God's name in vain is primarily a sin against God, hence it appears in the first table, but when joined with perjury it becomes also a sin against one's neighbor. The Anabaptists are

---

[31] III, xix, 7. To make the meaning clearer, I have stated in paragraph form what the original gives as a continuous passage. The same has been done in other long quotations.
[32] II, viii, 22.

wrong to take literally Christ's word to "swear not at all," for Jesus could not have meant to set aside what the Father elsewhere expressly enjoins.[33]

Calvin's interpretation is ethical as well as theological, and not very startling. He shows breadth of judgment in recognizing that blasphemy is a matter of thought as well as word, and that the commandment relates not merely to ordinary profanity but to a misuse of holy things. Whatever narrow element Calvin introduced came in his application of the injunction rather than in his theory.

However, in his application, he spoke in no gentle tones. While he did not directly recommend the use of the death penalty for blasphemy, he defended its use among the Jews, and he had no doubt of the duty of the state to mete out appropriate punishment. Not only must preachers preach against it; civil officers must bestir themselves. "Judges and magistrates ought not to slacken the rein when God is mocked, his name put in shame, his religion fouled under foot. We have seen heretofore that blasphemies were more grievously punished than murder." [34] Citing the injunction of Leviticus 24:16 for the stoning of the offender, he points out that this was not the people's own doings, but the will of Heaven.[35]

Calvin can think of plenty of uncomplimentary things to say about Geneva's blasphemers—wretches who are trying to bury the judgments of God and would like to have Geneva cast into the abyss. He remarks parenthetically that everybody knows who they are and there is no need to mention names—an adroit dig at Servetus, perhaps, and Calvin's Libertine opponents.[36] The rest must arouse themselves or be worse than brute beasts. If God lifts a heavy hand, it is to wake up those that are asleep.[37]

. . . .

[33] II, viii, 26.
[34] *Opera*, xxviii, 57. Ser. on Deut. 22:25-30.
[35] *Opera*, xxv, 212. Comm. on Lev. 24:13.
[36] Some of Calvin's friends, particularly Bullinger and Musculus, thought that he should have defended the execution of Servetus on the ground of blasphemy rather than heresy.
[37] *Opera*, xxxiv, 214. Ser. on Job 21:1-6

The most interesting evidence of Calvin's opinion and that of his Genevan contemporaries about the seriousness of blasphemy is found in the ordinances which relate to this offense. The records contain a double set of documents, the legislation Calvin proposed and that which the Council adopted.[38] In almost every instance the Council—perhaps fearing they might themselves get caught in the clutches of the law—toned down the penalties he wished imposed.

Punishments were graded according to the seriousness of the offense, ranging in an ascending scale from "frivolous oaths" through plain "blasphemy" to "defying and renouncing God."

For *frivolous oaths,* Calvin prescribed kissing the earth for the first offense; in case of refusal, being put in prison a day and a night on bread and water. If the offender laughed or refused to desist, three days' imprisonment. The Council's provisions are more explicit. One is not permitted to "swear lightly by the name of God" under penalty of:

For the first offense, to kiss the earth and cry to God for mercy.
For the second offense, to kiss the earth again on one's knees, crying to God for mercy, and pay ten sous.
For the third offense, to pay sixty sous and be put in prison a day and a night on bread and water.
For the fourth offense, the preceding penalty and exile from the city for three months.

For *blasphemies* (not specifically defined, but apparently a stage more serious than the preceding), Calvin and the Council agreed on the fitting penalty, except that Calvin wanted larger fines and wanted the kissing of the earth done at the door of the church nearest the scene of the offense. The provisions as adopted specify:

For the first offense, to be put in prison a day and a night on bread and water, to kiss the earth on one's knees asking God for mercy, and pay ten sous.
For the second offense, kissing the earth as before, two days in prison, and twenty sous.

[38] *Opera,* xa, pp. 59-63.

For the third offense, three days and sixty sous, also kissing the earth with head bared and asking for mercy in the place where the offense was committed.

For the fourth offense, the preceding penalty with exile from the city for six months.

For *defying and renouncing God,* there is a marked difference between Calvin's opinion and the Council's. Calvin thought such an offender ought to be put in the stocks for three hours; be put in prison on bread and water till the next Sunday; and then be led to the door of the church to ask pardon of God, torch in hand.[39] This for the first offense: for the second, to be branded and banished from the city. The Council, whether from greater liberality or greater fear of getting ensnared, said nothing of public humiliation at the church or of branding. Their edict reads like those for the less serious types, though with more days in prison and larger fines. The kissing of the earth is to be done in the presence of the officers of justice. Only at the third offense do the stocks appear, when the guilty party is to have three days in prison and three hours in the stocks, or banishment for one year from the city, at the discretion of the magistrates.

Other provisions made the enforcement of the penalties more certain. If one rebelled, or made fun of the penalty, he might be retaken as a rebel against God and justice and punished with a double penalty, according to the exigencies of the case. If anyone *overheard another* swear, blaspheme, or deny or renounce God, he was obligated to admonish the offender and report the case, under pain of being fined ten sous. Calvin, with the characteristic eagerness of the Calvinistic conscience to assume responsibility for others' sins, wanted the penalty for failure to admonish and report to be the same as for the offense itself.

Apparently swearing was more common in taverns then elsewhere, for inn-keepers were expressly forbidden to permit it. If they heard any, they must report to justice under penalty of sixty sous fine and a day's imprisonment for each time. Yet

[39] Cf. the penalty imposed on Pierre Ameaux, *supra,* p. 33.

apparently not many such reports were given. One suspects that they were sometimes obliged to close their ears or lose good customers.

The records also give the legislation enacted against blasphemy in the surrounding villages.[40] This is similar, and blasphemy is here defined as "swearing by the body or blood of our Lord, or similarly." To renouncing God is added the offense of renouncing one's baptism, for no sharp line was drawn between the honor due to God and to the Reformed faith. The use of imprisonment and the stocks is supplemented by an ominous provision for "more severe corporal punishment at the discretion of the *messieurs.*"

Of all the anti-sacrilege regulations, the quaintest is one which makes it an offense to go to church to pray at any save the appointed time of worship. After specifying the hours at which the churches shall be open for service the provision adds:

> The churches shall be closed for the rest of the time, in order that no one may, out of superstition, enter outside of the hour [of service], and if anyone is found making some particular devotion within or near there, he shall be admonished. If he be found unwilling to correct this superstition, he shall be punished.[41]

This is stamping out Catholicism with a vengeance—to make it a punishable offense even to go to church to pray except with the congregation! The Calvinists were great sticklers for doing things systematically. One wonders whether the Lord would have been as much offended as the Genevans at a prayer uttered out of season.

5. HERESY

In close proximity to the ordinance last cited there stands another which reads:

> If any one contradicts the Word of God, he shall be sent before the Consistory to be reprimanded, or before the Council to receive punishment, according to the exigencies of the case.[42]

40 *Opera,* xa, 55.
41 *Ibid.*
42 *Ibid.,* 56.

This sounds simple and trivial. There is no mention here of fines or imprisonment, of kissing the earth or banishment. But "punishment according to the exigencies of the case" was a phrase weighted with much meaning. With such latitude, a crime could be committed in the name of religion which will forever stain the annals of Geneva.

The problem of heresy, or conversely of religious liberty, is much too big to be treated with any adequacy in this brief survey.[43] That it loomed large in the history of Calvinism is obvious. We have already noticed the main outlines of the process which brought Servetus to the stake. This is paralleled by the execution of the Quakers who were hanged for heresy on Boston Common. Only a faith with iron in it, and a distorted sense of the will of God, could lead to such a consummation.

Men do not persecute very often because they love to see others suffer.[44] Only the sadist does that, and sadism is a form of mental abnormality which fortunately is rare. It takes either callous indifference or a strong sense of duty to nerve one to lead another to the stake or gallows. The normal individual will willingly die, or kill, only for a great cause.

Such a great cause is the glory of God. When one is convinced that God's glory transcends all earthly considerations, and when one is also convinced that God's glory is being fouled in the dust and men's minds poisoned by false doctrine, one can bring himself to kill for God. As national loyalty leads one both to endanger his own life and to take that of another "for king and country," so religious loyalty will lead a person convinced of the greatness of the cause and the futility of other means of remedy to use force and even to take life to uphold God's honor. To this motive is added the duty to protect one's brother. When wolves are about to devour the sheep, it is not only the most effective, but the kindest,

---

[43] Nikolaus Paulus, *Protestantismus und Toleranz im 16. Jahrhundert* (Freiburg im Breisgau, 1911), pp. 228-275, contains a valuable analysis of the Calvinistic attitude toward heresy.

[44] For the summary of Calvin's theory of persecution which follows, the author owes much to an unpublished manuscript by Professor Roland H. Bainton of Yale University.

policy to kill the wolves and save the sheep. When a serpent is poisoning men with venom, it would be false charity to take pity on the serpent and let men die.

This, in brief, is the kind of logic Calvin used. There is no reason to doubt that he was perfectly sincere, or meant to be when he said he felt no personal resentment toward Servetus. He would have treated any one else—even his nearest friend or kinsman—in the same way, if he had thought him guilty of persistently dishonoring God and ruining men's souls. God's glory must take precedence over every human affection.

The thirteenth chapter of Deuteronomy is Calvin's justification for much of his theory of the duty of exterminating heretics. Here in defense of the stoning of false prophets he observes:

We ought to trample under foot every affection of nature when it is a question of his honor. The father should not spare his son, the brother the brother, nor the husband his own wife. If he has some friend who is as dear to him as his own life, let him put him to death. . . . If we are not to put the cart before the ox, we must begin with God. . . . If then a husband loves his wife without regard for God, he is worthy to be classed among the brute beasts.[45]

To dishonor God is the worst crime any one can commit, and God is dishonored by false doctrine.[46]

If we rightly consider what it is to speak falsehood in the name of Jehovah, it will certainly appear to us to be more detestable than to kill an innocent man, or to poison a guest, or to lay violent hands on one's own father, or to plunder a stranger. Whatever crimes can be thought of do not come up to this; that is, when God himself is involved in such dishonor as to be made an abettor of falsehood. What, indeed, can more peculiarly belong to God than His own truth? . . . Now to corrupt pure doctrine, is it not the same as if to put the devil in God's place? [47]

Calvin never tires of pointing out that the heretic's sin against God is a worse crime than other offenses which get their punish-

[45] *Opera*, xxvii, 251. Ser. on Deut. 13: 6-11.
[46] *Opera*, xxiv, 360. First Precept on Deut. 13: 6.
[47] *Opera*, xliv, 348. Comm. on Zech. 13: 3.

ment by law. For robbery one gets hanged; shall he go scot-free if he robs God of his honor?[48] If a city suffers the least damage, reparations are demanded; shall God's honor be injured with impunity?[49] When a prince is injured, even by being spoken against, no one objects to the punishment of the offender; is God less than earthly princes? "If a revolutionary stirs up insurrection and tries to move the people to sedition, off goes his head and no one protests. Why? Because it is necessary to conserve the state and the police. Yet here is God who has sovereign empire, and a worm of the earth rises against him and endeavors to seize his honor, abase his empire and superiority, and it is a matter of indifference."[50] To fail to punish such offenses is to affront God and give support to Satan.

Calvin's doctrine of the absolute authority of Scripture is the source of much of his intolerance, for he believed with all the ardor of his soul that anything which contradicted Scripture was heresy. Vain curiosity and presumptuous pride, he says, have been the ruin of many, and have made them set up their own views in place of the Word of God. "Some have attempted to mix the Koran with the Bible, the dreams of the pagans and the superstitions of the Papists with the purity of the Gospel, and cull out the best. . . . But our Saviour will not so let men trust their own powers."[51] It is futile to try to substitute conscience for the authority of Scripture, for before conscience can be trusted, it must itself be brought into harmony with the word of God.[52] To say that heretics need not be punished because each may interpret Scripture according to his own judgment is to open the door to every kind of slippery practice and undermine the power of the Christian faith.[53]

---

[48] *Opera*, xxvii, 255. Ser. on Deut. 13:6-11.
[49] *Opera*, liii, 142. Ser. on I Tim. 2:1-2.
[50] *Opera*, xxvii, 244. Ser. on Deut. 13:2-5.
[51] *Opera*, xxvii, 233. Ser. on Deut. 13:1-3.
[52] Cf. Beza, *De Hæreticis*, 94.
[53] It is unnecessary to suggest that such reasoning is by no means antiquated. The difference between the present day and Calvin's is not so much in point of view as in consistency in carrying the point of view to its consequences. Servetus was burned at the stake; heretic preachers and professors today get "fired."

Calvin found no lack of Biblical justification for ruthlessness in stamping out the enemies of God. The Old Testament gave him plenty of such instances. Is it not recorded in God's Word, he asks, that God sometimes ordered whole cities to be utterly destroyed, and all the inhabitants thereof? But what of it? They were damned already. The little children might seem to be innocent; but by the judgment of God, all from greatest to least were under condemnation. Predestination joins hands with Old Testament ethics to make Calvin say, with rather startling confidence, of the children slain in the razing of an impious city, "We may rest assured that God would never have suffered any infants to be slain except those who were already damned and predestined for eternal death." [54]

.   .   .   .

To be a heretic was not merely to hold doctrine contrary to the (Calvinistically interpreted) Word of God; it was to be guilty of a lapse from the truth. Jews and Turks were not heretics, for they never had had the light. It is significant that the Protestant persecutors of Calvin's day left the Jews and Turks almost wholly undisturbed, and showed their disapproval even of the Catholics much more by word than action. The Catholics might be superstitious, and were under condemnation as idolaters, but they held to the fundamentals. It was heretic Protestants, such as Servetus and the Anabaptists in Europe and the Quakers in New England, that must die for the purging of the Church.

This tendency to show greatest severity toward heretics among the Protestant sectaries has several explanations. It was doubtless due in part to the fact that possessors of a Calvinistic conscience are prone to disturb the members of their own family more than they annoy the neighbors, simply because they feel a greater responsibility for their souls' welfare. It was due in part also to an environmental factor, for the Calvinists did not, to any great extent, live

[54] Opera, xxiv, 363. First Precept on Deut. 13:15. Professor Bainton makes this comment, "Calvin scarcely yields the palm to Arnold Amalric, the papal legate, who when there was doubt as to how to distinguish the Catholics and the Cathari, exclaimed, 'Kill them all. God will know which are his.'"

in close proximity to Jews, Turks or Catholics, and so felt less necessity for exterminating them. It was due, furthermore, to an intellectual concept of the nature of heresy. While all Christians were thought responsible in a general way for bringing light to those in darkness, the darkness of those who had never seen was looked upon as a misfortune, that of those who had seen and turned away, a sin.

Vigorous as was Calvin's condemnation of heresy, he never advocated the wholesale slaughter of heretics. He believed that for heresy to merit the death penalty, the lapse must be an obstinate and serious one. More broad-minded than many of his successors,[55] he recognized three grades of error—that which could be pardoned with a reprimand, that to be mildly punished, and that to be exterminated by death. A slight superstition, he said, might be corrected with patience; but when religion is shaken from the foundations then one must have recourse to the extreme remedy.[56] This is why Calvin took such pains to show that Servetus had been obdurate. His persistent refusal to recant seemed to Calvin to stamp him as an obstinate, stiff-necked heretic, defying God to the last and giving no evidence of repentance. Though Servetus prayed for his persecutors on the way to his execution while Farel belabored him for not repenting, and died calling on the Son of the eternal God, this to Calvin was evidence of obstinacy rather than martyrdom. As Calvin saw the incident:

At his death he showed a brute-like stupidity whereby one could see that he took nothing in religion seriously. . . . Although he gave no sign of repentance, neither did he say a word in defense of his doctrine. . . . He had no reason to fear that his tongue would be cut out. Why could he not state briefly why he obstinately refused to call on the eternal Son of God? Who will call this the death of a martyr? [57]

One is prompted to wonder why, if God is really the all-determining arbiter of human destiny Calvin thought him to be, the vindication of his honor might not safely be left in his own hands

---

[55] Beza in his *De Hæreticis* is less liberal.
[56] *Opera*, viii, 477. *Refutatio Errorum Michaelis Serveti.*
[57] *Ibid.*, 498 f. Cf. *supra*, p. 44.

without so much human intervention. But in Calvin's thought, to neglect to smite God's enemies would be to shirk a manifest duty laid upon the elect as God's lieutenants. "We are the vindicators of God against the impious." [58] Calvin's theory of persecution is implicit in the conviction that because God's will is inviolable, the elect must be his instruments to crush apostasy and defeat the wiles of Satan.

. . . .

Such is Calvin's view of heresy as an offense against God. But he believed it also to be an offense against man, and this reinforced the severity of his condemnation. The heretic who spreads the virus of false doctrine imperils the immortal soul of his brother— a crime infinitely worse than to injure his transitory body. Heresy is like an insidious disease—to be eradicated, if need be, by strong medicine or the surgeon's knife. "The mockers who would suffer all false doctrines and let any one disgorge what he likes are not only traitors to God but enemies of the human race. They would bring poor souls to perdition and ruin, and are worse than murderers." [59] Here again the heretic is more dangerous than the Jew or Turk, for the latter are open enemies while the heretic works subtly to corrupt the souls of his fellow-Christians. God will let loose his wrath upon the community that tolerates such contagion.

Though the facts did not always substantiate the charge, Calvin and his contemporaries believed that heresy would loosen the bonds of morality. We noted that an attempt was made in the trial of Servetus to prove him guilty of moral laxity, but this had to be dropped for lack of evidence. The connection between free-thinking and free-living in the Libertines was cited as evidence of the insidious effects of false views about God, the devil, and the soul. [60] The Anabaptists were freely anathematized with charges of communism, polygamy, free love, anarchy and treason. [61]

To justify or shield the sinner was to participate in the sin.

---

58 *Ibid.*, 362. First Precept on Deut. 13: 12.
59 *Opera*, xxvii, 245. Ser. on Deut. 13: 2-5.
60 *Opera*, vii, 153-248. *Contre la Secte des Libertins.*
61 *Opera*, vii, 53-142. *Contre les Anabaptistes.*

"Any one who objects to the punishment of heretics and blasphemers," Calvin says, "subjects himself knowingly and willingly to the like condemnation of blasphemy." [62] This was a dart in the direction of Castellio, whose *De Hæreticis* had criticized Calvin sharply for his part in the Servetus affair. Even more bluntly he remarks, "That they may be free to vomit their virus they plead for toleration and deny that heresy and blasphemy should be punished. Of such is that dog Castellio." [63]

6. THE CALVINISTIC THEORY OF PERSECUTION

If heresy is an offense against society, it follows that the strong arm of the law must be laid upon the offender for society's protection. To repress heresy is to protect the flock from the ravages of a wild beast. "Christ left his disciples as sheep in the midst of wolves. . . . Christ desires us to imitate his own meekness, but this is no reason why the magistrates should not protect the safety and tranquillity of the church. To neglect this is the deepest perfidy and cruelty." [64] It is the duty of pastors to gather the sheep into the fold and keep them there as best they can, "but if wolves and robbers come, they must cry, Wolf! Wolf!" [65]

Such is the doctrine that cost Castellio his position and brought Servetus to his death. It is the doctrine that caused the banishment from Massachusetts of Roger Williams and Anne Hutchinson. It is the doctrine that caused Quakers in the Puritan colonies to be whipped at the cart's tail, imprisoned, branded, banished, hanged.[66] In its major features, it is the doctrine that caused Europe to run red with the blood of martyrs, Protestant and Catholic. It does not excuse Calvin that he was no less a persecutor than others of his day—much less a persecutor, in fact, than Catharine

---

[62] *Opera*, viii, 476. *Refutatio Errorum Michaelis Serveti.*
[63] *Opera*, xl, 649. Lecture on Daniel 4: 1-3.
[64] *Opera*, xxiv, 357. First Precept on Deut. 13: 5.
[65] *Opera*, xxvii, 244. Ser. on Deut. 13: 2-5.
[66] "So far [to 1660], in the Puritan colonies, mainly in Massachusetts, over forty had been whipped, sixty-four imprisoned, over forty banished, one branded, three had had their ears cut off, five had had the right of appeal to England denied them, four had been put to death, while many others had suffered in diverse ways." James Truslow Adams, *The Founding of New England*, p. 272.

de' Medici or the Duke of Alva, whose victims were numbered by the thousands. To cause the death of one was to persecute too much. Calvin persecuted—but it was no mad frenzy that led him to it.

Calvin's doctrine of persecution was the coolly reasoned product of a theology which combined God's sovereignty, man's littleness, Biblical literalism, and Hebraic ethics. When God's glory must be upheld at any cost, it is not for a mere "worm of the earth" to raise an obstacle. When man is believed to be so inconsequential and so sunk in sin that he can be thought of as a worm, the natural restraints of human sympathy lose their hold. When many an example of the slaughter of God's enemies can be cited from an inerrant Bible, God's follower feels obligated to act as God's lieutenant to stamp out unbelief. When one's whole outlook on life is tinctured with the spirit of Moses rather than Christ, there is no mourning at the death of Pharaoh's cohorts. Lacking any one of these dominant beliefs, Calvin and the Calvinists could not have persecuted.

The doctrine of persecution was an outgrowth, too, of a factor which lay not in the theology, but in the temperament, of Calvin and his Puritan successors. This was the combination of an overwhelming sense of duty with the almost complete inability to see another's point of view. God's will *must* be done; God has revealed his will *to me*. Had Calvin and the Calvinists lacked either the Puritan conscience or the Puritan self-assurance, not even their theology could have made them persecute. But they had both the theology and the temperament, and the outcome was predestined.

CHAPTER VI

GOD, THE DEVIL, AND THE SABBATH

In the previous chapter we observed how Calvin and the Calvinists tried to glorify God by suppressing idolatry, blasphemy and heresy. We shall now look at two other aspects of the Calvinistic conscience; the fear of the devil—particularly that phase of the power of the devil displayed in witchcraft, and the imperative obligation to preserve the sanctity of the sabbath. The Puritan's horror both of magic arts and of sabbath-breaking root back in Calvin's teaching; yet in both, Calvin himself was more tolerant than his Puritan successors. He was austere enough, but his austerity was tempered with much shrewd sense, and even with magnanimity of a sort. The frenzy of the witchcraft persecutions and the silly literalism of the Puritan sabbath regulations were later developments. If Calvin was responsible for these excesses, it was only as any leader is responsible when he utters a principle that his less capable subordinates carry out of bounds.

I. MAN'S OLDEST ENEMY

The devil, to Calvin, was a very real person. Like Adam, he was so important that Calvin could not have got along without him. Again like Adam, he is responsible for the plight man finds himself in. Such subtle questions as where he came from, or why an all-powerful God should permit such a rival, did not trouble Calvin's thought. His was a theological, not a metaphysical, mind.

It is unnecessary to bore the reader with a rehearsal of all that Calvin has to say about Satan. There is much repetition. The central theme of all his observations is that Satan is a wily creature speaking smooth words and putting on an attractive front to catch men unawares and draw them into sin. To go after idols, superstitions, and heresies is to sacrifice to the devil and not to God. There is no middle ground at all between God and the devil—so Calvin asserts flatly. This tendency to sharp cleavage between good and evil characterizes much of Calvin's thought, and is responsible in large measure for Calvinism's lack of mercy for the sinner.

2. MAGIC ARTS

Calvin accepted the current notion of the existence of witches who had commerce with the devil. There was never in Geneva any such wholesale execution of witches as took place in Salem a century and a half later; but at the time of the panic over the plague, witches were put to death with his approval, as conjurers of disease.[1] This raises the question as to whether the Salem witch-exterminators could look to Calvin for authority.

Calvin said very little about witchcraft as such, and never prescribed the death penalty for witches, though he uttered many warnings against falling prey to the wiles of the devil in the form of magic arts. He was very sure that it is against God's will to have commerce with the devil, either to seek illicit knowledge or to try to communicate with the spirits of the dead; but his writings contain no definite statement of the appropriate penalty for such offenses.

This is probably due in part to the fact that it was not a very acute problem in Geneva. The alleged plague-spreaders were put to death for causing the death of others, and with credence granted to belief in the power of witches—a belief well-nigh universally held in that day—it was natural that they should receive capital punishment as murderers. However, it is significant that the records show no evidence of executing witches for minor offenses, and Calvin's reticence is itself an indication that he did not think the sin of witchcraft necessitated such a penalty. Heresy was clearly a sin to be extirpated root and branch; magic arts were offenses to be preached against.

[1] *Supra,* p. 30.

The kind of magic art which Calvin arraigns most sharply is that which tries to penetrate hidden mysteries and find out what it is not for man to know. Fortune-telling and spiritualism come in for more denunciation than witchcraft. Men have a natural curiosity, Calvin says. This got Adam into trouble, and men should learn from his example. Instead, they keep on trying to be like the gods and find out everything. Our nature is corrupted by two evils; an immoderate desire to know and the use of forbidden means. The light of intelligence is a singular gift of God, and we should be content to acknowledge our ignorance and ask God for needed light instead of having recourse to Satan. "From these sources, from a foolish curiosity and a licentious boldness, flowed all the superstition and error that has come into the world. So God dealt with these pests by forbidding magic arts. . . . The best kind of knowledge is sobriety, to be satisfied to know only what is expedient." [2]

But while God forbids all such superstitious practices as the work of Pharaoh's magicians or the Chaldean sooth-sayers, he gives to some of his chosen servants—Daniel, for example, the gift of divination. *Divination* itself means to get knowledge by divine aid—the more shame to those who seek it from the devil.[3] Most of our dreams have natural causes, such as our daily thoughts, the state of the body, too much eating or drinking, etc. But some dreams are under divine regulation, such as Nebuchadnezzar's and Calpurnia's.[4] Similarly, there may be something in astrology, but the seed of the father and mother is a hundred times more important than the stars in forming the traits of a child.[5] Such conjuration is not to be mistaken for true learning.

Calvin pays his respects to spiritualism in his observations on Saul's visit to the witch of Endor. In calling up Samuel from

---

[2] *Opera,* xxiv, 266. First Precept on Deut. 18:9.

[3] *Opera,* xl, 554. Lect. on Dan. 1:17.

[4] *Opera,* xl, 558 f. Comm. on Dan. 2:2. In general, Calvin had a poor opinion of the ancients, other than those who figure in Biblical or ecclesiastical history. It is the more surprising to find him here citing as example not only Calpurnia's dream but that of Augustus' physician.

[5] *Opera,* vii, 519. *Contre l'Astrologie.*

the dead, she showed herself in league with Satan. The devil's ministers profane the name of God and pretend to utter prophecies in his name, yet their art is wholly instigated by the devil. "Deluded by the foolish affections of nature," men are induced to inquire curiously about the condition of the dead in order to know that it is well with them in the new life—and Satan seizes this occasion. Not that affection itself is bad—the evil lies in what it drives men to. "To the higher affections is added a sort of stupid eagerness to speak with the dead . . . as if some great good were to come of such converse." [6] The devil, fostering this error, pretends to give us excellent advice about our enterprises, and claims to induce the dead to indicate their state to the living. But whether living or dead, we must depend on God alone and on his Word. Only so can we overcome the vice of curiosity and reject all the diabolical illusions by which Satan works his wiles.

.   .   .   .

Calvin is very clear about the evilness of magic arts. "God says in sum, *That if we want to be his people, we cannot be wrapped up in sorceries, or divinations, or enchantments, or conjurations with the dead, or conjurations with familiar spirits.*" [7] (Italics Calvin's.)

Calvin is not so clear as to whether he thinks the devil really does all the things he claims to do. He is sure that God's power is adequate to thwart Satan's; Christ holds him in check as if with his foot upon his throat. [8] Satan is a pretender. Yet he seems to ascribe to the devil a goodly measure of real power— much more than is consistent with an *all*-powerful God. From his Biblical premises came the belief in an all-powerful God and a semi-powerful devil, and Calvin never thought it necessary to try to reconcile these concepts.

Like Calvin, the Puritans attached great theological importance to the devil. James Truslow Adams has remarked that the devil

[6] *Opera*, xxx, 644. Hom. on I Sam. 28: 7-11.
[7] *Opera*, xxvii, 493. Ser. on Deut. 18: 9-15.
[8] *Opera*, li, 551. Ser. on Eph. 4: 7-10.

was the saving grace of the Puritan doctrine, for he supplied the melodrama in what would otherwise have been a fatalistic, legalistic system.[9] The finest English Puritan poem has Satan for its hero, and Satan appears on almost every page of American Puritan prose. But the real tragedy, with Satan as its leading character, lay not in literature, but in life. As one contemplates the turbulent frenzy of 1692 when two hundred persons in northeastern Massachusetts were accused of being in league with Satan, one hundred and fifty imprisoned, and twenty-nine put to death, one wishes that Calvin might have gone further in his rejection of superstition—and that his followers might even have gone as far as he.

3. FROM LORD'S DAY TO PURITAN SABBATH

In the matter of sabbath observance, there is a marked difference between Calvin's doctrine and that of the New England Puritans. The Puritans were sabbatarians, and the pharisaic literalism with which they insisted on the observance of the fourth commandment is familiar history. In the Massachusetts Bay Colony all labor must cease at three on Saturday afternoon, and woe unto him who engaged in any labor or frivolity before Sunday night! From fines and whippings for those caught walking or playing in the streets on Sunday, Massachusetts went on in 1727 to penalize even the holding of funerals on Sunday. "Connecticut had a kind of pre-Baumes sabbath law punishing Sunday burglary by one ear off, first offense; two ears off, second offense; and death, third offense." [10]   Connecticut punished by minor penalties any who went out of the house on Sunday "except for worship or necessity." New York—less rigid in general morality than the New England colonies—in 1659 passed a law against travel, labor, shooting, fishing, sporting, playing, horse-racing, frequenting ale-houses, etc., on the Lord's day. Laws of varying severity were passed in all the colonies. Even Rhode Island, home of religious liberty, forbade "gaming, tippling, immodesty and wantonness" on the sabbath.

---

[9] *The Founding of New England*, p. 82.
[10] Moehlman, *The Story of the Ten Commandments*, p. 156.

In Calvin, we find no such austerity. There was rigidity enough about the Genevan Sunday régime; but it was a rigidity concerned primarily with getting people to church. To absent oneself from sermon was a grave offense; what one did afterward was not a matter of such concern. To be sure, labor on the Lord's day was prohibited, but the prohibition of toil was never carried into such minutiæ of literalism as among the Puritans. Geneva never countenanced the free, loose, frolicsome Sunday approved by Continental Romanists and by England under the Anglican régime; neither did the laws or practice of Geneva approximate in severity those of early Massachusetts or Connecticut.

To discover how the early Reformation leaders looked upon the sabbath, it is necessary to go back some centuries in church history. Within a half-century after Jesus' death, Christianity had divided into two groups, Jewish Christians who observed a seventh-day sabbath and Gentile Christians who kept the Lord's day in commemoration of Jesus' resurrection. There was a general opinion among the fathers of the early church—Ignatius, Tertullian, Justin Martyr, Chrysostom and others, that the sabbath had been abrogated and the Lord's day given instead as a day of worship. For about five centuries the Lord's day was not identified with the sabbath. From the sixth century on, it began to be affirmed occasionally that the glory of the Jewish sabbath had been transferred to Sunday, but the identification of the two was by no means general. Even the early Protestant reformers drew a distinction between them, and their liberalism in regard to the keeping of the fourth commandment appears a bit startling to modern ears. Zwingli held that the ceremonial sabbath had been abolished and therefore anyone might work after attending divine worship. Luther considered the sabbath commandment an altogether external matter, and recommended the keeping of Sunday on grounds of expediency rather than necessity.[11]

Like the early fathers and Zwingli and Luther, Calvin insisted

11 *Ibid.*, pp. 149, 150. The Augsburg Confession (art. xxviii) repudiates the sabbath substitution theory.

that the ceremonial aspects of the sabbath had been abrogated. He placed the exact moment of its abrogation at the time when the veil of the temple was rent.[12] The sabbath was given, he says, to foreshadow the spiritual repose of the people of Israel, and with the coming of the Gospel all shadows were done away. But it was given also for two other reasons, as a day of worship on which to hear the Word and perform the rites of religion, and as a day of rest for servants—the last being added by Moses as a subordinate injunction. These last two reasons for its observance stand, and their significance has been transferred to the Lord's day. Therefore it is the Christian's duty to observe Sunday as a day of worship and repose.

Perhaps the most compact statement we can quote to show Calvin's view-point is from the Genevan catechism of 1545 in reference to the fourth commandment.[13]

Minister. What command is given about the keeping of this day?

Child. That the people assemble to be instructed in the truth of God, to make common supplication, and to give witness of their faith.

Minister. How do you understand that the commandment is given also for the relief of servants?

Child. To give some relaxation to those who are in the power of others. Likewise this serves the common good; for each is accustomed to work the remainder of the time, when there is a day of repose.

Minister. Now let us say how this commandment pertains to us.

Child. Regarding the ceremony, it is abolished; for it is fulfilled in Jesus Christ. (Col. 2:19)

Minister. How?

Child. Our old man is crucified by virtue of his death, and by his resurrection we live in newness of life. (Rom. 6:6)

Minister. Then what remains to us?

Child. To observe the order established by the Church, to hear the word of the Lord, to take part in the public prayers and the sacraments: and not to go contrary to the spiritual ordinances which exist among the faithful.

There may be a subtle utilitarianism in the suggestion that men will work more the rest of the time if there is a day of

---

[12] *Opera,* ix, 588.   [13] *Opera,* vi, 65 f.

repose, but there is sound sense. The Genevans were compelled by law to work six days in the week and refrain on Sunday; [14] likewise they were compelled by law to go to church on Sunday "to observe the order established by the Church."

In commenting elsewhere upon the proper observance of the sabbath, Calvin shows his usual shrewdness and a rather high ethical sense. He protests repeatedly against the narrowness and superstition of the Jewish observance of the day in the time of Christ. It was given as a day of sanctification, spiritual repose, and gratitude to God, and as such it should still be observed. To observe it rightly, we must govern our thoughts and appetites. "It is in vain for hypocrites to burden themselves and put on a fine show, for while they have covetousness, envy, rancor, pride, cruelty, and fraud in their hearts, they will certainly violate the day of repose." [15] Calvin would have no profiteer try to buy God's favor by going to church.

The day is given us to teach us to bridle our affections and worship God. This, of course, ought to be done every day, but "for our infirmity, even our laziness, a day had to be chosen." [16] It would be well for the people to assemble in the name of the Lord every day. However, Calvin remarks pathetically, it is hard enough to get them there on Sunday! A great part have to be constrained as if by force.

Calvin says nothing of mowing lawns or tinkering automobiles on Sunday, but apparently human nature then had some of its present tendencies. A great many, he says, think to have Sunday in which to attend better to their business, "and they reserve Sunday as if there were no other day in the whole week to think about this. The bell rings for church, yet they can think only about their work and take stock of this and that." [17] Others stay at home and gourmandize. Others prefer to go off and have a good time. (Considering the slight opportunity for Sunday diversion

---

[14] *Opera,* xxi, 211. *Reg. Con.* XXX, fol. 248; June 4, 1537.
[15] *Opera,* xxvi, 287 Ser. on Deut. 5: 12-14.
[16] *Ibid.,* 291.
[17] *Ibid.,* 292.

then afforded in Geneva, one wonders what Calvin would say of twentieth century practice.) After commenting on such desecrations he regretfully remarks, "All this is so common it is a great pity, and would to God it were harder to find examples." [18]

So much for Calvin. He wanted the Lord's day observed with religious reverence and fitting decorum, but there is little here, except the imperative obligation to attend church, which savors of the Puritan sabbath.

. . . .

For the real origin of the Puritan sabbath, we must look three decades after Calvin's death. In 1595 an English Puritan by the name of Nicholas Bownde [19] published a book entitled *The True Doctrine of the Sabbath, plainly laid forth and soundly proved.* He argued that the sabbath had existed from creation, that its observance was designed to be perpetual and universal, and therefore that the sabbath had not been abrogated. The Lord's day, though the first day of the week, must really be the sabbath, Bownde declared, and in it no work was to be done nor any recreation indulged in. The Jewish sabbath was thus made over into the Christian Sunday. The Puritans adopted and promoted this point of view, though the Church of England, always more lenient toward Sunday recreations, opposed it as the sabbatarian heresy.

Bownde's book had great influence among the Puritans. The attempt of Elizabeth and her prelates to repress it were in vain. What Bownde did was merely to put the capstone on a process which had been taking shape for centuries, and seal it with a Calvinistic rigidity. But it was the turning-point. Henceforth the Puritans were to be literalists in their observance of the Lord's day. When the *Book of Sports* for sabbath recreation was issued by the Stuarts and all clergy were required to read it in their parishes or surrender their benefices, this was no slight factor in depriving Puritans of their livings and Charles I of his head. The Puritans who came to America under such circumstances were bound to be

[18] *Opera,* xxvi, 293.
[19] Or Bound.

sabbatarians. It took a long time then for the pharisaism of a Jewish sabbath to drop out of the Christian Sunday. And when it dropped, in the anti-Puritan reaction, not much was left.

.   .   .   .

This chapter and the preceding one have dealt largely in negatives. We have seen what Calvin and his Puritan successors denounced. They did not approve, nor were they hesitant to say they did not approve, of what they called idolatry and blasphemy and heresy, of commerce with Satan and profanation of the sabbath. Yet in all these negatives there is a positive note. Calvin and the Puritans denounced these practices because they revered and honored God. In each of these offenses they saw an affront to God's majesty. "The glory of God" was no glib phrase; it was a driving and dominant ideal accepted and lived by as man's chief end.

The Calvinistic conscience drove Calvin to sacrifice himself and others to the uttermost. The verdict of history after four centuries is that his sacrifice of others, and sometimes of self, was austere to the point of cruelty. The same is true of his successors. Had the glory of God been tempered with a realization of the dignity of man, had the Calvinist's God been the God of the Sermon on the Mount, had Christian charity outweighed legalism, the outcome might have been different, and more admirable. Yet it scarcely becomes an irreverent age to think lightly of the Calvinist's reverence; and it may be doubted whether the glorification of comfort and the worship of prosperity is a more inspiring ideal than the glory of God.

PART III

THE CALVINISTIC CONSCIENCE AND MAN'S DUTY TO MAN

CHAPTER VII

DOMESTIC RELATIONS

In the previous chapters we have looked at Calvin the man and Calvin the theologian. We have seen what Calvin thought about man's duty to God, and how this overtowering sense of duty in matters of religion influenced social relations. Basic, powerful, relentless, such an all-dominating conviction of a transcendent God before whom man must utterly abase himself could not fail to have its effect for good and ill on moral living.

We must now see what Calvin had to say about man's duty to man. In this study of social ethics we shall not leave duty to God behind. This would be impossible in a system that made God the ever-present force controlling all human conduct. However, the view-point of inquiry will be the duties laid by God upon an elect Christian in his relations with his fellow-men.

We shall begin with a look at Calvin's theory of family and sex relations. This has been studied less than any other phase of Calvin's thought, and practically nothing has been written on it. Yet it is of much interest, both because of its contemporary significance and its later influence. Calvin's observations give a clear-cut statement of the Protestant theory of the family at a time when it had very recently become differentiated from the Catholic, and was still in process of taking form. His views upon the abrogation of celibacy by the clergy and the legitimacy of divorce were for that day heretical and revolutionary.

1. THE CONTEMPORARY SETTING

To understand Calvin's views on the ethics of family life it is necessary to try to see the situation from the contemporary standpoint. Protestantism has now so fully accepted the idea of a married clergy and the legitimacy of divorce under some conditions that it is difficult to realize that the Reformers instituted a radical innovation. Calvin married in 1541. It was only sixteen years earlier, in 1525, that Martin Luther had married Katharine von Bora, and set the tongues of the European world to wagging. Luther had been a monk, Katharine a nun, and both had taken vows of perpetual celibacy. Both had become intellectually and morally convinced that celibacy was an unnatural state not commanded by the Scriptures, and both felt that God had released them from their vows by showing them a better way. So they married, and begot children.

But though Luther was firmly convinced that the clergy ought to marry, he could never bring himself to sanction divorce for any cause other than adultery, and this but grudgingly. A famous case arose in which Luther was pressed to choose between advocating divorce and bigamy, and he cast his vote on the side of the latter. The landgrave Philip of Hesse had a wife. She apparently had faults—Philip said she did—but adultery could not be proved against her. And Philip had an uncomfortable combination: a conscience and an uncontrollable (or uncontrolled) desire for immoral relations with other women. Had he lacked the conscience, he would simply have indulged his desire, and raised no question. Since he had the conscience, he thought that an attractive wife would enable him to keep within the matrimonial bond. But he already had a wife. And what to do about it? He sent to Luther to find out. Luther of course recommended chastity and self-restraint; but Philip replied that this was to no avail. The only way out that would satisfy Philip's conscience was either bigamy or divorce. When the matter was reduced to such an alternative as this, Luther advised Philip to marry the second woman and not tell the world about it.[1]

That a great religious leader of honored memory should prefer bigamy to divorce strikes the modern mind as strange. But the reason is not difficult to find. It says plainly in the Bible that

[1] James Mackinnon, *Luther and the Reformation,* IV, p. 265 ff.

divorce is forbidden for any cause save adultery. It does not say that bigamy is forbidden; in fact, Abraham, Jacob, and other Old Testament characters practiced it and apparently enjoyed the favor of God. So if one must choose, it seemed clear in Luther's mind that bigamy was preferable.

Calvin was born just twenty-five years after Luther, and he did his work on the basis of a quarter century advance. By the time Calvin was ready to declare his views, the marriage of the clergy had become an accepted practice among Protestants. The question of divorce was still in a state of uncertainty and suspicion. Calvin was staunchly opposed to bigamy, or any other form of polygamy, but he went far beyond his times in the liberality of his views upon divorce. We shall see a little later what these were.

2. THE SIN OF ADULTERY

There was one point on which both Luther and Calvin were well agreed, the heinousness of the sin of unchastity. *The Scarlet Letter* has immortalized the New England Puritan's pitiless condemnation of adultery. In this the Puritans followed closely in the lead of their theological head. On page after page he condemns this grave offense. One almost suspects him of having a complex on the subject, for he lugs in his denunciation of *palliardise* in conjunction with almost every moral problem he discusses.

To the Calvinistic conscience, unchastity was the unpardonable sin against society. The adulterer, Calvin says, not only sins against his fellow-man but against God, for he profanes the holy temple of God and disfigures the body of Christ of which we have been made members. And to commit adultery is not merely to commit the overt act; it is to be guilty of immodesty in speech or dress or gesture.[2] It is for this reason that he so severely condemned dancing and "immoral" songs. His objection to the theatre was based not only on his aversion to having men assume feminine attire, but to a fear that such "mummeries" might lead spectators

[2] *Opera*, xxviii, 20, 59. Sers. on Deut. 22: 5-8, 25-30.

into paths of lewdness. He enjoins purity of thought as well as action, and in a statement which comes as near to the spirit of the Sermon on the Mount as one finds in Calvin he says, "I call continence not only keeping the body free from fornication but also keeping a chaste mind." [3]

In view of the severity of Calvin's condemnation of the offense, it is surprising to find the legislation of Geneva fixing penalties which are comparatively mild. If the sin of unchastity were committed by the unmarried, the punishment was to be imprisonment for six days on bread and water and the payment of sixty sous "for the bank." If either of the offenders was married, the imprisonment was to be for nine days and the payment according to the seriousness of the offense. Then, as if to leave no shade of doubt, the ordinance adds a third stipulation, "Those who are betrothed must not cohabit until the marriage is celebrated in the church, otherwise they will be punished like adulterers." [4]

Imprisonment for nine days on bread and water and the payment of a fine was nothing to be desired; yet it was far less terrifying than the stoning sanctioned by Deuteronomy or the branding practiced in New England. This raises an interesting, and so far as I know unanswered, question as to why the Genevan legislators were satisfied with such leniency. The best guess is probably that the Libertines, who by no means shared Calvin's scruples in the matter, were strong enough politically to prevent the passage of more drastic legislation. In any case it is clear that Calvin did not approve such mildness. In his sermon on Deuteronomy 22: 13-24 [5] which enjoins the stoning of those taken in adultery, he holds up to ridicule and scorn the idea of merely putting adulterers in prison for a few days, "as if one had carried off a glass of wine to say, 'Taste which is the better.'" When a person is accused of robbery he is tried and hung. But when one steals the bed of another, which is the worst kind of robbery, he merely gets put in

[3] IV, xiii, 17.
[4] *Opera*, xa, 58.
[5] *Opera*, xxviii, 41 f.

jail where he has as much freedom as one would have in a public tavern, while everybody comes to pay court to him and pity the poor prisoner! Adulterers might better not be punished at all, Calvin says, than by such procedure. "It is to expose justice to scorn and mock God and all his commandments." [6]

In the same sermon Calvin strongly suggests, though he apparently hesitates to say flatly, that adultery ought to be punished by death. He delivers a fierce invective against the adulteress:

She injures her husband, exposes him to shame, despoils also the name of her family, despoils her unborn children, despoils those whom she has already borne in lawful wedlock. When a woman is thus in the hands of the devil, what remedy is there except that all this be exterminated? [7]

Then he adds with reference to the stoning commanded in Deuteronomy 22:21:

And so it must be, in such a great extremity when the punishment is so severe, that the Lord wishes this to serve as an example to us, that those who have lived in such scandal in their lives may teach us by their death to keep ourselves chaste. [8]

Later, after saying that this is a worse offense than robbery which is punishable by death, he exclaims, "Do you not see that it is an insufferable crime, and one which ought to be punished to the limit?" [9] A literal reading of this injunction to punish *"jusqu'au bout"* can scarcely mean anything else than the death penalty. However, as he does not elsewhere in his condemnation of adultery say that the guilty parties should be put to death, he may mean here to justify the Deuteronomic practice and point out its stern moral lesson without clearly recommending the death penalty to the Genevans. As in the case of Catholic idolaters and witches, Calvin could not quite bring himself to say, in so many words, that such offenders merit death.

It was very clear in Calvin's mind that every individual had a

[6] *Ibid.*, 52.
[7] *Ibid.*, 51.
[8] *Ibid.*, 52.
[9] *Ibid.*, 53.

responsibility for the stamping out of such foul corruption. Nobody could be exempt by closing his eyes, going his own way, and living in decency himself. To permit adultery is to participate in the adulterer's guilt. "If we suffer them and let them be nourished by our indifference, we shall be held before God as brothel-keepers and procurers." [10] If the fires of adultery be not quenched, they will consume the whole city and country, and we shall all be under the curse of God. Calvin's sense of responsibility for others' sins was strong. The Calvinistic conscience has never been content to legislate for itself alone.

It is interesting to note also what Calvin says of venereal disease as a punishment of God upon the adulterer. God, he says, has raised up new maladies as punishment for wrong-doing. This one was not mentioned in Moses' law, or even known to our fathers of a hundred years ago. But within fifty years God has sent "this pox" to punish the adulterer. And apparently sterner measures still are necessary. "These mockers of God . . . only wipe their muzzles and laugh if God strikes them with an ugly disease so that they are eaten up with canker." But God has still more in his strong-boxes which he will let loose upon the earth if men will not cease from sin.[11]

Calvin was well aware of what Jesus said to the woman taken in adultery. But he staunchly refused to admit that this meant that any mercy was to be shown. What Jesus meant, he says, is merely that he did not wish to be the judge in the case, as he refused to divide an inheritance between two brothers. Jesus did not come "to abolish the law of God, his Father, annihilate all order, and make his church into a pig-sty." We are enjoined to live in chastity to the end of the world, and when marriages are thus maintained we may expect the blessing of the Lord to prosper us.[12]

If the Puritan was stern to the point of unfeeling cruelty in his denunciation of the sin of unchastity, it is not surprising.

[10] *Opera*, xxxiv, 653. Ser. on Job 31: 9-15.
[11] *Opera*, xxviii, 404, 465. Sers. on Deut. 28: 25-29, 59-64.
[12] *Opera*, xxviii, 53.

And there is still enough of Calvinism abroad in the land to make Hester Prynne's offense, in the eyes of "respectable" people, a sin which brands the sinner in deepest scarlet.

3. THE ABROGATION OF CELIBACY

Calvin had two reasons in joining with Luther in protesting against the vow of celibacy; the conviction that marriage was a holy institution ordained of God and therefore permitted to all, and the equally strong conviction that marriage was a very necessary human institution if unchastity was to be avoided. While the second may not have surpassed the first in his thinking, he says much more about it. His horror of adultery filled him with scorn at the current monastic practice, and he was more blunt than gentle in pointing out the futility of the vow of celibacy.

Continence, he says repeatedly, is a special gift of God, not granted to many.[13] "Continence is a remarkable gift, indeed a rare one, and bestowed upon very few."[14] It is therefore sheer presumption on the part of one who has not received this gift from God to think that he can live the celibate life. In fact, to take a vow of celibacy is "to act precisely as if any unlearned and illiterate person were to set himself off as a prophet or teacher or interpreter of languages."[15] In either case, a special endowment is necessary. No individual has a right to entertain a confidence that God will bestow upon him the gift of continence; and for such as do not receive it, God has provided a safe and legitimate remedy in marriage.[16] Marriage is a veil by which the fault of immoderate desire is covered over, so that it no longer appears in the sight of God.[17] To take the vow of perpetual virginity and reject the proffered remedy is to rebel against God.[18]

Calvin, as usual, is clear-cut in his reasoning. Answering a set

---

[13] *Opera,* v, 330; vii, 42, 670; xxviii, 131; xxxvi, 346; xlv, 533; xlix, 406 *et al.*
[14] *Opera,* vii, 664.
[15] *Opera,* xlix, 407. Comm. on I Cor. 7: 8.
[16] IV, xiii, 17.
[17] *Opera,* xlix, 406. Comm. on I Cor. 7: 6.
[18] II, viii, 42.

of articles put out by the faculty of the University of Paris, he neatly
analyzes in firstly, secondly, thirdly fashion the matter of taking
vows:[19]

> In regard to vows three things must be observed: first, whether what
> we vow is in our power; second, whether the end is good; third, whether
> it is pleasing to God. If these are lacking, or any one of them, the vow
> is invalid and of no account.
>
> In the first place, the Scriptures teach that perpetual continence is not
> in the power of everyone. For Christ testifies that not all hear this
> word. (Mt. 19: 11.) Also Paul suggests . . . that this is a singular
> gift, not granted to all (I Cor. 7: 7). Therefore he orders all who burn
> to take refuge in the remedy of marriage. Whoever cannot contain, he
> says, let him take a wife. Likewise to avoid adultery, let each have his
> own wife.

Calvin then goes on to show that in the monastic vow of
obedience the end is not good, and that the vow of poverty is displeasing to God. Therefore he concludes—Q.E.D.—that all three
vows of the monastic life are invalid and of no account.

Furthermore, he cites plenty of pragmatic evidence. Experience
shows, he says, that wherever this yoke has been imposed on priests
they have been shut up in a furnace of lust to burn with perpetual
fire. "It is scarcely possible to find one convent in ten which
is not rather a brothel than a sanctuary of chastity."[20] Opponents
of the true gospel may sing the praises of virginity, but this avails
nothing when they fail to practice it. "If one takes a wife, it is
regarded as a capital crime; if he commits adultery a hundred
times, it is atoned for with a small sum of money."[21] The vow of
celibacy has deprived the church of many good and faithful ministers, for pious and prudent men will not thus ensnare themselves.[22]
God has provided a remedy for all this in marriage; and those who
have already taken vows of celibacy ought to consider themselves
absolved by God from such a superstition. "For if an impossible

[19] Opera, vii, 42. Articuli Facultatis Parisiensis, cum Antidoto.
[20] IV, xiii, 15.
[21] Opera, vi, 498.
[22] Opera, xlix, 407. Comm. on I Cor. 7: 7.

vow be the ruin of souls, which it is the will of the Lord to save and not destroy, it follows that it is not right to persevere in it." [23]

On the other hand, Calvin could scathingly denounce the adulterer, and on the other, could assert that we should all be adulterers save for the grace of God and the saving remedy of marriage. This was a natural consequence of his theology. He was true to his predestinarian convictions when he declared that continence was a gift bestowed only by the grace of God. In Adam's sin all human nature was corrupted, and our sins are our own fault. Through God's mercy and free gift, not through our merit, we find release.

4. WHAT IS MARRIAGE FOR?

Calvin gives a clear, blunt statement of the purpose of marriage. His conception, like that of his contemporaries, savors more of the flesh than of the spirit. So far as I have been able to discover, neither Calvin nor Luther ever speaks of marriage as an institution established for the mutual companionship of husband and wife, though both say that the wife is given to be a helpmate for her husband. The two functions of marriage repeatedly affirmed are to beget offspring and serve as a remedy for incontinence. So essential did Calvin deem the physical aspect of marriage that he regarded a physical incapacity for sex intercourse as sufficient ground for the annulment of a marriage, and on his recommendation such a provision was written into the Genevan statutes.

With a frankness that is a bit startling even to a sex-hardened age, Calvin remarks:

The unsexed [24] and eunuchs, without virility, are excluded from marriage by Christ. . . . And certainly there is nothing more repugnant to sense than the error that the fidelity of a woman cannot be released when she thought she was marrying a husband and finds herself deceived. Indeed, such a frustration of union overthrows the very nature and end of marriage. For what else is marriage than the union of

---

[23] IV, xiii, 21.
[24] Literally, "the cold" (*frigidos*). It is unclear whether he means that a mere psychological lack of the normal amount of sex feeling is sufficient ground for the dissolution of a marriage.

male and female? Why, indeed, was it instituted except for these two ends, either to beget offspring or as a remedy for incontinence?" [25]

Calvin is clear in his conviction that a union which cannot fulfill the second of these two functions is no union at all, and therefore null and void. He is less outspoken on the question of sterility as a ground for divorce, and makes no provision for it in the divorce laws. In condemning Elkanah for taking a second wife because the first was barren, he says that when one desires to have children, he should earnestly pray about it, as Isaac did. Then if the prayer is not granted, he should accept the denial of his petition in all patience and humility, as the dispensation of an all-wise God in whose hand are both the giving and withholding of offspring.[26]

Marriage, as originally ordained by God, had only the one function of begetting offspring; it was through Adam's sin that it became a necessary remedy for incontinence. And through Adam's sin came all its evils—for Calvin recognizes that the married state has its limitations. "If our father Adam had remained in integrity, it is certain that marriage, as an instrument of God, would have been a perfect and angelic life." [27] But it is no longer a perfect and angelic life. Nor is it all unmixed sweetness. Answering the objection that it is arduous to have to live always with one wife, Calvin remarks—either cleverly or naïvely, "Let us remember that, since our nature was corrupted, marriage began to be a medicine; and therefore we need not wonder if it have a bitter taste mixed with its sweetness." [28]

Strong as was Calvin's opposition to ecclesiastical celibacy, he expresses much sympathy with Paul's position. When Paul says it is good for a man to refrain from connection with a woman, he does not mean, Calvin says, that marriage itself is evil, but only that it would be *expedient* to refrain because of the troubles,

[25] *Opera*, xa, 231. *Advices on Matrimonial Questions.*
[26] *Opera*, xxix, 260.
[27] *Opera*, xxviii, 159. Ser. on Deut. 24: 1-6.
[28] *Opera*, xlv, 532. Comm. on Mt. 19: 10.

anxieties and vexations of married life. It is as if one said, "It were good if one did not have to eat or drink or sleep," for then one could devote all his time to meditation on heavenly things; and since there are many impediments in married life which keep a man entangled, it were *good* on that account to be free.[29] True, it is better to marry than to burn. "It is not, however, without good reason that he [Paul] returns so often to proclaim the advantages of celibacy, for he saw that the burdens of matrimony were far from light."[30] One must not become despondent, Calvin says, if one marries and then finds troubles ensuing. Many promise themselves "unmixed honey" and then get disappointed. One wonders whether Calvin speaks here from his own limited domestic experience. In any case, this bachelor-widower was an astute observer of human affairs!

5. SACRAMENT OR CIVIL CONTRACT?

Calvin follows Luther in holding that marriage is not a sacrament. The Papists are in error, he says, in holding it to be such. As usual, he is more vigorous than gracious in pointing out their error. They have been ignorantly deceived by a mistranslation in the Vulgate. Paul says in Ephesians 5: 31-32, "For this cause shall a man leave his father and mother, and shall be joined unto his wife, and they two shall be one flesh. This is a great mystery: but I speak concerning Christ and his church." The Catholic church has fallen into the double error of rendering *mystery* as *sacrament,* and of holding this statement to apply to marriage when it really has reference to the mysterious union of Christ with his church. The blunder is the more inexcusable, Calvin thinks, because the same word is used elsewhere (I Tim. 3:9, 16; Eph. 3:9), and no claim made that this betokens a sacrament. "Let this oversight, however, be forgiven them; liars ought, at least, to have good memories." And if marriage is a sacrament, then why, with brain-

---

[29] *Opera,* xlix, 401. Comm. on I Cor. 7:1.
[30] *Opera,* xlix, 421. Comm. on I Cor. 7:32.

less versatility, do they stigmatize it as impurity and exclude priests from it?[31] Softness of speech was not among Calvin's virtues!

Marriage, of course, is a good and holy ordinance of God; on that all can agree. "And so agriculture, architecture, shoemaking, and many other things, are legitimate ordinances of God, and yet they are not sacraments."[32] A sacrament must not only be a work of God, but it must be an external ceremony appointed by God for the confirmation of a promise. That there is nothing of this kind in matrimony even children can judge. But, they say, it is a sign of a sacred thing, that is, of the spiritual union of Christ with his church. This too proves inadequate as an argument, for on such a basis there will be as many sacraments as there are similitudes in Scripture—even theft will be a sacrament, for it is written, The day of the Lord cometh as a thief. (I Thess. 5:2.) Calvin concludes that to hold marriage to be a sacrament on such reasoning would argue a want of mental sanity.

This denunciation of the Catholic position led the Dutch Calvinists, and through them the New England Puritans,[33] to regard marriage as a civil contract, to be entered into before civil magistrates. Yet Calvin did not advocate the solemnizing of marriages by a magistrate. Marriages in Geneva took place in church just before the sermon on a day when a regular service was being held. The civil authorities could determine the conditions under which marriage could be entered into and dissolved, but Calvin seems to have taken it for granted that it was the minister's business to perform the ceremony. It is God himself who joins male and female in holy union; it is to his ministers of the true faith that he gives authority to act for him in holy things.

Calvin highly disapproved of having a marriage celebrated with a Mass and paid for like any commercial transaction, though he did

[31] IV, xix, 36.
[32] *Ibid.*, 34.
[33] The Massachusetts Bay Colony in 1646 passed an edict that "no person whatsoever in this jurisdiction shall join any persons together in marriage, but the magistrate, or such other as the General Court or Court of Assistants shall authorize, in such place where no magistrate is near." Similar enactments were passed in New Haven and Rhode Island. Moehlman, p. 225.

not attempt to say that a Catholic marriage was not binding. He remarks indignantly:

> I ask you: the priest who sells a Mass, is he not committing a sacrilege? What then of him who buys it? Our Lord says a good wife is the special gift of Providence. When we ought to be grateful to Him and ask Him to consummate this gift by bestowing His blessing on the marriage, is it not to provoke His wrath to use such an abomination? [34]

Calvin does not express himself on the question of ministers' fees, but it is easy to guess his opinion. Marriage is a holy ordinance of God, and wives are free gifts of Heaven.

6. MARRIAGE REGULATIONS

The form of service sanctioned by the civil authorities of Geneva is given in full in the *Opera*. In general structure it is not unlike the modern Protestant service, though it contains more Biblical citations. There is, of course, no use of prayer-book or ring; this would savor too much of Romanism. The wife promises to obey, for it had not occurred to wife or husband yet to raise the question. In accord with Catholic practice, public notice must be given in advance, elopements thus being automatically eliminated. The introduction to the text of the ceremony reads:

> It is necessary to note that before celebrating the marriage, it is published in church for three Sundays: so that if anyone knows any hindrance, he can announce it early, or if anyone has an interest in it, he can oppose it.
> This done, the parties present themselves at the beginning of the sermon. Then the minister says: ——[35]

A set of ecclesiastical ordinances passed by the Council in 1561, apparently at Calvin's instigation, also throws light on marriage procedure in Geneva. The marriage could take place on any day when a regular service was being held *except* Communion Sunday. On this day there must be no extras, "in order that there be no

[34] *Opera*, vi, 556.
[35] *Opera*, vi, 203.

distraction and each be the better disposed to receive the sacrament." [36] And there must be no dallying on the wedding day! And no extravagance, or revelry, or anything else unbefitting Christians. The ordinance enjoins:

That the parties at the time they are to be married come modestly to the church, without tambourines or minstrels, maintaining the order and gravity suitable for Christians; and this before the end of the sounding of the bell, so that the marriage may take place before the sermon begins. If they are negligent and come too late, they shall be sent away.[37]

Thus speaks the disciplinarian. Promptness is a virtue to be observed in the least matters to the greatest! No instance is recorded of a couple's coming late and being sent ingloriously away. It did not happen where Calvin held the reins.

Nor was Calvin for dallying about getting married after the pair had made up their minds to it! Another ordinance—one which today would be considered a grave infringement on personal liberty—has to do with the term of engagements. It reads:

After the promise is made, the marriage is not to be deferred more than six weeks. Otherwise, the parties are called to the Consistory to be admonished, and if they do not obey, they are to be sent before the Council to be compelled to celebrate it.[38]

Woe unto the couple who tell the world too lightly that they expect to marry! For there is no retracing of steps. Six weeks is time enough to get a trousseau ready, and there is no need of time to conjure up pomp or vain display.

Two circumstances only could release the betrothed from a promise once made. If a girl is taken for a virgin and it is discovered that she is not, the pledge of the fiancé is void. The bond is already broken. Also—and this indicates a eugenic and sanitary provision far in advance of the times—if one of the parties has a contagious or incurable disease, the other is absolved from

---

[36] *Opera*, xa, 109.
[37] *Ibid.*, 108.
[38] *Ibid.*, 107.

the betrothal promise. Difficulties over the dowry, money matters, or other external accessories cannot interrupt the marriage.[39]

Calvin did not believe in allowing youngsters to marry at will. In fact, he seems in some passages to imply that all the choosing is to be done by the parents. Hagar is commended for getting Ishmael a wife. "Since marriage forms a principal part of human life, it is right that in contracting it, children should be subject to their parents and should obey their counsel."[40] It is preposterous that youths and maidens should acquire spouses for themselves for lust.[41] Minors in Geneva who married of their own accord "through folly or flightiness" were to be chastised, and the marriage rescinded upon request of their parents or guardians.[42] Calvin knew something of the psychology of adolescence; and refers to the years from twelve to twenty as "a tender and slippery age," during which a lack of the gift of continence might make it necessary for parents to give their consent.[43]

Actually, however, Calvin's policy was less drastic than his words would indicate; probably less drastic than that of his Puritan successors. The consent of parents was desirable, but not obligatory, for those who had attained years of discretion. The Genevan ordinance specifies that those above legal age (eighteen for woman, twenty for man) may take the matter to the Consistory, if the parents will not consent, and the Consistory are to call in the parents and admonish them to do their duty. If they still refuse, the marriage can take place anyway. The parents can be compelled to give a dowry as if they were pleased with the match, the amount to be set by the Council in conference with the parents.[44]

Furthermore, the consent of parents was a principle that worked both ways. If adolescents could not marry at will, neither could parents force them to marry against their will. Marriage was to be

[39] Ibid.
[40] Opera, xxiii, 306. Comm. on Deut. 21:20.
[41] Yet according to Calvin's theory of marriage, this would seem to be permissible for older people!
[42] Opera, xa, 105.
[43] Opera, xlix, 424. Comm. on I Cor. 7:36.
[44] Opera, xa, 105 f.

entered into only by free consent. In a day of rigid restriction of personal freedom, it is significant that this principle of non-coercion was written into the Genevan legislation.[45]

. . . .

On degrees of relationship permissible between the contracting parties, Calvin takes a position mid-way between the Catholic and the modern Protestant position. He speaks with scorn of the idea "that no marriages are lawful between persons related, even to the seventh degree," [46] and holds that while first cousins may not marry, marriage is permissible beyond that point. But he stands staunchly with the Catholic view that one may not marry one's deceased wife's sister or one's brother's wife.[47] To marry one's brother-in-law or sister-in-law is forbidden, he thinks, by the provisions of Leviticus 18:16-18, where one is prohibited from marrying any in-law or step-relative.[48] Yet Deuteronomy 25:5 says that if a man dies childless, his brother shall take his wife and beget him offspring. How reconcile this difficulty? Calvin here displays the ingenious logic which he was able to muster for the interpretation of any troublesome passage. The word translated "brother" in Deuteronomy must really mean "relative," he says, for God would not permit here what he forbids elsewhere. The marriage of Ruth and Boaz is cited as example.

Another problem of relationship was even more acute in those early Reformation days—one of which the legacy has persisted to the present. This was the question as to whether one of the "true" faith (i.e., a Protestant) might marry an "unbeliever" (i.e., a Catholic). Calvin here, as usual, combines intolerance with shrewd sense. Such marriages, he says, are not to be contracted, for trouble

---

[45] *Opera*, xa, 106.

[46] IV, xix, 37.

[47] *Opera*, xa, 233, 235.

[48] In general, the Puritans adhered to Calvin's principle. Yet one of New England's greatest divines was the offspring of a marriage which Calvin might not have approved. The Cottons and Mathers were curiously interrelated. Richard Mather's second wife was Mrs. John Cotton, who had a daughter Mary. Richard Mather had a son Increase by his first marriage. Increase Mather married Mary Cotton, his step-sister. Cotton Mather was their son. Sawyer, *History of the Pilgrims and Puritans*, iii, 224.

inevitably results. A wife who is an unbeliever will be like deadly poison unless she renounces her past life. Bad company must be avoided: one who associates with a drunkard gets to drinking and becomes a devil—how much worse the state of that man who is tied to an unbelieving wife for life and death! [49] Yet such a marriage, once contracted, is to be maintained in all but the most extreme cases. Only when it is very clear that one must choose between fidelity to God and fidelity to wife can difference in religion afford ground for the severing of the marriage tie. [50]

7. POLYGAMY

Calvin, as we noted earlier, was staunchly opposed to polygamy. This does not surprise us. But his rejection of it was somewhat hard to reconcile with his Biblical literalism and Old Testament ethics. The patriarchs—very worthy gentlemen like Abraham and Jacob—practiced polygamy by God's permission. Calvin knew that as well as anybody. And how oppose polygamy without opposing the patriarchs and the Word of God?

Calvin was never without a resource in matters of Biblical interpretation. Adam was a great help. Polygamy is contrary to the will of God, he says, for when God created a wife for Adam, he made only *one* wife. "What would have hindered him from creating two wives for Adam if he had wanted to? But God was content with one." [51] Lamech, who introduced bigamy, was of the house of Cain, and polygamists ought to be ashamed of their prototype. "In the beginning" there was one Eve; and, to the end, God wills that a man be the husband of one wife.

But what of Abraham? The answer is near at hand. God gave Abraham a special dispensation because of Sarah's barrenness, that the promise might be fulfilled and his seed transmitted. Isaac had sons by his first wife, and there was no need of a second. But the problem of Jacob is more baffling. His first wife bore him sons;

---

49 *Opera*, xxvii, 656. Sermon on Deut. 21: 10-14.
50 *Infra*, p. 151.
51 *Opera*, xxvii, 666. Ser. on Deut. 21: 15-17.

yet he had another wife and two concubines. Here Calvin flatly refuses to uphold him, and the romantic beauty of Jacob's courtship of Rachel receives a jolt. In Rachel, Jacob indulged his lust. One cannot excuse his conduct. But he got his punishment—God saw to that. He lived in quarrelsome contentions all his days, when with one wife he might have enjoyed peace and harmony.[52]

Polygamy ever breeds domestic strife. The example of Elkanah reinforces that of Jacob. Even Abraham did not do quite right in marrying Hagar, and he was compelled to suffer the penalty in giving up his son and driving him forth into the wilderness with only a little bread and water. He ought rather to have trusted God to remedy Sarah's sterility.[53]

Thus Calvin proves from Scripture—out of the mouth of God —that polygamy is wrong. Our modern moral sense agrees with him in this conclusion. But Calvin never realized that it was *his own* moral sense and the customs of civilized society which led him first to reject polygamy, and then to find authority for his rejection in the Scriptures.

8. OFFSPRING

Sterility was something to be remedied by God. This raises a further question. To what extent did Calvin look upon large families as evidence of God's favor?

In common with Catholicism and other forms of early Protestantism, Calvinism recommended the begetting of children, and looked upon a numerous progeny as a blessing from God.[54] Yet I have not been able to find any passage in which Calvin himself explicitly urges his followers to beget large families. Perhaps he thought that a man who had spent all but eight years of his life as bachelor and widower and would die childless could not graciously enjoin others to "be fruitful and multiply." It is more likely that he did not say whether families should be large or small

---

[52] *Opera*, xb, 258 f.; xxix, 259 f.
[53] *Opera*, xxix, 259. Hom. on I Sam. 1:6-8.
[54] Troeltsch, *Protestantism and Progress*, pp. 93 ff.

because he believed so firmly that the giving and withholding of children was in God's hand. God makes the grass to grow; God fecundates the beasts; God gives human progeny. Fertility, like continence, is the gift of God. "So it ought to be noted that there is no natural strength in us for generating, unless God bless us with his great bounty so that we bear a large progeny, received from him alone." [55]

Thus it follows that when one does have a large family, it is an evidence that God has signally blessed the parents. Job, for example, had seven sons and three daughters. This indicates that God had placed his blessing upon him to prosper him in all his ways.[56] Lamech sinned in taking matters into his own hands and marrying two wives, perhaps because "impelled by an immoderate desire to augment his family, as proud and ambitious men are wont." [57] All is to be left in God's hands, and God will bless with large families those whom he chooses so to bless.

Calvin does not say very much about this evidence of God's favor, or its implications. But his followers held this doctrine firmly, and it had far-reaching consequences which Calvin could not foresee. In his time, the problem of birth control had scarcely arisen. When it emerged, it had to face the opposition of religious scruples not only from Catholics but from large bodies of Protestants of Puritan extraction. If to limit one's family is to interfere with the work of God, artificial restriction is anathema. The battle still is on, and the Calvinistic heritage is no slight contributor to the forces of opposition.

For God to give Job a large family was to prosper him. But Calvin apparently saw no problem of poverty and economic struggle arising from such "prospering." Catholic and Calvinist have joined hands in regarding a large family as evidence of God's favor, and have fostered a fierce economic competition—which can scarcely be thought to receive God's favor—in the struggle for food

[55] *Opera*, xxix, 260.
[56] *Opera*, xxxiii, 37. Ser. on Job 2: 2-5.
[57] *Opera*, xxiii, 999. Comm. on Gen. 4: 19.

for these many mouths. Child labor and the clash of labor with capital for a living wage are in part a Calvinistic legacy.

9. COMPANIONATE MARRIAGE

Calvin believed firmly that marriage was neither to be entered into nor dissolved lightly. He went beyond his times in permitting divorce for some causes, but he stood like a rock for the sanctity of the marriage relation. "Companionate marriage" would have received short shrift from Calvin.

As a matter of fact, it did. The Spiritual Libertines,[58] though probably not so black (or so up-to-date!) as Calvin painted them, had a much less rigid conception of marriage than he, and advocated a relation which was the practical equivalent of "divorce by mutual consent." We shall let Calvin describe it:

> They call it a "spiritual marriage" when each is satisfied with the other. So if a man takes no pleasure in his wife, according to their view, he can look elsewhere where he can find satisfaction. However, that the wife may not be dispossessed, they give her leave also to try to better her condition and to take any chance that is offered her. If someone asks what will become of marriages which are considered indissoluble if it is permitted thus to withdraw at will, they answer that a marriage contracted and solemnized before men is carnal unless there is real agreement of spirit. They say that the only obligation which ought to hold among Christians is that of mutual agreement.
>
> Yet this tenure is not permanent. The day after tomorrow, if an adulteress falls out with her paramour, she can change to a new one if one offers himself who pleases her better. A debauchee can nose around here and there to get new spiritual wives and take them when he finds them. . . . Now consider what will be left of safety in the world—of order, of loyalty, of honesty, of assurance—if marriage, which is the most sacred union and ought to be most faithfully guarded, can thus be violated?[59]

There is not much doubt that the Libertines were right in charging an element of the carnal against Calvin's orthodox idea

---

[58] Karl Müller, "Calvin und die 'Libertiner,'" in *Zeitschrift für Kirchengeschichte*, N. F. III, 1922, maintains that Calvin totally misrepresented them. Wilhelm Niesel in the same periodical, I, 1929, questions this.

[59] *Opera*, vii, 212 f. *Contre la Secte des Libertins*.

of marriage. Had there been more of "mutual agreement" in the Calvinistic conception, it would have profited. But Calvin, like the opponents of companionate marriage today, saw the foundations of permanent marriage undermined by the proposal to let the relation terminate at will. So he set himself sturdily against it. The Calvinists after him did likewise. Not till the present day has his view of the binding nature of marriage been challenged on any wide-spread scale.

10. DIVORCE

Yet Calvin sanctioned divorce, with permission to the innocent party to remarry. Old Testament ethics again appears. God, speaking through Moses, permitted divorce, not because he approved it, but because he was dealing with a perverse and rebellious people.[60] The same situation holds. It is undesirable, yet a practical necessity. Calvin uses a homely figure to illustrate both its undesirability and necessity. If one's finger or arm becomes infected, he says, one does not cut it off right away. But if the infection be such that the whole body will be poisoned, it is better to lose a member than to lose one's life.[61] The twain are one flesh; but the union may be broken.

The most obvious cause by which the union is broken is adultery. In some of his sermons Calvin seems to say that this is the only legitimate ground for divorce. The two are joined as one—the husband the head, the wife the body—and can no more be severed than one can cut oneself into two parts.[62] Christ objected to divorce because he who divorces his wife tears away a part of himself and breaks a bond more sacred than that of child to parent.[63] But the act of adultery severs the bond.

Elsewhere Calvin admits three other grounds, physical incapacity for sex intercourse, desertion, and extreme religious incompatibility. All of these carry the privilege of remarriage for the innocent party but not for the guilty. Separation without remar-

---

[60] *Opera,* xxviii, 140; xlv, 528.
[61] *Opera,* xxviii, 139. Ser. on Deut. 24: 1-4.
[62] *Ibid.,* 144.
[63] *Opera,* xlv, 528. Comm. on Mt. 19: 4.

riage is recommended for those who are hopelessly incompatible but cannot claim divorce. The wife has as much right to divorce her husband as the husband his wife.

Again, the Genevan legislation is valuable source material. Here we can be sure that we have Calvin's own view, for we have a copy both of the projected ordinances which he compiled and of those actually passed. They were adopted almost exactly as he proposed them, differing only in slight changes of form, though some reluctance on the part of the Council is indicated by the fact that sixteen years elapsed between their proposal and adoption.[64]

Reference has already been made to Calvin's conviction that a person incapable of consummating the conjugal union should not be allowed to marry. He went further, and declared that in such a circumstance the marriage, if performed, was void and could be set aside without the necessity of getting a divorce.

The first provision in the ordinances for the dissolution of a marriage refers to such an annulment. It reads as follows:

For what causes a marriage may be declared null:—

If it happens that a woman complains that he who has taken her in marriage is malformed by nature, being unable to have intercourse with his wife, and this is proved true by confession or examination, the marriage shall be declared null. The wife shall be declared free and the man forbidden to misuse any woman further.

Likewise, if the man complains of not being able to cohabit with his wife because of some fault in her body, and she does not wish to permit it to be remedied, after the truth of the matter has been found out the marriage shall be declared null.[65]

Apparently it did not occur to Calvin or his contemporaries that there was anything carnal about such a provision. It was simply a natural consequence of their theory of the nature and purpose of marriage. The Freudians had not yet arisen to point out a connection between the rigidity of the Calvinistic conception of chastity *outside* the married state and the excessive emphasis on the

[64] Proposed Nov. 10, 1545; adopted Nov. 13, 1561.
[65] *Opera*, xa, 110.

physical *within* it. But "compensations" existed for centuries before psychologists gave them a name. Nor is it an unknown phenomenon still for a person to be very "puritanical" in the outward forms of chastity and very carnal in matters which fall within the law.

. . . .

Then follows in the legislation a statement of "for what causes a marriage may be rescinded." The first of these, naturally, is adultery. The case being duly proved, the innocent party may secure a divorce and may remarry, though he is urged to pardon his wife instead. Forgiveness is better than a ruptured home, but "no insistence shall be made to constrain him beyond his good pleasure." A wife has the same right, for according to the word of Paul the obligation pertaining to the marriage bed is mutual. No divorce may be granted to either if the adultery occurs through the fault of the one ostensibly sinned against, or if there is some connivance for the purpose of securing a divorce.

The most surprising thing about this provision is the completeness with which the wife is put on a par with the husband. Calvin was by no means an advocate of sex equality—of that we shall say more later. But in matters relating to sexual union, he holds to a strict equality. The provision reads:

Formerly the right of the wife was not equal with that of the husband in cases of divorce. But since according to the witness of the apostle the obligation is mutual and reciprocal in reference to cohabitation of the bed, and in this the wife is no more subject to the husband than the husband to the wife, it follows that if a man is convicted of adultery and the wife asks to be separated from him, and they cannot be reconciled by good admonitions, it shall be authorized.[66]

Calvin treats elsewhere of this mutuality in the sex relation, maintaining that it is as much the duty of the husband to fulfill the desire of the wife as the reverse. This conviction of equality he draws from the words of Paul in I Corinthians 7:4. However, as if fearful that somebody might think he meant to affirm the wife

[66] *Opera*, xa, 110.

her husband's equal in all things (awful heresy!), he takes pains
to say:

> But it may be asked why the apostle here puts them upon a level,
> instead of requiring from the wife obedience and subjection. I answer
> that it was not his intention to treat of all their duties, but simply of
> the mutual obligation as to the marriage bed.[67]

Had Paul and Calvin carried this mutuality further, it might
have been better for human progress. But at least, the women of
Geneva had Paul to thank for securing them equality in matters
of divorce.

.   .   .   .

The next set of provisions [68] marks a radical step beyond contemporary procedure. In a day when divorce was grudgingly
granted for any cause, it is very surprising to find Calvin and the
Genevans granting it for desertion.

The first clause is a sort of "Enoch Arden" provision. After ten
years' disappearance, if the party who disappeared has not been
heard from, divorce may be granted to the one who remains.

The rest of the items refer to abandonment. If a man leaves his
wife "through debauchery or bad affection" the wife is diligently to
search for him. Having located him, she can serve on him a summons to return or take the consequences. If she can not make him
come back, public announcement of the case is to be made three
times in church at two-week intervals, also in court, and his nearest
friends and relatives are to be notified. If this, too, is fruitless, she
can apply to the Consistory for separation and receive her freedom, the rebellious husband being banished forever from the city.
If he appears, they are to be "reconciled harmoniously and in the
fear of God."

If a man makes a practice of thus leaving his wife to travel
around the country, he is to be brought back and punished. If he
repeats the offense, he is to be reprimanded and imprisoned on bread
and water, and still more severely punished if he goes the third

---

[67] *Opera*, xlix. Comm. on I Cor. 7: 4.
[68] *Opera*, xa, 111 f.

time. After the third offense with no sign of improvement, the wife of the vagrant husband shall be free.

If the wife goes away and her husband wants a divorce, she is to be notified and her character investigated. The divorce will be granted or withheld according to what is found out about her. If she fails to appear within a specified time, the same procedure is followed as with a husband who disappears.

. . . .

The legislation does not distinctly specify the conditions under which divorce may be given for differences in religion. It is, perhaps, subsumed under the question of abandonment, for it was expected that marriage to a Catholic would form a ground for divorce only if the Protestant party were forced to migrate because of religious persecution and the wife or husband refused to go peacefully along. However, there is historical evidence that Calvin approved of granting divorce with privilege of remarriage on this ground. When the Italian Protestant Caracciolo had migrated to Geneva to escape persecution, and his Catholic wife had refused to change her religion or accompany him, Calvin consented to his being given a divorce and allowed to marry again.[69] Furthermore, in a set of *Advices on Matrimonial Questions* in reply to certain inquiries, he favors separation under such conditions as a last resort. He does not say definitely whether he would carry this separation to the point of divorce, but implies that he would. Possibly he hesitated to make flatly a statement so far removed from current practice.

There is an interesting difference of emphasis in the advice which he gives to a woman married to a Catholic husband, and to the man who has a Catholic wife. When asked if a woman who was persecuted by her husband for her religion should leave him to go to Geneva or to some other church where she could live in repose of conscience, Calvin replied that she ought not to do so because of the binding nature of marriage. She ought rather to

---

[69] M. Young, *Life and Times of Aonio Paleario*, II, p. 446. *Opera*, xvii, 509.

rely on God and try to convert her husband. Finally, however, the advice ends with a grudging concession:

If after having tried the aforesaid things she sees herself in imminent peril, even in danger that the husband may persecute her to death, then she shall use the liberty which our Lord gives to all His own to escape the fury of wolves.[70]

But if a man is married to a Catholic wife who makes things uncomfortable for him, he is apparently not obliged to put up with so much. He shall, of course, do his best to win his wife to the true faith, laboring with her daily and praying God to change her heart. But if he does not succeed and has to emigrate for freedom of worship or to escape persecution, he is justified in going without her, and no fault is to be imputed to him.

Calvin enjoins him also to take the children along, as the best treasure God has given him. If he leaves them behind, they will be held in such captivity that he will all his life regret having left them. Calvin was no more anxious than his Catholic neighbors to have the children reared by those of another faith.

· · · · · · ·

A note which resounds through Calvin's utterances upon separation and divorce is the obligation to do everything possible to settle differences before permitting the home to be broken. There was no "Court of Domestic Relations" at Geneva, but there was a Consistory. And it was expected that when husband and wife could not agree, the Consistory should do something about it. The law provided that when there were "quarrels and debates together," they should be called before the Consistory to be admonished. The records show that in numerous instances this was done. For wife-beating, the husband was to be sent before the Council and "forbidden under sure punishment." There is a fragment of an ordinance, written by Calvin but apparently never passed, which provides that in case of separation there should first be an inventory and division of goods, and every effort made to reconcile the parties. This proving unavailing, they are "each to withdraw peacefully

[70] *Opera,* xa, 241.

under pain of returning to the previous condition." Calvin was for peace—whether in marriage or separation—but not for peace at any price. The closing words of this projected ordinance set forth of a principle of liberty which one would scarcely expect to find in so puritanical a moralist:

> Whenever it happens that for the release or convenience of the two parties or of one, it seems good to them to divide and separate, as to that we leave them to their liberty.[71]

11. WOMEN'S RIGHTS

With a brief word on the place which Calvin ascribed to woman, we shall conclude this survey. In an earlier chapter we noted what Calvin thought about the kind of woman worth marrying. A wife must be chaste, frugal, patient, and solicitous for her husband's health and prosperity. Yet we have seen too that he permitted to the wife a certain kind of sex equality.

But Calvin's theory of sex equality did not go very far. Again Adam comes to the fore. "The twain shall be one flesh"—this all depends, Calvin says, on the fact that the wife was formed of the flesh and bone of her husband.[72] This being the case, there is no slightest doubt as to which is superior.

Furthermore, God made woman as a helpmate for man. This ought to keep her from hindering her husband, *comme une diablesse*. A man may not leave his wife. "And the woman on her part will also recognize, 'This is my husband who is my chief: he has authority over me, and God compels me.'"[73] Since God gives woman such a command, she disobeys not man but God if she gets haughty and chafes against the yoke. The husband, to be sure, is not to tyrannize over his wife. But he is to be the master. "Let the husband so rule as to be the head, and not the tyrant, of his wife. Let the woman, on the other hand, yield modestly to his demands."[74]

---

[71] *Opera*, xa, 144.
[72] *Opera*, li, 227. Comm. on Eph. 5:31.
[73] *Opera*, xxviii, 149. Ser. on Deut. 24:1-4.
[74] *Opera*, xlv, 529. Comm. on Mt. 19:5.

According to Paul's injunction, there is to be equality as to the
marriage bed. But still, *not quite* equality. The man who commits adultery is to be punished, like the woman. Nevertheless,
adultery is more shameful in a woman than in a man. Calvin was
too consistent a thinker to declare flatly, in the face of Paul's words,
that an adulteress sins more grievously than an adulterer. But the
double standard ingrained in the concepts of his time, as of ours,
put a strain upon his logic. "Indeed he pollutes himself who cor-
rupts the wife of his neighbor: but on account of the modesty of
the sex the contamination seems greater in a woman than in a
man." [75]

So much for woman in the home. What of woman in public
life?

The problem was not very prominent as yet, for it had occurred
to relatively few women to try to hold any position outside the
home. Still less had it occurred to men to let them.

The question first came conspicuously to the foreground in reference to the right of women to rule. Before Calvin's death, Mary
Stuart was ruling in Scotland and Elizabeth in England. Calvin's
arch-Calvinistic disciple, John Knox, was irate at such a scandalous
state of affairs, and caused a great commotion by publishing a
war-whoop entitled *The First Blast of the Trumpet Against the
Monstrous Regiment of Women*.[76] This made trouble for Calvin,
for it was published in Geneva without Calvin's knowledge or permission while Knox was staying there as an exile from Mary's persecutions. Though Calvin was not responsible, it hurt his cause
in England, for it prejudiced Elizabeth against everything proceeding from Geneva.

Calvin did not approve of women's ruling, but he was much
milder in his opposition than was Knox. He was too good a
Biblical scholar to forget that Deborah once ruled by God's permission. The law of nature and the law of God, Calvin says, orders
woman to submit and not to rule—that is clear in the Scriptures.

[75] *Opera*, xl, 428. Lect. on Ezek. 18: 5-9.
[76] Geneva, 1558.

But if a woman becomes queen by permission of the laws of the kingdom, as Deborah did, she is not to be dislodged. Philip was given no order to disturb Candace, queen of the Ethiopians. Though government by a woman is a sign of God's anger, it is to be endured till God removes it. And God will dispose of women tyrants in his own way—witness the fate of Athaliah.[77]

Though Calvin gave a qualified approval to letting women have their thrones, in another sphere he stood rock-ribbed. It is by no accident that the Presbyterian church has refused to ordain women, or to open to them anything like equality with men in religious offices. Calvin would have none of it. He denounces roundly the then-common practice of allowing midwives to baptize infants about to die.[78] It is not a woman's business, and the child might better die unbaptized.[79] A still more heinous offense is for a woman to assume to speak in meeting. Not only Paul, but Tertullian and Epiphanius set the stamp of their authority against it. "It is not permitted to any woman, Tertullian says, to speak in church, nor to teach, nor to baptize, nor to offer sacrifice: neither to lay claim to the lot of any man or of the priestly office."[80] Not till the Catholics corrupted things did this practice appear. "It is the height of impudence to urge here the approval of earlier times, for it is plainly evident that this abuse did not become implanted except with the barbarous confusion of the whole of Christianity."[81]

With such a stand on the part of their spiritual father, it is not surprising that the Calvinists of Boston less than a century later banished Anne Hutchinson for daring to think for herself and assemble the women to hear her rehearse the sermon of the previous Sunday. "Let the aged women be teachers of good things,

---

[77] *Opera,* xv, 92, 125.
[78] *Opera,* vii, 684; xi, 625, 706.
[79] Calvin did not hold, as some of the later Calvinists did, that baptism was necessary for salvation. He thought that through God's promise to Abraham the children of the faithful became sharers in salvation. However, he held of infants, as of adults, that some were elect and some were not. This led to the Puritan distinction between elect and reprobate infants.
[80] *Opera,* vii, 684.
[81] *Ibid.*

that they may teach the young women," she quoted (Titus 2: 3, 4), but this word of Paul was crushed by the weight of the more familiar word, "It is a shame for women to speak in the church." In a man-made world, it was dangerous business to let women meet together in conclave to be taught by another woman. So they called her a Jezebel and banished her from the colony.[82] We have covered some ground since then. But the legacy of restriction upon woman's freedom left by Paul and Calvin will not soon be done away.

[82] Some other factors were involved. She taught religious tolerance in opposition to the current attitude, and offended many of the ministers by saying that they preached under a "Covenant of Works" rather than a "Covenant of Grace."

CHAPTER VIII

THE MIDDLE CLASS VIRTUES

1. CALVINISM AND MIDDLE CLASS MORALS

This chapter is a study in the middle class virtues. Why not "the aristocratic" or "the proletarian" virtues? Because of the nature of the group that Calvin's teaching gripped and molded. Calvinism has always been primarily a middle class religion. This does not mean that it has not embraced in its ranks the very rich and the very poor, the aristocracy and the proletariat. It has had adherents at opposite economic poles, and at every intermediate station. Yet those at either end of the economic scale are few in comparison with the numbers whose fortunes lie in the ranks of the comfortably well-to-do.

The term "middle class" is somewhat ambiguous. It has two meanings, related but not identical. Sometimes it is used to refer to those in the middle income groups, the not-very-rich and not-very-poor. Here are included the owners of small private enterprises, wage earners of moderate income, well-to-do farmers, educators, clergy, and in general most of those in the learned professions. In ordinary parlance, all whose income is sufficient to live in modest comfort but not luxury are of the middle class. The early settlers of America were largely of this type, and it has continued to be the back-bone of American life. Most of the Calvinists, whether of Puritan, Dutch, or Scotch Presbyterian lineage, have belonged to this group, though it would be impossible to say conversely that most of the middle income group have been Calvinists.

A second use of the term identifies the middle class with the *bourgeoisie,* and in some respects runs counter to the first. Historically, the middle class arose in European society when a new

157

commercial class emerged with interests which could not be identified with those of either the landed aristocracy or the peasants. As the medieval feudal system in agriculture and the craft-gilds in industry gave way to a more complex capitalistic organization, it was inevitable that radical changes should take place resulting in the emergence of a new social stratum. When domestic consumption and the exchange of goods by barter and fairs passed over, with the improvement of means of communication, into continental and world trade, the merchant class came into power and prominence. Bankers arose to supply the capital and credit needed for large-scale enterprises. As the wage system replaced private craftsmanship, the fellowship of the old master-apprentice relation gave way to an economic cleavage of employer and employed. Then with the coming of machinery and the industrial revolution, the cleavage was further widened, and merchant and financier joined hands with manufacturer to form an employing, capitalistic *bourgeoisie*. This merchant-banker-employer group is often spoken of, from its historical origin, as the "middle class," though actually it is now a long way from the middle both in wealth and influence. It possesses; it governs; it dominates not only industry and business, but politics, education, religion and practically every form of social relationship. Through financial power, it has become the upper class. In this second sense also, Calvinism is conspicuously a middle class religion.

In surveying of Calvin's life and personal traits we saw certain virtues repeatedly exemplified; reverence, chastity, sobriety, frugality, industry, honesty. These are not the only Calvinistic virtues, or the only middle class virtues. But these were the dominant Puritan virtues, and through Puritanism they became the dominant virtues of middle class America. To fear God and keep the sabbath; to shun scandal and do a sober, honest day's work; to live simply, invest shrewdly and put by for a rainy day—this to many a "substantial" citizen still sums up the whole duty of man. These are the virtues above all others which mark their possessors as "respectable." These are the virtues which make the descendants of the Puritans esteem highly their cultural heritage and look askance at the coming of immigrants with a different cultural background. It was the preference of the majority of American voters for this set of virtues which caused the defeat of Smith and the election of Hoover to the Presidency in 1928. These virtues are epitomized in Calvin's most famous namesake, formerly President of the United States and now a highly esteemed middle class citizen of Northampton, Mass.

Two of these virtues with their ramifications we have treated in earlier chapters. The virtue of reverence, we saw, carried with it for Calvin and his successors a high regard for orthodoxy; a horror of profanity, the Pope, and the devil; and a strict sense of the obligation to go to church regularly and remember the sabbath day to keep it holy. It permeated the whole of life among those whose chief duty was to glorify God. The virtue of chastity also reached far in its influence, for with a conviction of the sanctity of marriage went also a merciless lack of sympathy for sexual sins and the grounds of a deep-seated aversion to any artificial limitation of the family. It remains for us now to consider those virtues which are most closely bound together by an economic reference; sobriety, frugality, industry and honesty.

2. SOBRIETY

When Calvin enjoined sobriety, he meant by the term both moderation in the use of intoxicants and general simplicity of living. To live soberly meant to avoid excess of any kind. Following Paul, he summarized the virtues of a well-regulated life as sobriety, righteousness and godliness. (Titus 2:11-14.) Then, with his usual precision, he defines his terms:

'Sobriety' undoubtedly denotes chastity and temperance, as well as a pure and frugal use of temporal blessings, and patience under poverty. 'Righteousness' includes all the duties of equity, that every man may receive what is his due. 'Godliness' separates us from the pollutions of the world, and by true holiness unites us to God. When these virtues are indissolubly connected, they produce absolute perfection.[1]

A large claim, that! But Calvin was modest enough about his own shortcomings and those of his fellow-men to say that absolute perfection is never found in this mundane sphere.

We shall see first how Calvin stood on the temperance question, then take a look at his view of sobriety as the "pure and frugal use of temporal blessings."

Calvin, as we noted earlier, was by no means a total abstainer, either in theory or practice.[2] He says plainly, "We are nowhere . . . forbidden to drink wine."[3] Upon occasion he drank himself, in moderation. But he stood like a rock against the sins of gluttony and drunkenness. The passage just quoted is followed at once with a qualification. "This indeed is true; but amidst an abundance of all things, to be immersed in sensual delights, to inebriate the heart and mind with present pleasures,—these things are very far from a legitimate use of the Divine blessings." Any sort of "inebriation," whether of mind or body, was to Calvin the mark of the beast.

His sermons ring with condemnations of the man who, made in God's image, pollutes himself with gluttony and drunkenness till he falls to the level of the brute. If such people do not know any better, they should be restrained.

No slight punishment awaits the intemperate, who, by cramming their bellies, waste their strength. Such persons need not only to be advised, but to be kept back from their fodder like brute beasts.[4]

We noted Calvin's somewhat ill-starred attempt at prohibition.[5] Though he was not a total abstainer, there is little doubt that were he living now, he would stand for the full enforcement of the law.

[1] III, vii, 3.
[2] *Supra*, p. 27.
[3] III, xix, 9.
[4] *Opera*, lii, 320. Comm. on I Tim. 5: 23.
[5] *Supra*, p. 28.

The grounds on which Calvin attacks the evil of intemperance are sensibly taken. He objects to it principally because it injures the health, dulls the sensibilities, interferes with working efficiency, wastes money, and—worst of all in Calvin's mind—interferes with the worship of God. We quote a few characteristic statements:

Drunkards are so bereft of their senses that they kill themselves, as if they wanted to cut their own throats. When they come to the table they sit down like dogs and get up like hogs.[6]

If a man gives himself over to drunkenness and gluttony, he puts himself in his grave before his death. For we see drunkards who are like corpses, they are half-rotted. And why? It is their pay for gourmandizing, and abusing God's handiwork. Some turn to adultery, others to thieving and plundering. However much they think they are gaining profit, they are only heading toward perdition . . . where they will have accomplished nothing except to heap up a pile of wood for the fire of God's wrath to consume.[7]

Intemperance is like a tyrant which so overcomes all the senses and feelings of men that there is no freedom in them.[8]

Let us see now what intemperance involves. If a man so gorges himself as to become useless, his nature is changed. He acts as if he were trying to defy God and nature and all order. . . . When a man is so stupefied that he has no more strength, he changes himself into a beast, effacing the image of God. Furthermore, God is cast into forgetfulness. Is not this the ingratitude of a monster, and a mixing of heaven and earth?[9]

What will become of thanksgiving, if you overcharge yourself with dainties or wine, so as to be stupefied or rendered unfit for the offices of piety and the duties of your calling?[10]

These arguments have a familiar sound. One must be temperate for the sake of preserving one's personality intact, doing one's daily work, and honoring God. But there is a conspicuous omission. The argument is self-regarding and God-regarding, but it lacks the note of concern for social welfare and seems not to recognize

[6] *Opera*, liv, 441. Ser. on Titus 1:7-9.
[7] *Opera*, xxxiv, 379. Ser. on Job 24:1-9.
[8] *Opera*, xxxvii, 652. Lect. on Jeremiah 6:10.
[9] *Opera*, li, 718. Ser. on Ephesians 5:15-18.
[10] III, x, 3.

that intemperance may have social causes. This is significant, for Calvin's middle class followers have often prided themselves on their own temperance, and have enjoined temperance upon others as a service to God and business, with slight regard for conditions of social and economic injustice which foster intemperance and crime.[11] There is still much more enthusiasm among the people of Protestant churches for prohibition than for a living wage.

On the mode of punishing drunkenness in Geneva we have less precise information than in the matter of unchastity. However, the records contain a set of provisions drawn up for the outlying villages and these reflect Genevan opinion. No one was to ask another to drink under penalty of three sous. (Apparently it was assumed that there would be less drinking on the "Dutch treat" basis!) Taverns were to be closed during the time of sermon, the tavern-keeper and the one entering each to be fined for violating the law. If one were found in a tavern during sermon he was to pay three sous and be sent to the Consistory; for the second offense, five sous; for the third, ten sous and be imprisoned. These edicts on drinking in the taverns end with a curious provision, "No one shall make rhymes under penalty of ten sous." Perhaps, the overjoyful had too often burst forth in ribald verse, with Calvin as the theme!

3. FRUGALITY

As we noted, sobriety to Calvin meant also frugality. He observed the sins of the drunkard, the spendthrift and the adulterer to be closely intertwined, and we often find him roundly denouncing the three in one breath. The "pure and frugal" use of goods is constantly enjoined. Economy was a dominant trait in the Calvinistic conscience. Calvin lived simply and frugally himself, and laid on his followers an aversion to extravagance and luxury,

---

[11] Illustrated among the New England Puritans by the three-cornered rum trade. Molasses was brought from the West Indies to New England to be distilled into rum. The rum was taken to Africa to be exchanged for slaves, and the slaves in turn were brought back to the West Indies to be exchanged for cargoes of molasses. While this was by no means approved by all the Puritans, it was tolerated without much protest.

the effects of which still persist. The Scotch (and many others) are of Calvinistic lineage.[12]

A common misunderstanding should be corrected. Calvin was not in theory an ascetic. He never taught that one should deny himself the ordinary pleasures of life, or live so frugally as to injure bodily well-being. He always counseled moderation, and the avoidance of both austerity and indulgence. Many gifts, he says, are bestowed upon us by the Creator, not for our necessity but for our pleasure. The beauty of flowers, foliage, and fruit, the delicate tints of ivory and marble, are given to delight the senses. It is our privilege and duty to use them for enjoyment. We must therefore discard that "inhuman philosophy" which would make no use of the Creator's gifts except for absolute necessity, despoiling man of all his senses and reducing him to a senseless block.[13]

Equally essential is it to guard one's health. Paul advises Timothy to use a little wine for his stomach's sake. This is because Timothy was frugal to the point of retrenching even on food, and Paul had to reprove him.

Timothy was, indeed, upright in his aims. But because he is reproved by the spirit of God, we learn that excessive severity of living was faulty in him. . . . While we ought to be temperate in eating and drinking, every person should attend to his own health. And this not for the sake of prolonging his life, but that, so long as he lives, he may serve God and be of use to his neighbors.[14]

If Calvin thus condemned "excessive severity of living," this raises the question as to why he opposed so many forms of enjoyment now generally recognized as wholesome. Frugality and simplicity certainly took an ascetic turn. We have seen how staunchly opposed he was to dancing. Card-playing could be permitted only with rigid reservations. The theatre was anathema. Songs must pass the censor, and instrumental music was banned from the

---

12 It may not be out of place to suggest a connection between this trait of the Calvinistic conscience and the middle class tendency to make economy in government a political touchstone.

13 III, x, 2, 3.

14 Opera, lii, 320. Comm. on I Tim. 5:23.

churches. Churches and dwellings must be plainly furnished. The Puritans after him, both in England and America, were still more rigorous, and art suffered severely. One who visits the cathedrals of England finds it hard to forgive Cromwell for having smashed so many acres of priceless medieval glass. There was an unimaginative practicality about Calvinism which was hostile to the spirit of the Renaissance. It was too ascetic to permit the elevation of artistic feeling into a philosophy of life, as Catholicism did with its richer emotional appeal. Troeltsch says that the rise of modern art, as symbolized by Ruskin, marks the end of the sway of Puritan asceticism.[15]

The solution of this apparent contradiction is not hard to find. "All things that are connected with the enjoyment of the present life are sacred gifts of God, but we pollute them when we abuse them."[16] Calvin believed that if such recreations and adornments were to be permitted, they would be abused. The heart might be set on earthly things and not on God. Dancing and the theatre breed adultery and lewdness. Card-playing wastes time and fosters gambling. Adornment of person and sumptuous living encourage pride and arrogance. Adornment of church or ritual bears the taint of Romanism, and detracts from the pure worship of God and the hearing of the Word as expounded in the sermon. The only safe course is to eschew all vain display.

A second answer is found in the conception of this life as mere preparation for the next. Nobody ever believed more firmly than Calvin that

> I am a stranger here,
> Heaven is my home.

In terms that seem at times to contradict his injunction to enjoy God's bounty, he enjoins the *contemptus mundi*:

The mind is never seriously excited to desire and meditate on the future life, without having previously imbibed a contempt of the present.

---

[15] *Protestantism and Progress*, p. 169. He holds that in its attitude toward art, the demarcation of early Protestantism from the modern world is sharper than at any other point.

[16] *Opera*, xlix, 420. Comm. on I Cor. 7: 29.

There is no medium between these two extremes; either the earth must become vile in our estimation, or it must retain our immoderate love. Wherefore, if we have any concern about eternity, we must use our most diligent efforts to extricate ourselves from these fetters.[17]

So we must regulate our lives like pilgrims traveling toward another land. If the terrestrial life be compared with the celestial, it is to be despised and accounted of no value, for the summit of felicity is to enjoy God's presence. While we are yet here, we must endure patiently its trials and keep our souls uncorrupted by the vain pleasures of the world.[18]

Such a view of the future life as man's true destiny could scarcely fail to have its effect on matters of practical concern in the present life.

He who commands us to use this world as though we used it not, prohibits not only all intemperance in eating and drinking, and excessive delicacy, ambition, pride, haughtiness, and fastidiousness in our furniture, our habitations, and our apparel, but every care and affection which would either seduce or disturb us from thoughts of the heavenly life, and attention to the improvement of our souls.[19]

Holding this doctrine, Calvin and the Calvinists came naturally to fear the corruption of "worldly" things. They saw no medium between two extremes.

. . . .

The limits of space forbid an exhaustive treatment of the protests of the Calvinistic conscience against extravagance and worldly softness. The general outlines are familiar.

Plain living in foods is commended, both as to quantity and quality. As we take away food from greedy children, God does the same with grown men. Those who have to be catered to with delicate morsels and special cooks encourage a shameful extravagance.

Those who have devised much variety in order to satisfy the appetite have surely offended God, and ought to be despised—however

[17] III, ix, 1, 2.
[18] *Ibid.*, 3-6.
[19] III, x, 4.

much they are lauded by people who exclaim, "Oh! what a fine cook; oh! what a capital inn-keeper!" They glory in having invented many viands and concocted new dainties to please the palate of those who demand too luxurious service. All this is detestable, and it could be wished that such people had died before they were born.[20]

All earthly possessions are gifts of God. But not all recipients of God's bounty are grateful—not even grateful enough to return thanks for their food! Calvin has no patience with the person who is in too much of a hurry to say grace before he eats:

Those things which God has appointed for our use . . . require us to offer praise to Him. . . . Hence it follows that they who swallow them down without thinking of God are guilty of sacrilege, and profane God's gifts. And this instruction is the more worthy of attention because we daily see a great part of the world feeding themselves like brute beasts.[21]

Semper idem!

Likewise God enjoins simplicity in dress. "Indeed, if we look well at the origin of clothes, we ought not to be so given to superfluous display as we are." Every time we put on shirts or dresses, it should remind us of Father Adam's sin, and call us to a true humility.[22] And Calvin has slight respect for those who spend everything on their backs:

It is certain . . . that if it were not for ambition and pride, extravagance would not be so common as it is. There are a great many people who prefer to endure hunger and thirst in their bodies in order to use their money on things which are of no use to them except for pomp and vanity. . . . And we see this today more than ever before.[23]

This sounds so modern that one wonders whether Calvin had not seen a girl in a five hundred dollar fur coat lunching on a ten cent sandwich and five cent cup of coffee. He had not, but

---

[20] *Opera*, xxviii, 35. Ser. on Deut. 22: 9-12.
[21] *Opera*, xlvii, 132. Comm. on John 6: 11.
[22] *Opera*, xxviii, 20. Ser. on Deut. 22: 5-8.
[23] *Ibid.*, 21.

he had seen women in Geneva dressing beyond their means. And men too. With playful sarcasm, he suggests that the great lords and fine dandies who want to attire themselves like dolls to be gazed upon, ought all to be forced to become dress-makers. Then they would have plenty of chance to try on all the costumes and use their ingenuity devising new ones.

. . . .

Calvin had a deep insight into the perils of prosperity. We cannot blame God for sending scarcity and want, he says, for when he sends us plenty we misuse these gifts. If there is abundance of wine, people get drunk and cannot be restrained—what is worse, they blaspheme the name of God. Similarly, in abundance of wheat, people get intoxicated by prosperity. Pride arises and they will bear neither admonition nor discipline. Besides, there is cruelty each toward the other, and he who possesses most tyrannizes over his neighbor and has no pity for those in need. Since this is our conduct in abundance, God has to change his policy and send us want to bring us to a true humility.[24] The inebriation of prosperity is man's undoing.[25] Again one notes Calvin's keenness in analyzing a practical situation. Could he have looked some centuries ahead, he might have pointed to a civilization shaped in large measure by the ideals of his spiritual descendants as a striking illustration of this inebriation of prosperity.

Elsewhere, Calvin suggests that when God sends prosperity, "the affluence of our blessings is to try our frugality."[26] When God pours forth what is needful with a liberal hand, he tests our temperance to see whether we will use these gifts with frugality and gratitude. To restrain ourselves in the midst of abundance is a virtue well-pleasing to God, and reveals a grateful heart. Calvin might have added, though he did not, that this is also an excellent way to lay up treasures upon earth as well as in heaven.

---

[24] *Opera,* xxviii, 445. Ser. on Deut. 28: 46-50.
[25] *Opera,* xxxix, 230. Lect. on Jer. 42: 13-17.
[26] *Opera,* xliv, 280. Comm. on Zech. 9: 15.

His followers were not slow to avail themselves of this practical implication.[27]

4. INDUSTRY

We come now to the virtue on which Weber in his *Protestant Ethic and the Spirit of Capitalism* lays greatest stress as Calvin's major contribution to the growth of the capitalistic spirit.

I can agree only partially with Weber's view that Calvin is the source of the *Berufsethik* which made industry a dominant Puritan trait.[28] There is no doubt that Calvin himself was an unusually hard-working person who prized highly the virtue of industry. Also, it is true that most of his disciples, both contemporary and subsequent, were hard-working people. The Puritans could not have established themselves in New England, nor the Scotch-Irish Presbyterians in the second tier of colonies, if they had not been willing to labor long and hard in the face of obstacles. The Calvinistic temper is opposed to softness of any kind, and idleness is a form of softness. All this had its effect upon the attainment of prosperity, and eventually on the piling up of fortunes and the establishment of capitalism. But when one searches Calvin's own words, one finds comparatively little about the duty to labor. Denunciations of the blasphemer, the adulterer, the drunkard, and the spendthrift, appear on almost every page. Also, of the avaricious person who covets his neighbor's goods and amasses riches dishonestly. But one must seek diligently to find references to the sin of idleness, or praises for the virtue of toil.

There are several possible explanations of this relatively slight emphasis. Perhaps he took it for granted that people ought to work hard, and therefore did not think it necessary to say so. This, however, seems unlikely. Calvin did not take anything for granted. Even if he did, he hammered away for double emphasis.

---

[27] Cf. *infra*, pp. 184-187. Had the frugality practiced by the Calvinists been universal, economic progress would of course have been retarded by the diminution of trade due to under-consumption. It was because others were furnishing markets by living in luxury that the Puritans were able to amass wealth.

[28] To be discussed in the next chapter.

A more reasonable explanation may be that idleness was not a sin very much practiced in Geneva, and therefore he did not think it necessary to say very much. Probably it is true that idleness was a less conspicuous evil than drunkenness or unchastity or extravagance. Yet it can hardly be supposed that there were not many lazy people, both rich and poor, within hearing of Calvin's tongue. Human nature has not changed materially since then. Among the rich, at least, whose avarice and extravagance he continually denounces, there must have been much idleness. But the sin of inactivity among those who could afford to refrain from work seems never to have impressed him greatly. Idle servants receive much more of his condemnation.

I believe that the explanation is to be found mainly in Calvin's theology. God is the sovereign Lord of all. God dispenses riches and poverty as he will. It is not man's merit, or man's toil, that gets a person riches. Rather, it is God's grace. Some get riches as an evidence of God's favor. Some get them in order to furnish, by their punishment, an awful example to the wicked of the sin of avarice. But both the giving and withholding of riches are in God's hand.

A few citations from Calvin's words will make this clearer:

As the Psalmist shows, it is in vain to rise up early in the morning, and go to bed late, and drink water [*sic*] and eat only half enough bread; that will advance one not at all unless God extends His hand and bounty. On the contrary, goods sometimes come to His children as they sleep. And this shows that men err if they think they enrich themselves by their own merit.[29]

Reversals, like accessions, of fortune are God's doing. Later in the passage just cited Calvin comments upon the fact that people who think they have got rich through their own effort or shrewdness blaspheme God, and then God has to take their wealth away to punish their ingratitude. There is an interesting reference here to the rising commercialism of Calvin's day, also to the losses

[29] *Opera*, xxvi, 627. Ser. on Deut. 8: 14-20, referring to Ps. 127: 2.

which many of the landed gentry were suffering in the transition to a new economic order:

> If we are perverse and rob God of His right, we must be impoverished and constrained by necessity to come to Him. From this proceeds the change in fortune we see when a rich and apparently impregnable house loses all its money and is crushed. I do not speak solely of the *maisons bourgeoises*. There are also the great houses of the lords, whose thousand-pound rents are cut in half, then to a third, and finally they dwindle to nothing.[30]

Calvin is conscious of the enervating power of riches. His injunction, however, is not on this account to work harder in one's secular calling. Rather, it is man's duty to strain every nerve to perform his duty to God and render him due homage.

> Let us walk always in the fear of God, rendering gratitude and homage to God for the goods we possess, knowing we cannot enjoy them unless it pleases Him to continue His grace toward us. Then riches will be a blessing, and like honors, delicacies and the like, will not intoxicate men or put them to sleep, but rather will make them more vigilant in placing everything in God's hands.[31]

Calvin believes, of course, that people ought to labor. But he does not think that they ought to labor all the time, or become so wrapped up in their work as to forget God in the pursuit of riches. The people of Amos' time, he says, were unwilling to quit work even on the sabbath or the new moon, for they thought that to rest even one day was to lose time. The prophet had to reprimand them, and people of the present should take warning.

> For we see that the avaricious grow weary, as their cupidity ever excites them, for they are like an oven: and since they are thus hot, if an hour is lost, they think that a whole year has passed away; they calculate the very moments of time. "How is it," they say, "there is no merchant coming? I have now rested one day, and I have not gained a farthing."[32]

---

[30] *Opera*, xxvi, 627 f.
[31] *Opera*, xxxiv, 309. Ser. on Job 22: 18-22.
[32] *Opera*, xliii, 145. Comm. on Amos 8: 5.

This goes on till the mania for labor which goes with avarice becomes a "disease of the mind." Again, could Calvin have looked into the future he would have seen plenty of minds thus "diseased" among his spiritual descendants.[33] If Calvinism itself was a primary factor in the development of the spirit of feverish haste which has possessed the Western world, this is a strange paradox.

. . . .

All these passages have a somewhat negative sound. Already Calvin was perceiving the evil which comes from working too much in the pursuit of this world's goods. But there are other passages which enjoin the positive virtue of industry. Father Adam again appears. The labor of man is necessary as a punishment for sin. It is necessary, too, simply because God in his wisdom ordains that man should toil—though of course, Calvin hastens to add, God could nourish us with our arms crossed if he wanted to.[34] Yet it pleases God that men should work, each one in the estate to which he is called. Calvin, like Luther, seems here to accept the functional view of society which had prevailed in the Middle Ages, holding that everybody should perform the duties of his station without murmuring.

There are many occupations honorable in the sight of God, and everybody ought to pursue the kind in which he can be most helpful to his neighbors.[35] Manual labor is commended (I Thess. 4: 11) but this does not mean that no other kind is lawful. The main thing is to labor diligently at something, and conduct oneself honorably in the eyes of God and men. "For nothing is more unseemly than a man that is idle and good for nothing—who profits neither himself or others, and seems born only to eat and drink." [36]

It is in conjunction with Paul's rule that "if any would not work, neither should he eat," that Calvin's condemnation of idleness appears most plainly. "It is certain that idleness and indolence

---

[33] This term is used broadly to indicate all who were influenced by Calvinism, not necessarily those affiliated with Calvinistic churches.
[34] *Opera*, xxviii, 379. Ser. on Deut. 28: 9-14.
[35] *Opera*, li, 211. Comm. on Eph. 5: 28.
[36] *Opera*, lii, 164. Comm. on I Thess. 4: 11.

are accursed of God." [37] It is taught by the Scripture and recognized even by the heathen that man was created to do something. Paul's principle is wholly reasonable, and idleness is not to be encouraged by supplying the lazy with food. Calvin elsewhere enjoins almsgiving as a religious duty, but never the feeding of the shiftless. For "idle bellies that chirp sweetly in the shade" [38] he had no sympathy.

However, it was not in Calvin's precepts, but in his example, that we find his most potent influence. As we saw in surveying his life, he labored incessantly, and labored in the face of obstacles that would have daunted any soul of softer fibre. In spite of ill health such as would, in many men, have justified complete idleness, he did an amazing amount of work. His writings in the fifty-nine volumes of the *Opera* constitute alone a literary output such as few other men could have produced in a life-time, if they had done nothing else. When one adds to this the time consumed in preaching and lecturing nearly five hundred times a year, if Beza's account is at all to be relied upon, and the time devoted to counseling those in need, in admonishing offenders, in fighting his way through the almost incessant controversies of the first twenty years of his ministry, the herculean tasks which he accomplished give evidence of an astounding industry which speaks far louder than any words.

So we find in Calvin a double emphasis; an injunction to labor, and a warning against laboring too much in the pursuit of gain. It was the injunction to labor which impressed itself most firmly on Calvin's followers, whether in Scotland, England or America. And the injunction bore its fruits. The combination of frugality with industry made for thrift—and thrift for the amassing of riches. Then with the heaping up of riches came the care of this world and the undoing of much for which Calvin labored. As minds became "diseased," his followers forgot the timely warning of their leader.

[37] *Opera*, lii, 213. Comm. on II Thess. 3:10.
[38] *Opera*, xb, 64.

5. HONESTY

We come now to the last of the middle class virtues which we shall survey, the virtue of honesty. This is a very broad term, sometimes virtually inclusive of all the rest. An "honest" person, in common parlance, often means a "respectable" person. And a respectable person is one who does not get drunk or run with women or swear to excess, one who goes to church regularly and contributes generously, one who does an honest day's work, pays his bills, and piles up a neat bank-account. If he meets these requirements, he is one of Middletown's leading citizens and it matters little how he exploits his employees through the week.

Werner Sombart in tracing the rise of business morality suggests the genesis of this conception of an honest citizen. Among the Florentine traders, where capitalism had its rise, the virtue of *onestà* came as early as the fourteenth century to be highly prized, This meant then, as its derivative now, not merely business honesty but respectable living according to the accepted canons of one's group. "In essence, this meant—eschew all irregularities; appear in respectable society; avoid drinking, gambling and women; go to church regularly; in a word, always wear the aspect of true respectability, and all for the sake of your business. Such a moral rule of life will ensure your credit." [39] One finds in the commercial circles of this early day "a perfect picture of Benjamin Franklin, the incarnation of the spirit of respectable citizenship." [40] Sombart cites as example Leone Battista Alberti in the fifteenth century, whose *Del governo della famiglia* extols the then unusual virtues of thrift, business foresight, and economy of time. Daniel Defoe's *Compleat Citizen* in the seventeenth follows the same pattern, and leads on to Franklin's familiar almanac philosophy in the eighteenth. Sombart agrees with Weber that Calvin contributed to the emphasis upon these virtues, but points out that

[39] Sombart, *The Quintessence of Capitalism*, p. 123.
[40] *Ibid.*, p. 104.

he was by no means the first to give them religious or popular sanction.[41]

There is little question that Calvin had much to do with the development of the virtues which make up honesty in this Rotarian sense. But with one present day feature of business respectability Calvin stands completely out of joint. It is now quite possible to be "honest" in the sense of keeping business contracts, maintaining a good name, and breaking no law of state or society, and still be deceptive and avaricious. Calvin could find no approval of such practice in God's word, and he never tired of thundering against the sins of avarice and deception.

The Decalogue, for Calvin, summed up the whole of moral law. Therefore it is not surprising to find him staunchly enjoining the last three commandments and denouncing theft, lying and covetousness. First, a look at the ninth, then together at the eighth and tenth.

Calvin is almost Kantian in his insistence that a lie is always wrong. He has trouble here, for the Bible says Rahab lied to shield the spies and Rebecca to help Jacob get the birthright, and the record stands apparently with God's approval.[42] Calvin was too honest himself either to dodge the evidence, or to admit these acts to be virtuous. So he got around the difficulty by saying that there was a fault here, but the fault was suppressed by the kindness of God. He insists repeatedly that lying is wrong because it is contrary to God's nature. God is truth, and before him no untruth can find favor. "Those who hold what is called a dutiful lie to be altogether excusable, do not sufficiently consider how precious truth is in the sight of God."[43] Lying cannot be justified unless we want to mix heaven and earth, or call black white, or change light to darkness. And a lie is doubly grievous if it harms another person, for then God is offended and our neighbor

---

[41] *Infra*, p. 187.
[42] *Opera*, xxv, 440; xxiv, 19. Comms. on Josh. 2: 8; Exod. 1: 18.
[43] *Opera*, xxv, 440.

also suffers injury. There are grades of lies, some worse than others, but none is blameless in the sight of God.[44]

Calvin is surprisingly broad-minded in seeing the range of injury covered by the command, "Thou shalt not bear false witness." A lie, he says, is more than a saying of untrue words. When Paul forbids lying, he condemns every sort of cunning and all base artifices of deception.[45] We are forbidden to engage in backbiting or tale-bearing, or in any way to injure the reputation or interests of our neighbor. God's command against bearing false witness applies as much to private conversation as to perjury under oath. To steal another's reputation is as bad as to steal his purse. One's mind leaps to Shakespeare (born the year Calvin died), as one finds him saying:

For if a good name be more precious than any treasures whatsoever, a man sustains as great an injury when he is deprived of the integrity of his character as when he is despoiled of his wealth.[46]

God forbids the hearing, like the spreading, of detraction. And God hates not only slander in the tongue but malice in the heart. "An unreasonable propensity to unfavorable opinions respecting others" can never find favor in God's eyes. Calvin rises to the spirit of the Sermon on the Mount as we find him urging charity in judgment, and the placing of "fair constructions on every man's words and actions."[47] The pity of it is that this advice was not more often followed by himself.

Calvin spoke in no uncertain terms against the sins of avarice and rapine. His whole personality was set like flint against any chicanery or double dealing to which the love of money might entice the weak. While he did not condemn riches as such, he was well aware of the temptations which the love of riches offer the soul, and his sermons resound with warnings against plunder, fraudulence, and greed.

[44] *Opera*, xxx, 327. Hom. on I Sam. 19: 17-21.
[45] *Opera*, lii, 120. Comm. on Col. 3.
[46] II, viii, 47.
[47] *Ibid.*, 48.

Calvin's theory of property rights follows directly and simply from his theology. Everybody holds his possessions by the dispensation of the supreme Lord of all. Private property is thus a sacred trust, and "therefore no man can be deprived of his possessions by criminal methods, without an injury being done to the Divine dispenser of them." [48] To steal another's goods or defraud him of his just due is to commit a more heinous offense than any ordinary injury to one's neighbor, for it is to affront God.

As in the bearing of false witness, Calvin holds that there are many kinds of theft other than what is commonly so labeled. No fraudulence is to be glossed over with fair terms or covered by some trick of the civil law. Man may be deceived: God cannot be. He analyzes so clearly the current practice—contemporary and subsequent—that we shall let him speak for himself:

The species of theft are numerous. One consists in violence, when the property of any person is plundered by force and predatory license. Another consists in malicious imposture, when it is taken away in a fraudulent manner. Another consists in more secret cunning, where any one is deprived of his property under the mask of justice. Another consists in flatteries, where we are cheated under the pretense of a donation. But not to dwell too long on the recital of the different species of theft, let us remember that all artifices by which the possessions and wealth of our neighbors are transferred to us, whenever they deviate from sincere love into a desire of deceiving, or doing any kind of injury, are to be esteemed acts of theft. This is the only view in which God considers them, even though the property may be gained by a suit at law.[49]

Nor does avarice pertain only to the acquisition of another's material possessions. To fail in service to one's neighbor, whether the service due be that of kind office or paid employment, is to rob our fellow-man and offend God.

And this kind of injury relates not only to money, or to goods, or to lands, but to whatever each individual is justly entitled to; for we defraud our neighbors of their property, if we deny them those kind

[48] II, viii, 45.
[49] *Ibid.* Subsequent quotations are from the same section.

offices, which it is our duty to perform to them. If an idle agent or steward devour the substance of his master, and be inattentive to the care of his domestic affairs; if he either improperly waste, or squander with a luxurious profusion, the property intrusted to him; . . . and if, on the other hand, a master inhumanly oppress his family,—God holds him guilty of theft.

.   .   .   .

In general, the Puritans and other early Calvinists accepted this view of the sinfulness of chicanery and avarice. Fair dealing toward master, servant, or peer was a virtue highly prized. Honesty of spirit—not simply the appearance of honesty as an economic asset—characterized the Puritan conscience. Though covetousness existed, it was condemned. It was not "respectable" to be avaricious or to defraud one's neighbor.

This is still true—in a measure. It is bad business tactics to get a reputation for being dishonest. Yet there is not the cleavage between respectability and avarice which once prevailed. The doctrine that "business is business" has led to the heaping up of fortunes by ostensibly religious people through more than one of the processes which Calvin bluntly labeled theft.

This change has come about through an interplay of many complex forces. Yet in principle, the reasons are not difficult to uncover. As the competitive system expanded, competition became sharper and the struggle for economic supremacy loosened moral restraints. As machinery mechanized the processes of industry, men too became mechanized. The duty to God and neighbor for which Calvin pleaded became entangled in the machine and lacerated almost beyond recognition. Under the influence of Calvin's injunctions to sobriety, frugality and industry, his followers waxed rich and became inebriated with prosperity; and an age beset with the love of things and riches clung to the semblance of honesty as an economic asset but forgot the heart of Calvin's message. An all-powerful materialistic system replaced, in men's thinking, an all-powerful deity. In the next two chapters we shall examine further the processes by which this came to pass.

CHAPTER IX

"THE PROTESTANT ETHIC AND THE SPIRIT OF CAPITALISM"

We have had occasion to refer a number of times to a famous essay by Max Weber, *Die protestantische Ethik und der Geist des Kapitalismus*.[1] In this treatise Weber has pointed out the close concomitance between the growth of Calvinism and of capitalism and has tried to analyze the relationship between the two. He maintains that the capitalistic spirit may virtually be regarded as the child of Calvinism. The essay is richly suggestive, and has been productive of so much controversy[2] that any treatment of Calvinistic ethics or of the middle class virtues would be incomplete without reference to it. A summary and brief discussion of it will be included here for the light which it throws on the economic ethics of Calvinism.

1. THE SPIRIT OF CAPITALISM

Weber starts his inquiry from the empirical fact that the possessors of capital, the more highly educated workmen, and the more

---

[1] Published serially in 1904-05 in the *Archiv für Sozialwissenschaft und Sozialpolitik* (vols. xx and xxi). Republished in book form in 1922 as the first study in Weber's *Gesammelte Aufsätze zur Religionssoziologie* (J. C. B. Mohr, Tübingen). Translated into English by Talcott Parsons and published by Scribner's, New York, 1930.

[2] Among the most important books and articles discussing Weber's thesis are the following: Ernst Troeltsch, *Die Soziallehren der christlichen Kirchen und Gruppen*, Tübingen, 1923; Lujo Brentano, *Die Anfänge des modernen Kapitalismus*, München, 1913, translated by M. Epstein and published as *The Quintessence of Capitalism*, London, 1915; R. H. Tawney, *Religion and the Rise of Capitalism*, New York, 1926; also his foreword to Parsons' translation of the essay; Gerhard von Schulze-Gaevernitz, "Die Geistesgeschichtlichen Grundlagen der Anglo-Americanischen Weltsuprematie. III. Die Wirthschaftsethik des Kapitalismus" in *Archiv für Sozialwissenschaft und Sozialpolitik*, Bd. 61, 1929; F. Rachfal, "Kalvinismus und Kapitalismus" in *Internationale Wochenschrift*, 1909, i, III; H. Sée, "Dans quelle mesure Puritains et Juifs ont-ils contribué au Progrès du Capitalisme Moderne?" in *Revue Historique*, t. CLV, 1927; Kemper Fullerton, "Calvinism and Capitalism" in *Harvard Theological Review*, July, 1928.

highly trained directors of technical and commercial undertakings, are prevailingly Protestant. Catholic higher education is humanistic rather than technical, and in industry Catholic employees tend to remain in subordinate positions while skilled workmen and entrepreneurs are recruited mainly from Protestant ranks. Furthermore, the countries in which capitalism has made greatest headway are prevailingly Protestant countries. During the sixteenth and seventeenth centuries the expansion of capitalism and Protestantism—particularly Calvinism—went hand in hand, and trade flourished best in Huguenot, Dutch and Puritan areas. The Spanish early noticed this connection and said that heresy (i.e. the Calvinism of the Netherlanders) favored the commercial spirit. Historically and contemporaneously, the connection is too widespread to be accidental.

Weber's first problem is to define the spirit of capitalism. He takes as a point of departure Benjamin Franklin's *Advice to a Young Tradesman*,[3] since this expresses the capitalistic spirit in classic purity and without religious connections.

Remember that *time* is money. He that can earn ten shillings a day by his labour, and goes abroad, or sits idle one half of that day, though he spends but sixpence during his diversion or idleness, ought not to reckon *that* the only sixpence; he has really spent, or rather thrown away, five shillings besides. . . .

Remember that money is of a prolific and generating nature. Money can beget money, and its offspring can beget more. Five shillings turned is six, turned again it is seven and threepence, and so on till it becomes an hundred pounds. . . . He that kills a breeding sow, destroys all her offspring to the thousandth generation. He that murders a crown, destroys all that it might have produced, even scores of pounds.

What Franklin advocates here, Weber says, is not mere business shrewdness, but an ethic—a sense of moral obligation for activity in one's calling. Franklin quotes Proverbs 22:29, "Seest thou a man diligent in his business? He shall stand before kings." The

[3] Written in 1736. Weber quotes also from Franklin's *Necessary Hints to Those That Would Be Rich*, 1748. Cf. *Works*, ed. of 1793, II, p. 55 ff.

Alpha and Omega of Franklin's ethic is an efficient diligence in business for utilitarian ends.

It is this feeling of moral duty to labor to increase one's capital which, according to Weber, most sharply differentiates the modern commercial spirit from the "traditionalism" of the Middle Ages. In all ages men have desired to make money, and have done so without restraint of moral scruples. But in the medieval period, money-making was not regarded as a duty. The tradesman of that day, like the peasant, lived frugally and saw no use of working harder than was necessary to meet his simple needs. He was content with little and preferred restfulness to riches.[4] To the pre-capitalistic man, the feverish, money-mad rush of modern life would have appeared incomprehensible. This ethical indifference to the obligation to work to increase one's profits was a barrier which had to be overcome before the capitalistic spirit could make headway.

The spirit of capitalism is characterized also, Weber says, by a tendency to ascetic self-discipline. The term *ascetic* is used by Weber to connote a life of strict ethical discipline lived, not apart from, but in the world. *Innerweltliche Askese* means the willingness to sacrifice personal comfort for the sake of an end in the pursuance of the duties of one's calling. Men who became masters of business and brought about the transition from traditionalism to capitalism were not, Weber says, mere speculators and economic adventurers. "On the contrary, they were men who had grown up in the hard school of life, calculating and daring at the same time, above all temperate and reliable, shrewd and completely devoted to their business, with strictly bourgeois opinions and principles."[5] To the present, after a complete sundering of this discipline from its earlier religious backgrounds, its characteristics are evident in the successful capitalistic entrepreneur.

[4] Fullerton cites an apt contemporary illustration of "traditionalism" in a Damascus shop-keeper who was accustomed to shut up shop, whatever the hour, when he thought he had made enough money for the day, and then go home to smoke his narghile and enjoy himself. *Harvard Theological Review*, July 1928, p. 167.

[5] *Gesammelte Aufsätze zur Religionssoziologie*, p. 53 f. In general, quotations from the essay follow Parsons' rendering, but I have made a few minor changes.

So here we have the spirit of capitalism—an ethical obligation to labor diligently to make money and an ascetic self-discipline which drives one to unflagging activity. This constitutes what Weber calls *economic rationalism*. Such conscientious devotion to business effort is an acquired ethic rather than a mere acquisitive impulse, and is irrational from the standpoint of eudæmonistic self-interest. To discover its sources he turns to early Protestantism.

2. THE PROTESTANT ETHIC

The central theme of Weber's essay is the idea that in economic rationalism, one's secular calling took on a religious significance which gave a moral dynamic to business activity. The term *Beruf,* or *vocatio,* he maintains, acquired a new meaning with the Reformation. Historical study shows that neither Catholic peoples nor those of classical antiquity have possessed a word for a calling in the sense of a life-task, while all the predominantly Protestant peoples have had one. The origin of the term, Weber thinks, is in Luther's use of *Beruf* to translate $\xi\rho\gamma o\nu$ and $\pi\acute{o}\nu o\varsigma$ in Ecclesiasticus 11:20, 21. When he wrote "Trust in the Lord and abide in thy *Beruf,*" it marked the emergence of a new concept—the religious significance of one's daily task.

In Luther's use of the term, one's *Beruf* is the work he accepts as God's decree. Furthermore, God decrees that man fulfil his calling, not in a monastery, but in the world. The concept is intertwined with one of Luther's most fundamental contributions, the setting aside of the distinction between the cloister and secular life as spheres of religious activity. All men, he said, are equally obligated to do God's work, and every legitimate calling is of equal value in the eyes of God. Man must labor at his *Beruf,* not away from the world, but in it.

However, to serve God *within* one's calling is not the same as to serve God *by* one's calling, and this last step Luther was too much of a traditionalist to take. Both his social and economic conservatism and his predestinarian theology made him look upon each man's *Beruf* as the station in life where God had placed him, to be humbly and patiently acquiesced in, not to be climbed out of. He never passed beyond the medieval functional view of society. Before the new *Beruf* concept could enact economic changes, a further step must be taken.

According to Weber, Calvin took this step. The obligation to glorify God in one's daily toil passed from service *in vocatione* to *per vocationem*. The change had theological roots. Predestination took a different turn in Calvin's thought, for Luther was a mystic, Calvin an intellectualist. Luther believed it possible to fall from grace and be reinstated through penitential humility and trust in God's word and sacraments. For Calvin, God's will is absolute, and God's grace is unavoidable for the saved, unattainable for the lost. The result, in Calvinism, is a doctrine of the isolation of the individual. Each man must travel his way of life alone. No preacher, no sacrament, no church can alter the inevitable destiny ordained of God.

Weber points out two important historical results of this doctrine of man's isolation. One is the ascetic note of Puritanism. It became the ground for the negative attitude of the Puritan toward all sensuous, æsthetic, and emotional elements in culture and religion. In the second place, it is the root of the pessimistic, other-worldly individualism of people of Puritan background. An example appears in that masterpiece of Puritan literature, *Pilgrim's Progress*. As Christian flees from the City of Destruction on his pilgrimage to the heavenly city, his weeping wife and children cling to him, but stopping his ears with his fingers and crying "life, eternal life," he staggers forth.

Calvinism thus tends toward individualism. But, says Weber, it also shows marked superiority in social organization. How reconcile the two? The answer is in the divine sovereignty. The world is designed solely for God's glory, and the elect must honor him by obedience to his will in the social order. For God's glory, society must be served. But this is a rationalized and impersonal social service, not one actuated by brotherly love or concern for humanity. It finds its foremost expression in *fidelity to the duties of one's daily task.* "Brotherly love, since it may only be practised for the glory of God and not in the service of the flesh, is expressed in the first place in the fulfillment of the daily task given by the *lex naturæ;* and in the process this fulfillment assumes a peculiarly objective and impersonal character, that of service in the interest of the rational organization of our social environment." [6]

By still another channel, Calvinistic theology became an incentive to activity. In an age when the life beyond was considered both more important and more certain than the interests of the present life, the primary question for every believer was "Am I of the elect?" For Calvin himself, this was not a problem, for he was sure that he was a chosen agent of the Lord. But as Calvinism developed, the question became acute. Outwardly, the elect did not differ from the damned. The same subjective experiences were possible except the perseverance of the saints, and this lay in the future which was veiled to human eyes. Yet not only one's peace of mind, but admission to the Communion table and much of one's social standing depended on the crucial question of one's state of grace.

Two related answers were given. On the one hand it was held to be an absolute duty to consider oneself chosen, and to combat all doubts as temptations of the devil. On the other, intense secular activity was recommended as the most suitable means of banishing doubt and attaining certainty of grace. The faith of the believer must be *fides efficax*—must confirm itself in outward deeds. This quest for assurance of salvation readily reinforced the obligation to glorify God by diligent toil. Not election, but assurance of election, could thus be won. Good works could save no man; but good works could give clear evidence, to the believer and his associates, that God had chosen him for salvation. Weber thus sums up this somewhat paradoxical doctrine:

Only one who is of the elect has really the *fides efficax*. Only he is able, by means of his regeneration and the resulting sanctification of his

[6] *Gesammelte Aufsätze*, p. 100 f.

whole life, to increase God's glory by really, not merely apparently, good works. . . .

In practice this means that God helps him who helps himself. Thus the Calvinist works out his own salvation; or more properly, the assurance of it. This is not, however, as in Catholicism through the gradual laying up of merit in individual good works, but through a life of systematic self-discipline.[7]

3. THE OUTCOME

In the final section of the essay, Weber traces the influence of this "Protestant asceticism" upon the growth of the capitalistic spirit in English Puritanism. He finds in Richard Baxter a type of the seventeenth century Puritan. His *Christian Directory, Saints Everlasting Rest,* and other voluminous writings give evidence of the practical effects of a century of Calvinistic thought.

Baxter's writings, like those of other Puritans, abound in warnings against the entanglements of riches. However, to avoid the moral relaxation which comes with their possession, *every man must labor.* The saints' everlasting rest is in the next world only. Waste of time is in principle the deadliest of sins. Work is necessary both as a defense against sexual temptation and as a means of glorifying God. Aquinas had held that the wealthy were under no obligation to labor; Baxter would exempt no one. "It is for action that God maintaineth us and our abilities; work is the moral as well as the natural end of power. . . . It is action that God is most served and honoured by." [8]

Now appears another paradox. This God-given obligation to labor, though it might be urged as a prophylactic against the corrupting influences of riches, could scarcely fail to lead to their accumulation. Furthermore, Baxter held that the usefulness of a calling must be judged not only by moral criteria but by its profitableness. In an oft-quoted passage he remarks:

If God show you a way in which you may lawfully get more than in another way (without wrong to your soul, or to any other), if you

---

[7] *Gesammelte Aufsätze,* p. 110 f.
[8] *Christian Directory,* Pt. I, Ch. X, Tit. 1, § 7, 3; p. 448.

refuse this, and choose the less gainful way, you cross one of the ends of your Calling, and you refuse to be God's Steward.[9]

Even the Puritans' repudiation of fleshly indulgence became an economic boomerang. Such means of enjoyment as were permitted must not cost anything. The theatre was taboo. Worldly feasts were forbidden and religious art suppressed, both from fear of superstition and fear of extravagance. Fine clothes and personal adornment were frowned upon. Sports were shunned as a waste of money and a temptation to forsake one's daily task. With the characteristic Calvinistic emphasis on sobriety, frugality and thrift, it was inevitable that consumption be curtailed. And this meant the laying up of this world's goods.

So the Puritans found themselves in an economic dilemma. On the one hand, they feared the soul-corrupting influence of riches. On the other, their diligence in business and asceticism in expenditures made them rich. A vicious circle was formed, comparable to the struggle of the monastic orders to cope with the secularizing effects of wealth. One of John Wesley's sermons indicates the fruits this policy had borne by the eighteenth century:

I fear whenever riches have increased, the essence of religion has decreased in the same proportion. Therefore I do not see how it is possible in the nature of things for any revival of true religion to continue long. For religion must necessarily produce both industry and frugality, and these cannot but produce riches. But as riches increase, so will pride, anger, and love of the world in all its branches. . . . Is there no way to prevent this—this continual decay of pure religion? We ought not to prevent people from being diligent and frugal; *we must exhort all Christians to gain all they can and to save all they can; that is, in effect, to grow rich.*[10]

Wesley's solution is that those who gain all they can, and save all they can, must also give all they can. But this failed to stem the tide. From a life of methodical self-discipline which looked upon industry, frugality, and profit-getting as God-given duties

[9] *Christian Directory*, Pt. I, Ch. X, Tit. 1, § 24, 9; p. 450.
[10] Southey, *Life of Wesley*, Ch. 29. Ed. New York, 1855, II, p. 308. Italics Weber's.

by which to glorify God and win assurance of salvation, the emphasis passed to money-making as an end. Devotion to one's calling took the place of devotion to the glory of God. A utilitarian worldliness replaced the search for the Kingdom of Heaven. The expanding industrialism of the eighteenth and nineteenth centuries transformed the economic order; but before this happened, religion had consecrated profit-seeking. As Weber puts it, "What the great religious epoch of the seventeenth century bequeathed to its utilitarian heir was above all else a gloriously, one might even say a pharisaically, good conscience in money-making." [11]

Other elements in the ascetic ideal were turned to profitable ends by captains of industry. All ascetic literature is saturated with the idea that faithful work, even with low wages, is pleasing to God. The workman must labor for conscience' sake: his rewards will be in the next life. Poverty is a discipline for godliness. It is the duty of workmen to labor soberly, and be content with their wages. It is the employer's duty to make profit, for he thereby obeys and honors God. Weber grimly remarks, "One sees how the interest of God and the interest of the employer merge together at this point in a curious way."

So workmen must labor contentedly for conscience' sake; and employers must gain profit for conscience' sake. The outcome is obvious. Weber summarizes compactly the result:

A specific middle-class economic ethic had arisen. With the consciousness of standing in God's full grace and of being visibly blessed by Him, the middle-class employer, as long as he kept within the bounds of formal correctness and his personal morals were unimpeachable and the use he made of his riches was not offensive, could follow the course most profitable to him, and regard this as his duty. Furthermore, the power of religious asceticism placed at his disposal sober, conscientious, uncommonly industrious workers who clung to their work as to a life purpose willed by God. It gave him, also, the comforting assurance that the unequal distribution of the goods of this world is a special dispensation of the providence of God, who pursues His hidden ends, in these matters as in grace, in ways inscrutable to us.[12]

[11] *Gesammelte Aufsätze*, p. 198.   [12] *Ibid.*, p. 198 f.

By the help of religious asceticism, external goods have now gained an almost inescapable power over men. We are caught in the toils of the system. "The Puritan *desired* to be a man of calling; we *must* be." [13] The life of rationalized self-discipline built upon the glory of God and the assurance of salvation has passed, but its capitalistic heritage of a life built upon the motive of amassing profits, and ever more profits, remains in its stead. Wall Street is the final result of the doctrine of election. [14] Capitalism occupies the shell from which the religious spirit that created and animated it has fled. "Like a ghost of its former religious content, the thought of *Berufspflicht* haunts our lives." [15]

4. AN ESTIMATE OF WEBER'S THESIS

This, in brief, is Weber's analysis of the connection between Calvinism and capitalism. I believe that he has over-stated his case. Capitalism existed, both in form and spirit, before Calvin's day. As Brentano, Sombart and Tawney have ably pointed out, economic forces outside the stream of religion contributed to its growth before the Reformation. The capitalistic spirit was strong in Venice, Florence, South Germany and Flanders in the fifteenth century, though these were Catholic areas. The development of capitalism in England and Holland was due in large measure to economic causes, particularly the territorial discoveries and the opening up of new lands to colonization and trade. Religious and economic factors were so intertwined that it is impossible to say categorically that either produced the other. In the next chapter we shall give some indication of their connection.

The moral forces which Weber ascribes to Calvinism were by no means exclusively Calvinistic. Calvin's emphasis on the middle class virtues was not new, for similar injunctions to industry and thrift are found in ancient philosophy and in medieval Catholicism. Sombart points out that the Stoics, particularly Seneca, Cicero and Marcus Aurelius, enjoined these virtues, and that they form a

---

[13] *Ibid.*, p. 203.
[14] Fullerton, p. 194.

[15] *Gesammelte Aufsätze*, p. 204.

prominent element in the Roman writings on husbandry.[16] Aquinas' emphasis on abstemious living, with his condemnations of extravagance, debauchery, idleness and dishonesty, gave a marked incentive to middle class thrift. While the idea of secular calling as divine vocation took on a new color with the Reformation, it was not a new idea.[17] The early and medieval church regarded physical work as a God-imposed duty, and the Vulgate uses *vocatio* in the sense of one's station in life.[18] The political thought of the Renaissance also had a greater influence on the spirit of capitalism than Weber appears to recognize, for as Brentano and Tawney point out, Machiavelli's exaltation of egoism was at least as influential as Protestant asceticism in the disintegration of medieval economic scruples.

I believe also that Weber overestimates the uniqueness of Calvinism in the development of a subsequent Protestant asceticism. Looking forward from Calvin's day, one finds clear evidences of economic assiduity among the Quakers, Baptists, Methodists, Anglicans, and in fact, in practically every Protestant sect.[19] While Weber admits the existence of this spirit among the Quakers and Baptists, and traces it to their own ascetic character, he dismisses too casually their contribution to the formation of a capitalistic *Berufsethik*. The same may be said of the Jews, whose stimulus to economic progress was based not merely on economic shrewdness and acquisitiveness, as Weber seems to imply, but at least in part on an ethical motivation grounded in religion.

Some of Weber's contentions, though true, appear to me to be far-fetched and one-sided. For example, his analysis of the ascetic, individualistic implications of predestination, and of the "impersonal social service" resulting from it, gives a true picture of one side

---

[16] *The Quintessence of Capitalism*, p. 224 f.

[17] While Brentano is right in saying that Basil, Augustine, Benedict and Aquinas recognized a divinely given duty to labor, I believe he misses an essential point of Weber's *Beruf* argument; namely, that with the coming of the Reformation the superiority of monastic labor was denied.

[18] *Die Anfänge des modernen Kapitalismus*, p. 137.

[19] It should, however, be recognized that Calvin's influence spread far beyond the borders of the Calvinistic churches.

of Calvinism. The Calvinists feared the "creature-worship" that would follow from placing human happiness before God's glory, and this bred an ascetic spirit which contributed indirectly to capitalism through frugal and industrious living. Society was in a measure served impersonally by the economic progress which resulted from diligent toil. However, this kind of service was by no means in the forefront of the Puritans' consciousness. They served men, to be sure, for the glory of God, but such service was, to them, far from being "impersonal." They had a warm personal concern for the souls, and often for the general welfare, of their neighbors. Both in Calvin and the Calvinists, the duty of fighting the devil and delivering men from evil living bulked much larger than fidelity to secular calling in their concept of social service.

Similarly, though it is true that the Calvinists labored zealously to find assurance of election through good works, a false inference is drawn if these good works are identified with "good work" in industry or business. A disciplined life of "worldly asceticism" does not necessarily bring economic efficiency in its train. While Weber probably did not intend to pass from good works to good work by an ambiguous use of terms, his transition is insufficient to banish a suspicion of confusion at this point.

I agree with Tawney that Weber greatly oversimplifies Calvinism. This seems to me his most serious error. It is doubtful whether he ever made a first-hand study of Calvin, for while the essay abounds in carefully annotated references to English Puritanism, its references to Calvin's own works are very meagre, and include nothing outside of the *Institutes*.[20] His argument is weakened not only by failure to distinguish adequately between Calvin and Calvinism, but to differentiate among the various classes of English Puritanism, and among the various types of Calvinism in different countries. Tawney aptly remarks, "As Cromwell discovered, there

---

[20] Weber protects himself by saying he is not studying the personal views of Calvin, but Calvinism. However, I question whether Calvinism can be properly understood apart from Calvin.

was no formula which would gather Puritan aristocrats and Levellers, land-owners and Diggers, merchants and artisans, buff-coat and his general, into the fold of a single social theory." [21] Troeltsch, who agrees in general with Weber's thesis, calls attention to his inadequate mention of the Huguenots, who were closer to the real spirit of Calvin than were the Calvinists of the Netherlands, England, or America.[22] Moreover, in view of the economic assiduity and influence of the Scotch and Scotch-Irish Presbyterians, it is strange that Weber says nothing about this branch of Calvinism.

However, to question the adequacy of Weber's thesis is not to reject it wholly. In spite of these limitations, I believe that his main points stand. His position seems to me to be significant and true in these respects:

(1) There is an historical correlation, which cannot be explained by an accidental conjunction, between the growth of Calvinism and the growth of capitalism. Capitalism was in the field before Calvinism appeared and was the product of many complex forces. But Weber nowhere contends that capitalism owes its *form* to Calvinism. Nor does he say that it owes its spirit solely to Calvinism, though his emphasis upon Calvinism's influence suggests this and has caused him to be so interpreted. He contends rather that Calvinism was a major influence in the development of the spirit of industry and self-discipline which caused the capitalistic classes to labor zealously for pecuniary ends, and to claim divine sanction for their acts. In this I believe he has made his case.

(2) His analysis of the spirit of capitalism as a *sense of obligation* to make money, rather than a mere greed for gain, is also sound. Even now, when the "ascetic" element is largely superseded by a profit motive far removed from its original religious significance, the typical middle class capitalist feels himself driven by a moral—almost a religious—obligation to keep on working to

---

[21] *Religion and the Rise of Capitalism*, p. 317.
[22] *Die Soziallehren der christlichen Kirchen und Gruppen*, p. 657 n.

"build up the business." To call the business big enough, and to stop to enjoy the fruits of one's labor, would be to transgress a moral code instilled through generations of Calvinistic ancestry.

(3) With Luther and Calvin, *Beruf,* or vocation, came to have a religio-economic significance that it did not formerly possess,[23] and it was a stimulus to economic progress when the distinction between the cloister and the market place, as spheres of God-serving activity, was broken down. However, I believe that Weber reads into the concept of "calling" more than properly belongs there, and exaggerates the difference between the Lutheran concept of service *in vocatione* and the Calvinistic *per vocationem*. Of this I shall say more in the next chapter.

(4) Weber's picture of the processes by which the economic virtues led to the amassing of wealth, and prosperity to the undoing of the religious asceticism that had given it birth, is essentially correct. The Calvinistic temper is not the only source of the present day exploitation of labor and exaltation of economic power, but it is one source. Many non-moral factors—machinery, steam and electric power, rapid transit, foreign trade, mass production and a host of other economic forces, would have brought about changes if Calvin had never lived. But Weber's major contention is for a recognition of moral and spiritual forces in the economic process, the effects of which persist after their religious roots have atrophied. In this I believe his conclusions to be sound.

. . . .

In part, Calvin was an unwitting contributor to the undoing of that for which he labored. Calvin's emphasis upon the economic virtues bore fruit in furthering the development of a soulless system in which economic expediency came eventually to supplant ethical idealism. But before Calvin was born, forces were in operation which were calculated inevitably to bring about a transition to a new economic order. To a survey of these forces, and how Calvin tried to meet them, we turn in the following chapter.

[23] Cf. Karl Holl, "Die Geschichte des Wortes Beruf," in *Gesammelte Aufsätze zur Kirchengeschichte* (Tübingen, 1928), pp. 189-219.

CHAPTER X

ASSETS AND LIABILITIES

The period of the capitalistic revolution roughly parallels that of the Reformation. Both came to a head in the sixteenth century, though both were being prepared for earlier and both have been unfolding their consequences through all the centuries since. Both were manifestations of a new individualism. Both were promoted by the contemporary political situation, with its rising nationalism and emergence of new states. Both were spread by the geographical expansion which came with explorations and the opening up of new territories. Each influenced the other; and neither directly caused the other.

We have seen how Calvin tried to curb man's natural appetite for self-indulgence and material possessions by an appeal to religion and moral idealism. No man ever labored more zealously to stem the tide of economic materialism. In large measure his warnings were futile, and the very virtues by which he sought to bring men to right living turned to ensnare their possessors. But the boomerang lay not in the virtues themselves. Rather, it lay in the combination of these virtues, reinforced by a powerful religious sanction, with a complex set of economic forces, reinforced by man's natural greed for gain. Before we say more about Calvin, it will be necessary to turn aside and get a picture of the economic situation in the midst of which he labored.

1. ECONOMIC BACKGROUNDS

The dominant factor in the capitalistic revolution was the change from a natural economy to a money economy. This took place some centuries before the sixteenth, and paved the way for a new era. It was not until the twelfth century that money was in common use in the cities, and its use did not spread to the rural sections to any marked degree till the fourteenth and fifteenth.[1] But its effect, when it came, was revolutionary. With the substitution of money payment for barter, the processes of buying and selling were so much facilitated that there was a great stimulus to the production of more goods. When payment for labor in money took the place of a return in services and maintenance, the resultant wage system broke down the household economy which had prevailed in the master-apprentice relation in industry and the overlord-villein relation in agriculture. The change, on the one hand, was in the direction of greater simplicity. But it brought with it a host of complex problems which had not troubled the relatively simple economic régime of a day when little was produced and little needed, and life was shaped along family lines. With the use of money came the possibility of hoarding and profiteering, large-scale commercial transactions upon credit, large-scale investments in distant areas, large-scale production, monopolies, and a concentration of power in the hands of the monied few.

To write the story of the rise of the capitalistic system lies outside the province of this book. Calvin had a part in fastening it upon his spiritual descendants, but Calvin originated neither the capitalistic system nor the capitalistic spirit. A brief survey of the forces of transition which broke down the feudal, agricultural economy of medieval Europe and introduced a new commercial, industrial régime may suggest the inevitability of the process. It was a rising tide against which Luther and Calvin might fulminate, but which they were wholly powerless to stem.

Medieval agriculture consisted mainly of subsistence farming in connection with the great baronial estates. While the work of the medieval craftsman and the labor in the monasteries are not to be discounted, the center of economic life for the vast majority of people in the Middle Ages was this feudal agricultural system. With minor variations, the system prevailed throughout western Europe.

[1] Smith, *The Age of the Reformation*, p. 517.

The manor was the unit for the collection of taxes and organization of agriculture. No money payments were made, but the peasants or villeins held their lands in fief from the overlord, paying in services and kind. The domain farm was managed for the lord by a bailiff and worked by the peasants. The waste lands used for pasturage were held in common, but there was an approximation of individual ownership in the fact that each peasant usually had an arable strip assigned to him which he could work for himself in his own time. These holdings were not permanent, and life was largely on a communal basis. Agriculture was stationary, for no more employment was possible, and there was little incentive to produce more than was needed for subsistence.[2] While the peasant did not own the land and must always give part of his time and produce to the overlord, he was relatively free and comfortable under his régime,[3] and he was spared the emotional upset of seeing others of his class suddenly enriched by some turn of fortune's wheel.

However, forces far removed from the life of the peasant farmer began to alter materially his status. The period from the thirteenth to the sixteenth centuries witnessed great economic progress and a radical change from the medieval system. The introduction of money and the rise of the credit system coöperated with increased facilities for travel to stimulate production and exchange. The Crusades brought West and East together, and the energy of the Florentine traders became a pervasive force. More demands for luxuries developed; more goods were made or imported to satisfy these demands. The medieval gilds began to disintegrate and give way to a wage system. Joint stock companies were formed, and money was invested in textiles, mining and foreign trade. Great financial houses arose and monopolies came into being, fostered not only by the business acumen of shrewd money-getters but by the

---

[2] Cunningham, *The Progress of Capitalism in England*, p. 41.

[3] Schapiro, J. S., *Social Reform and the Reformation* (Columbia Univ. Studies in History, Economics and Public Law, 1909), pp. 48, 54. Coulton in *Five Centuries of Religion* says that there was much more suffering at this period than has commonly been supposed.

favor of princes who saw a chance to borrow from them. In Italy the house of the Medici amassed a fortune as the Pope's bankers and seized the reins of government, while in Germany the Fuggers and the Welsers secured concessions, sent their ships everywhere, and became the J. P. Morgans of their day. The movement of population from rural sections to the towns and the increasing political importance of these towns gave evidence that a new "burgher" or "bourgeois" class had come into being.

By the end of the fifteenth century, the foundations of the old régime had broken down and a new merchant-banker class had emerged, which by holding the purse-strings of the nation was destined to be more powerful than princes. Once started, the process grew by its own momentum, for "money begot money," and the monied classes, holding the financial resources needed by the princes for the carrying on of incessant wars, reaped a rich harvest in lands, concessions, and trade monopolies.[4]

This growing capitalism influenced the whole social structure. Wherever commercial enterprise made its way, new markets were opened up. This reacted both favorably and unfavorably on agriculture. Farming being no longer solely on a subsistence basis, the opportunity for sale of produce stimulated increased production. More land was cultivated and greater care was taken in bailiff farming in order to supply outside markets.

However, an economic ferment was in the air which fared hard with the peasant farmer. The commercial classes saw that there was money in supplying these new markets. Many of the nobles were "land poor" and wanted money. Particularly was this true in Germany, where the lower nobility were being crowded to the wall by the rising power of the princes. The result was that the monied commercial classes bought up many of the estates of the nobles for more intensive cultivation, and the serfs were rudely dispossessed of the lands of which they had enjoyed possession, if not ownership, for generations.

[4] Cf. Ehrenberg, Richard, *Capital and Finance in the Age of the Renaissance* (London, 1928), p. 25 ff.

Another capitalistic encroachment which caused much hardship was the practice of enclosures. The pasture lands had formerly been held in common, and used by the peasants. But as the wool-trade increased, sheep-raising became profitable; and it was decidedly to the interest of the owner, whether baron or absentee capitalist, to fence in these common lands. This was done extensively, the lands thus enclosed being used not only for stock-raising but for increased tillage and for sport. From the standpoint of general economic progress this marked a step in advance; for more and better stock, and more and better crops, were raised under the profit incentive than on the old communal, subsistence basis. However, the process worked great hardship to the peasants, depriving them of grazing lands to which they had formerly had free access, and it helped to breed a discontent which finally burst forth in Germany in the Peasants' War.

Even when the peasant did not suffer from direct dispossession or enclosure, he was obliged increasingly to submit to irksome requirements which curtailed his freedom and financial resources. The dues and services which he had to render his lord grew steadily; and as they rose the peasant, formerly comparatively free, saw himself being reduced to serfdom.[5] The same amount had to be paid or given in produce if the crops were injured, and the peasant thought that the lord should stand the effects of "fire, flood and the devil" as well as he. The death-dues were particularly irritating. When the head of a family died, the lord took from the widow her best cow, horse, or other most valuable possession—in some cases all she had [6]—and the peasants naturally rebelled at the lord's inheriting from them and leaving their families penniless. Another source of annoyance was the hunting in which the lord engaged. The peasant's crops were destroyed by the chase; he often had to leave his work and assist by beating the bushes or furnishing

[5] Schapiro, p. 54 ff. The examples cited refer to the German peasantry. The English villein fared better, though he too suffered from dispossession and enclosures.

[6] This was true in Germany of the *Leibeigene*, or lowest class of serfs. The *Hörige*, who were free except for dues and services, usually had to surrender only their best article.

horses and wagons; and he was himself forbidden to kill the game that was destroying his crops. The peasant, reduced to abject poverty, frequently had to borrow of the capitalist, paying an exorbitant rate of interest and then losing all his possessions through foreclosure of a mortgage. This situation was so common by the time of the Reformation that Luther remarked that "any one who had a hundred gulden to invest could gobble up a peasant a year with no more danger to his life and property than there is in sitting by a stove and roasting apples."[7]

In Germany the troubles of the peasant were particularly intensified by the transition from the old German law to Roman law. The former consisted of uncodified local customs, and recognized communal ownership. Roman law did not, and the nobility as they seized the peasants' holdings appealed to Roman jurists to legitimatize what they accomplished by force. Under Roman law, the peasants could be ousted if they could not show documentary proof of ownership, and few could produce such evidence. Legal redress was practically impossible, for a peasant could not sue his own overlord, and when a peasant protested the Roman jurist decided in favor of the lord. The princes and nobles were quick to take advantage of the situation, and through appointment of the jurists controlled both courts and law. So it is not surprising that the proverb became common:

> Das edle Recht ist worden krank,
> Den Armen kurz, den Reichen lang.

It was revolt from exploitation of this sort which led to the Peasants' War of 1525. The peasants were largely the victims of circumstance. But so too, in a measure, were the nobility who oppressed them. The lower aristocracy were suffering themselves, and turned to the peasants as the only weaker ones whom they could exploit to get money. This was due in part to the growth in power of the great princes, to the loss of their own military importance which came with the invention of gunpowder, and to the drain

[7] Quoted by Schapiro, p. 63.

of constant division of estates through inheritance. But it was also due largely to forces which came with the new economic order. As values shifted from land to commerce, the landed aristocracy lost money, and were driven to extort from the peasants to regain what they could. As the merchant classes waxed rich and powerful and lived in luxury, the old families became envious of these *nouveaux riches* and resolved not to be outdone. In such a situation, human nature was still too unregenerate to be restrained by many moral scruples.

2. ETHICAL IMPLICATIONS

In such a period of economic upheaval, it was inevitable that an ethic adapted to an earlier day should undergo change in practice, if not in theory. The Middle Ages were not freer from the natural human desire to acquire profit than any other era. But the opportunities for acquiring profit at the expense of others were far more limited in Aquinas' day than in Luther's and Calvin's. In a relatively simple social order built largely upon a subsistence economy, the medieval church could with at least partial success promulgate its doctrine of the just price and reinforce it with denunciations of the sin of avarice.[8] When this same social order had become very complex, with the profit motive its dominant principle, adjurations calculated to restrain the operation of the profit motive were bound to fall upon deaf ears.

The main elements in medieval economic ethics, as sanctioned by Aquinas and the Church, were the doctrine of the just price, the curbing of the sin of avarice, the prohibition of usury, and the functional view of society. To these should be added another emanating from the unhurried spirit of the times rather than from religious sources, pride in craftsmanship and the duty of turning out a good product, however much time it might take to make it.[9] The just price was that which gave to the producer only what was necessary to pay him for his labor and enable him to

[8] Tawney, *Religion and the Rise of Capitalism*, p. 31 ff.
[9] Sombart, *The Quintessence of Capitalism*, p. 19.

subsist in his station in life. It was determined by the need of the producer rather than by competition, and the law of supply and demand had little to do with it. To claim more than a just price was avarice; and however much the medieval clergy practiced avarice, they roundly denounced it in theory. The taking of interest was forbidden by both ecclesiastical and civil law, though the ban on usury was dodged by many subterfuges, and the monasteries and papal collectors were among the earliest to evade it.[10] The functional conception of society tended to perpetuate social and economic cleavages by maintaining that every man should labor contentedly in the place where God had placed him. Social conservatism reinforced this stratification; and while the acquisitive instinct brought about violations in the other principles mentioned, it did not dislodge them from the accepted Christian mores.

When Luther and Calvin came upon the scene, the pre-capitalistic ethic was still accepted in theory, but was fast breaking down in practice. The principle of the just price, formulated in a simple economic order where there was little exchange and production was largely for subsistence, was beginning to sound old-fashioned in an order that offered to the enterprising trader alluring opportunities for profit. Avarice was still denounced, and increasingly practiced. Christians could not afford to let their Jewish neighbors reap all the harvest of a lucrative banking business, and easily found ways to harmonize their religious scruples with money-lending and interest-taking. It was still expected that peasants should retain their God-given place in the lowest stratum of society, but no such scruple restrained the man who wanted to amass wealth in a mercantile or banking business. With the voyages of discovery and consequent foreign trade which developed in the later fifteenth and early sixteenth centuries, capitalistic enterprise forged ahead by leaps and bounds; and with the growth of capitalism came a corresponding decline in the power of the medieval economic ethic.

Luther never understood the new economic order in which he

10 Ehrenberg, *Capital and Finance in the Age of the Renaissance*, p. 42 ff.

found himself. His economic concepts were those of Aquinas, and he failed to see that Aquinas' day was past. To cite Tawney's analogy, Luther's attitude to the new commercialism of his day was like that of a savage who stands before a dynamo or steam-engine he has never seen before, fearful, perplexed, annoyed, and possessed with the idea that there is a devil in it.[11] In his earlier writings, Luther denounced vigorously the rapacity of the princes and nobles, and gave the peasants some hope that they might find in him a champion of their cause. But Luther was as funda-mentally conservative in his social views as he was radical in his theology. When the peasants rose in revolt, he turned against them and used all the power of his tongue and pen to defeat their cause. In the invectives which he leveled against the "peasant rabble" there is little of the spirit of Christian brotherhood and it is not surprising that in the anger of disappointment they called him "Doktor Lügner." Many factors influenced him to take this stand, chief among which is probably the fact that the establishment of the new religion was his supreme concern, and he was enough of an opportunist to see that he could bring this about more effectively by the help of the princes than the peasants. But he was influenced not a little by a deep-seated conviction of the divine origin of social classes. To serve God in the place where God had placed one was the clear duty of man, and any attempt to rebel was a sin against God and the state, to be suppressed by any means that might prove necessary. Luther could denounce avarice, but he saw no obligation to alter the social status of those who were suffering most keenly as its victims.

The only religious agency which proved able to cope in any successful manner with the new situation was Calvinism. Catholic, Lutheran and Calvinistic churches continued to thunder against avarice, while avarice (i.e. the profit motive) grew apace and the just price became an interesting medieval relic. However, Calvinism not only thundered against the new order, but in considerable measure adapted itself to it. Calvin no more created

[11] *Religion and the Rise of Capitalism*, p. 89.

the commercial enterprise of his day than the Pope created the empire of Charlemagne; but like the Pope he greatly furthered what was already in process of development by conferring upon it a divine sanction.

3. THE LIFTING OF THE BAN ON USURY

Calvin made a contribution to the growth of the capitalistic system which Weber scarcely mentions,[12] though it had far-reaching consequences. This was through his recognition, under certain strictures, of the legitimacy of taking interest on loans.

To see anything striking in Calvin's attitude, his position must be viewed against the background of earlier religious sentiment. Usury was, of course, forbidden by the medieval church, and in general the secular authorities reinforced this verdict.[13] The grounds on which the taking of interest was condemned were numerous. Foremost among these was the Scriptural prohibition. A close second was the economic doctrine that money was barren. Since money could not produce, it was thought unjust to take pay for a loan, though rent for the use of land, because of the productivity of the latter, was considered legitimate. A passage in Aristotle's *Politics* was cited as authority for this view.[14] Various other considerations reinforced the accepted doctrine. Tawney in his *Religion*

12 Weber's disregard of Calvin's recognition of the legitimacy of usury may be due to the fact he does not pretend to be discussing Calvin himself, but Calvinism. However, as it had its chief influence in subsequent thought, it seems strange that he passes over so important a solvent of the traditional mores.

13 Tawney, *Religion and the Rise of Capitalism*, p. 37, says, "Florence was the financial capital of medieval Europe; but even at Florence the secular authorities fined bankers right and left for usury in the middle of the fourteenth century, and, fifty years later, first prohibited credit transactions altogether, and then imported Jews to conduct a business forbidden to Christians." Cf. also Doren, *Studien aus der Florentiner Wirthschaftsgeschichte*, i, 173-209.

14 *Politics*, I, iii, ad. fin. 1258ᵇ. Aristotle's statement reads: "Of the two sorts of money-making, one . . . is a part of household management, the other is retail trade: the former necessary and honorable, the latter a kind of exchange which is justly censured; for it is unnatural, and a mode by which men gain from one another. The most hated sort, and with the greatest reason, is usury, which makes a gain out of money itself, and not from the natural use of it. For money was intended to be used in exchange, but not to increase at interest. And this term usury (τόκος), which means the birth of money from money, is applied to the breeding of money because the offspring resembles the parent. Wherefore of all modes of making money, this is the most unnatural." Jowett's Translation.

and the Rise of Capitalism thus summarizes the objections urged: "To take usury is contrary to Scripture; it is contrary to Aristotle; it is contrary to nature, for it is to live without labor; it is to sell time, which belongs to God, for the advantage of wicked men; it is to rob those who use the money lent, and to whom, since they make it profitable, the profits should belong; it is unjust in itself, for the benefit of the loan to the borrower cannot exceed the value of the principal sum lent him; it is in defiance of sound juristic principles, for when a loan of money is made, the property in the thing lent passes to the borrower, and why should the creditor demand payment from a man who is merely using what is now his own?" [15]

Certain charges which, to the modern mind, appear to be on a par with interest-taking were regarded as permissible. In addition to rent, mentioned above, one might lawfully take the profits of partnership, provided one assumed also the partner's risks. One might loan money, and if the principal were not paid at the appointed time, one could demand compensation for loss. One might purchase an annuity, and receive an annual income in return for the payment of a capital sum. However, in rent, profits, compensation for loss, or annuity, there was an element of uncertainty which in current opinion formed a line of demarcation between these legitimate modes of income and interest-taking. Interest as a fixed payment to be made for the use of money *without risk to the lender* was frowned upon as an offense against God and nature. So gross a sin was interest-taking that in the papal indulgences, money so gained was ranked with stolen goods.[16]

Yet in spite of such condemnation, at the end of the Middle Ages interest-taking had been common for centuries. The first step toward a recognition of its legitimacy was with regard to loans made to princes and cities, considered to be for the common good. The monasteries were early loaners of money capital, and the first Christians to take usury were Italian merchants acting as papal collectors.[17] What was sanctioned in high places soon spread

[15] *Op. cit.*, p. 43.
[16] Ehrenberg, p. 42.
[17] *Ibid.*, p. 50.

to the masses, and many ingenious subterfuges were devised by which interest could be taken without being called usury. Sometimes interest was smuggled into the price of the bill. Sometimes commodities were loaned in place of money and charged for at a high rate. Sometimes interest payments were made in services. Sometimes loans were made in the form of deposits. Sometimes, as in the case of the loan of the Fuggers to Albrecht of Brandenburg, a charge was made to cover "trouble, labor and expense." Some got around the prohibition by saying that it was all right to borrow and loan again, but not to loan one's own money.[18] Interest was frequently taken in all but name through gratuities, rewards, and other innocent-sounding emoluments. By the end of the thirteenth century, evasions of the prohibition had become so common that special instructions had to be given by the Church to confessors for the handling of difficult usury cases.[19]

While the Church still opposed usury among the rank and file, it increasingly condoned the practice when this was for its own advantage. In the beginning, the Jews were the principal moneylenders. But as trade developed, Christian merchants supplanted them in the higher circles of Church and State. Italian merchants rose to power and prominence, not simply as traders, but as international financiers and collectors of revenue for the Pope. In Germany the Fuggers, powerful merchant-bankers of Augsburg, acquired vast mineral concessions through loans to Maximilian, and provided the funds by which Charles V bought his crown. Through a loan to Albrecht of Brandenburg enabling him to purchase from the Pope the archbishopric of Mainz, the Fuggers became involved in the events leading to the Reformation, for by private arrangement with the Pope, Albrecht was to get the money to pay the Fuggers by selling indulgences and taking half the proceeds.[19a] When Luther's opponent, Doctor Eck, went to Italy to

[18] Ehrenberg, p. 42, reports the case of one Lazaro Doria, who stated in his will that he had no load upon his conscience, for he had never used his own money in a business partnership, but had borrowed on bills all he had used for such dealings.
[19] Tawney, pp. 48, 296 f. St. Raymond's guide to the duties of an archdeacon (*Raimundi de Penna-forti Summa Pastoralis*) gives many questions to be asked for the detection of usury.
[19a] Mackinnon, *Luther and the Reformation*, I, p. 290 f.

ask the University of Bologna for confirmation of the doctrine that interest could lawfully be taken among merchants, the Fuggers thought it worth while to finance an expedition likely to prove so lucrative.[20] Jacob Fugger, the head of the firm, built a church and endowed an almshouse in his native city, and as Tawney sums up his career, "he died in the odor of sanctity, a good Catholic and a Count of the empire, having seen his firm pay 54 per cent [annually] for the preceding sixteen years." [21]

. . . .

Calvin lived in a day when loans upon interest were becoming accepted in practice, if not in theory, as an essential medium of trade. As business expanded, the borrowing of capital became an economic necessity, and those who had money to loan would not loan it without some profit in its return. Against "usury" in the present day meaning of the term, Calvin set his face like flint. There must be no interest-taking in which the rich could wrest money from the poor, or batten on the poor man's necessity. Yet Calvin saw, as Luther did not see, that in spite of grievous miscarriages of justice, the taking of interest was justified.

Calvin's fullest and clearest statement on the question is found in a letter which he wrote to his friend Sachinus in 1545 in reply to an inquiry made by Sachinus for someone else. This document is of such historic importance that I shall quote it almost in full.[22]

While I have had no experience myself, I have learned from the example of others how dangerous it is to give an answer to the question on which you ask my advice. For if we wholly condemn usury, we impose tighter fetters on the conscience than God himself. Yet if we permit it in the least, many under this pretext will take an unbridled liberty which can then be held in bounds by no restriction. If I were

---

[20] Tawney, p. 81.
[21] Ibid., p. 79.
[22] Opera, xa, 245. Sachinus' letter of inquiry (Opera, xii, 210) is dated November 7, 1545. Calvin's reply is undated and its heading is merely "De usuris. Jehan Calvin a quelquun de ses amys"; yet the content indicates that the two go together.
Calvin's letter in full may be found in Economic Tracts, series of 1880-81, pp. 32-36, Society for Political Education, New York, 1882. The translation there given is free and not wholly accurate.

writing to you alone, I should have no fear, for I know well your prudence and restraint: but since you are asking for another, I fear that he may gather a little more permission from my words than I wish. However, since I have no doubt that you will act with discretion according to the nature of the man and the circumstances, I will tell you how the matter seems to me.

In the first place, by no testimony of the Scriptures is usury wholly condemned. For the meaning of the saying of Christ, commonly thought to be very clear, i.e., 'Lend, hoping for nothing again' (Luke 6: 35) has been perverted. As elsewhere in speaking of the sumptuous feasts and ambitious social rivalry of the rich he commands rather that they invite in the blind, the lame and the poor from the streets who cannot make a like return, so here, wishing to curb abuses in lending, he directs us to loan chiefly to those from whom there is no hope of receiving anything. . . . The words of Christ mean that he commends serving the poor rather than the rich. Thus we do not find all usury forbidden.

The law of Moses (Deut. 23: 19) was political, and should not influence us beyond what justice and philanthropy will bear. It could be wished that all usury, and even the name, were banished from the earth. But since this is impossible, it is necessary to concede to the common good.

We have passages in the Prophets and Psalms in which the Holy Spirit inveighs against usury. Thus a city is described as wicked because usury is found in its market-place and streets. (Ps. 55: 11.) But as the Hebrew word here means *fraud* in general, the passage can be otherwise interpreted. Even if we grant that the prophet speaks explicitly of usury, it is not surprising that among the great evils of his time he should mention it, for with an improper use of usury, cruelty and many evil deceptions are often joined. . . .

It is said in praise of a holy and God-fearing man that 'he putteth not out his money to usury.' [23] Indeed, it is a very rare thing for a man to be honest and at the same time a usurer. The prophet Ezekiel (Ezek. 22: 12) goes even further, for in enumerating the crimes which inflamed the wrath of the Lord against the Jews, he uses two Hebrew words, Nesec and Tarbit: one of which means *usury* and is derived from a root meaning to *consume*, while the second signifies an *increase* or *addition*, doubtless because each man contriving to further his own gain takes or rather extorts it at his neighbor's loss. . . .

[23] Psalms, 15: 5.

Now it is said that today, too, usury should be forbidden on the same grounds as among the Jews, since there is a bond of brotherhood among us. To this I reply, that in the civil state there is some difference; for the situation in which the Lord had placed the Jews, and many other circumstances, made it easy for them to engage in business among themselves without usury. Our relationship is not at all the same. Therefore I do not consider that usury is wholly forbidden among us, except it be repugnant to justice and charity.

Calvin's recognition that a change in economic situation justified a change in policy with regard to usury is most significant. So is his willingness to interpret the Biblical prohibitions, not in terms of a literal reading, but in terms of "justice and charity." At this point, he almost ceases to be a literalist. In the next part of the letter he attacks squarely, and demolishes, the Aristotelian idea that interest must not be taken because money is barren.

The reasoning of Saint Ambrose and of Chrysostom, that money does not beget money, is in my judgment too superficial. What does the sea beget? What does the land? I receive income from the rental of a house. Is it because the money grows there? The earth produces things from which money is made, and the use of a house can be bought for money. And is not money more fruitful in trade than in any other form of possession one can mention? Is it lawful to let a farm, requiring a payment in return, and unlawful to receive any profit from the use of money? . . .
How do merchants derive their profit? By their industry, you will say. Certainly if money is shut up in a strong-box, it will be barren—a child can see that. But whoever asks a loan of me does not intend to keep this money idle and gain nothing. The profit is not in the money itself, but in the return that comes from its use. It is necessary then to draw the conclusion that while such subtle distinctions appear on the surface to have some weight, they vanish on closer scrutiny, for they have no substance. *I therefore conclude that usury must be judged, not by any particular passage of Scripture, but simply by the rules of equity.*[24]

Calvin then cites an example to show that borrowing money to buy a farm and paying interest to the lender who holds a mortgage

[24] Italics mine.

is no more reprehensible than leasing a farm and paying rent. He ends his positive argument with an injunction to consider the situation in its real nature and not to be led astray by words.

However, the letter does not stop at this point. Calvin realized that he had said surprising things which could easily be turned to base purposes. He concludes with a note of caution. It is necessary, he says, to be careful, for people seize upon a little word to justify unlawful usury. So he makes the following exceptions.

(1) Interest must not be taken from the poor.

(2) One must not be so bent on gain as to neglect the necessary offices, scorning his poor brethren.

(3) One must not go beyond the bounds of equity. These are to be ascertained by the Golden Rule.

(4) He who borrows must make as much or more gain from the money borrowed. (Apparently to prevent the possibility that the money borrowed might actually be "barren.")

(5) We must not judge what is equitable according to "vulgar custom" or the iniquity of the world, but take our rule from the Word of God.

(6) We must regard the transaction, not as a private affair, but for the good of the public.

(7) One must not go beyond what the laws of the region permit. This is not always a sufficient rule, for they often permit what they cannot restrain. It is better to ask too little than too much.

The seventh provision arouses curiosity as to whether usury at that time had become sufficiently sanctioned by the civil authorities to cause a legal rate to be fixed. This is partially answered for Geneva by the ordinances passed in 1547 for the governance of the surrounding villages. Here we find the statement:

Let no one take usury or profit above five per cent under penalty of confiscation of the principal, or being compelled to make other amends according to the exigencies of the case.[25]

25 *Opera,* xa, 56.

In Calvin's sermon on Deut. 23: 18-20, he speaks of the lawful rate as five per cent, but he warns against taking this amount from the poor.[26] Further light is thrown on the question in a letter to Calvin from John Utenhovius written from London November 26, 1549,[27] though unfortunately there is no record of a reply. In this letter he asks Calvin whether it is permitted to a Christian man to entrust his money to the merchants for a yearly return, and he says that ten per cent is permitted by the English king. Remarking that he has some money which he would like to place with some good man, lest it perish entirely useless with him, he ends piously, "Nevertheless I would rather beg my bread than do anything against my God."

In another letter written by Calvin to Morel some years later,[28] Calvin answers the question as to whether it is permitted to ministers to loan their money at a profit. Calvin is more cautious here than in his earlier statement. He says he thinks it would be better not to, since so many scandals arise. However, he admits that it would be impossible to condemn money-lending entirely without too great rigor; but he recommends that instead of drawing a definite return, the money be placed with some just man for a share in his profits. One must then be content with an equitable return according as God prospers this person. This suggestion (which might be interpreted as approving common stock above preferred) reflects both the medieval idea of the legitimacy of an uncertain return and Calvin's ever-present conviction that all human affairs are governed by God's hand.

In his sermons and commentaries upon the Scripture passages commonly interpreted as forbidding usury,[29] Calvin admits the legitimacy of a moderate rate of interest but denounces severely the gaining of excess profits and the exploitation of the poor. With his usual ability to penetrate all sham, he points out that there is no

---

[26] *Opera*, xxviii, 121.

[27] *Opera*, xiii, 462.

[28] In its Latin form it is dated in the *Opera* January 10, 1560, but the same thing is given in French under date of January 10, 1562. *Opera*, xa, 263; xix, 245.

[29] *Opera*, xxviii, 117 ff; xl, 429; xxiv, 679 ff; xxxi, 147.

virtue in the subterfuges by which men seek to take interest under other names. It is a mockery, he says, to refuse to take usury in money but take it in wheat or wine. "Such coverings no more avail than Adam's fig-leaves." [30] People try to disguise usury by calling it a contract, but one cannot blind the eyes of God under the shadow of a piece of paper or sheep-skin. It is puerile to maintain, as some do, that profit in goods is legitimate, but not in money. To loan wheat and demand sixty sous for it when it is worth only forty is usury before God, and all such profit is larceny. However, when interest is just, there should be no scruple in taking it. Trade consists of buying to sell again, and my throat is cut if I am hindered from carrying on my business. Usury is subject to grave abuses, yet men cannot engage in business without it, and men must make a living.

.   .   .   .

Was Calvin, in these admissions, merely capitulating to current practice and invoking religious sanctions to justify what was economically inevitable? If so, he did it without conscious deception; for whatever his faults, he was too honest to justify any view for the sake of mere expediency and too unmercenary to make concessions for economic gain. With his practical grasp of public affairs and his ability to see beneath practices to principles, he saw, as Luther failed to see, that the Scriptural prohibitions needed reinterpreting and that the "barren money" theory was fallacious.

The consequences of Calvin's doctrine were far-reaching and significant. Tawney states that both its critics and its defenders were correct in regarding Calvin's treatment of capital as a watershed.[31] Its significance lies not in its originality, but in its effect in placing the stamp of religious approval on a practice already widely prevalent. Before Calvin, Protestants as well as Catholics were taking interest, but were doing so either with a guilty conscience or with scruples profitably suppressed. After Calvin, trade with the loaning and borrowing of capital could be engaged in by adherents

[30] *Opera,* xxviii, 118.
[31] *Religion and the Rise of Capitalism,* p. 107.

of the Reformed faith without other moral strictures than those imposed by Calvin's exhortations to judge the matter by the principles of justice and charity. Limited as was his recognition of propriety of interest, he took the question out of the sphere of ecclesiastical restrictions and made it rest on the Golden Rule. And since the Golden Rule is very broad in its application—so broad it is easy to forget it in specific cases—Calvin's followers found it easy both to take interest with a clear conscience and to forget about the principles of justice and charity.

4. SECULAR VOCATION AS DIVINE CALLING

In view of all that Weber has to say about the religious significance in Calvinism of one's secular calling, one is surprised upon searching Calvin's writings to find that he has very little to say about the economic aspects of one's *vocatio*. He has a great deal to say about *vocatio* in its religious meaning, in reference to the calling (i.e. the election) of God's chosen saints. He enjoins industry, provided preoccupation with worldly tasks does not ensnare the soul. Yet when one combs Calvin's works for specific references to *vocatio* in its double meaning of secular vocation and divine calling, not many of these appear.

However, these are not wholly lacking. Where they do appear, they reinforce the functional view of society held by Aquinas and Luther—that every man is to labor faithfully in the station wherein God has placed him. Calvin rejects the medieval idea of the monastic life as a superior vocation, but I am unable to detect any marked divergence from the Lutheran conception of man's place in society.

One of his clearest uses of *vocatio* in its double meaning is with reference to I Cor. 7:20, Let every man abide in the same calling wherein he was called. "A calling," he says, "in Scripture means a lawful mode of life, for it has relation to God as calling us." [32] Paul's admonition does not mean that one cannot change his occupation, for it would be a hard thing if a tailor could not learn

[32] *Opera*, xlix, 415. Comm. on I Cor. 7:20.

another trade or a merchant betake himself to farming. It signifies only that one should not change his occupation in sheer restlessness, without any proper reason. Each man is to consider what is suitable to his calling, and avoid the uneasiness which prevents an individual from remaining in his condition with a tranquil mind.

This recognition of the propriety of changing one's calling for due cause might be interpreted as a break from the functional view of society, did not Calvin elsewhere distinctly affirm that it is every man's duty contentedly to serve God and do his work in the station where God has placed him. The following passage combines the use of vocation in a "vocational" significance with a clear affirmation of the functional conception.

Lastly, it is to be remarked that the Lord commands every one of us, in all the actions of life, to regard his vocation. For he knows with what great inquietude the human mind is inflamed, how insatiable is its ambition to grasp different things at once. Therefore, to prevent universal confusion being produced by our folly and temerity, he has appointed to all their particular duties in different spheres of life. And that no one might rashly transgress the limits prescribed, he has styled such spheres of life *vocations* or *callings*. Every individual's line of life, therefore, is, as it were, a post assigned him by the Lord. . . .

He that is in obscurity will lead a private life without discontent, so as not to desert the station in which God has placed him. . . . All, in their respective spheres of life, will bear and surmount the inconveniences, cares, disappointments and anxieties which befall them, when they shall be persuaded that every individual has his burden laid upon him by God. Hence also will arise peculiar consolation, since there will be no occupation so mean and sordid (provided we follow our vocation) as not to appear truly respectable, and be deemed highly important in the sight of God.[33]

Calvin thus argues, in words that could equally well have been written by Aquinas or Luther, that God demands contentment within one's divinely ordered station, however humble or distressing that may be. But he staunchly repudiated the idea that *every* vocation (i.e. occupation) was of the Lord. Such an idea would make any manner of living good, though condemned by the Word

[33] III, 10, 6.

of God. A papal priest might justify himself for chanting Masses, for that is his vocation! With a sarcasm more pointed than delicate, he remarks, "A monk ought to remain in his cloister like a pig in his trough, for that is his vocation. . . . Let a brothel-keeper, they [the Libertines] say, ply his trade—let a thief steal boldly, for each is pursuing his vocation." [34] In a passage which indicates by its irony how keenly he was aware of the economic evils of his day he observes:

If a lawyer wants to get fine fees, if he helps one party oppress the other, if he crushes the good cause to favor the wrong, he is not to blame! For each must follow his vocation. If merchants destroy the world with monopolies, if they counterfeit and disguise their goods, if they perjure themselves every hour to defraud and circumvent, if they plunder and consume all they can snatch, let nobody speak! For that would blaspheme the vocation of the Lord. [35]

The apparent contradiction here between God's placing every man in his predestined vocation and the repudiation of certain vocations as anathema in the eyes of God, is typical of the deep-seated inconsistency inherent in Calvinistic doctrine. In spite of predestination, neither Calvin nor the Calvinists could bring themselves, in a concrete case, to admit that God made men sin. Had Calvin been challenged to define his terms more sharply, he would probably have said that a secular calling displeasing in the eyes of God was not a true "vocation," but a form of human perversity.

. . . .

What is to be gleaned from these statements? First, Weber's contention that Calvin gave *vocatio* (or *Beruf*) a combined secular-religious significance is substantiated. He did not use the term in this sense extensively. The use of *vocatio* in its theological connotation, referring to election, is its usual, but not its only, meaning.

Second, Calvin did not depart materially from Luther in regard to the functional view of social organization. Calvin clearly en-

---

[34] *Opera*, vii, 211. *Contre la Secte des Libertins.*
[35] *Ibid.*, 212.

joins contentment with one's lot, service to God *in vocatione*. Whatever of the idea of service *per vocationem* is present in Calvin's thought arises from his injunctions to industry. Both by example and precept, he inculcated in his followers the practice of untiring diligence. It is through this channel, rather than through any distinct change in the *Beruf* concept, that he paved the way for the marriage of Calvinism with capitalism.

Finally, Weber overlooks an important element. Calvin's followers undoubtedly attached more importance to the double meaning of *vocatio* than did Calvin. But Weber seems to me inadequately to recognize the significance of language in the transition. To the present, "calling" may mean either the calling of the Lord to a godly life, or it may mean one's occupational calling. "Vocation" has the same double meaning, though its secular connotation now predominates. Once the double meaning had been established in the language, identifications were bound to be made, either implicitly or overtly, through forces psychological and philological rather than theological.

5. PROFITABLE SERVANTS

Calvin's repeated admonitions to be patient in adversity, and to submit humbly to the poverty sent by God, undoubtedly had the effect, as Weber says, of making workers the more content to labor at low wages. While Calvin delivered imprecations in plenty against the oppressors of the poor, these were never taken so seriously on either side of the economic chasm as were the injunctions to docile and diligent toil. There is some justice in the charge that Calvinism made religion an opiate.

Calvin believed to the last letter that those in any sort of subordinate position must obey the higher powers. Of this we shall see more evidence in the next chapter, when we look at his political theory. Applied to the economic order, this meant that he would permit no exception to the Scriptural injunction, "Servants, obey your masters." To do otherwise, in his judgment, was a flat violation of a divine command. If the master oppressed the servant, that, of course, was a sin on the master's part—to be preached against and punished by the divine wrath. But it in no wise absolved the servant from the duty of obedience. Every man is where he is by the dispensation of Providence, and to rebel against one's lot is to rebel against God.

"The poor ye have always with you"—this is to test our charity and our courage. With a directness which has not always characterized the rationalizations of those who have since justified the *status quo* by this word, Calvin says:

> Why then does God permit some to be poor here below, if not that He wants to give us an occasion to do good? So let us not attribute it at all to fortune when we see one rich and another poor, but let us recognize that God so disposes, and it is not without reason. We cannot always see why God enriches one and leaves another in poverty. . . . Therefore God wants us often to lower our eyes to do Him honor, since He governs men according to His will and inscrutable wisdom.[36]

There is nothing here which directly sanctions the payment of low wages. But in practical application, such an injunction to docile acceptance of one's lot meant that the wage-earning poor man must take patiently whatever amount his employer, in God's inscrutable wisdom, vouchsafed to give him. "The interest of God and the interest of the employer merge together at this point in a curious way."

6. EXPLOITATION AND UNEMPLOYMENT

In fairness to Calvin, it should be understood that he no more condoned the mistreatment of servants by their employers than he countenanced sloth or restlessness in the servants. One is not to withhold the wages of a poor man, he says, for by this means he earns his living. (Calvin immediately hastens to say that it is really the blessing of God, rather than his own industry, that sustains the worker.) "If I compel a poor man to work for me and I pay him only half his wage, it is certain that I defraud him of his labor."[37] And to defraud a poor man of the labor of his hands is

---

[36] *Opera,* xxvii, 337. Ser. on Deut. 15: 11-15.
[37] *Opera,* xxviii, 189. Ser. on Deut. 24: 14-18.

ASSETS AND LIABILITIES 215

worse than to plunder a field, for he has no other foundation or inheritance.

In this connection also, Calvin gives the employing classes some straight talk on the matter of exploiting the necessitous condition of workers in seasons of unemployment. This passage is worth quoting, both as an evidence of current practice and as indication that Calvin saw clearly the difference between the lack of opportunity to work and the unwillingness to work. In fact, he saw this distinction, with its moral implications, far more clearly than have many of his spiritual descendants.

If I bargain with some one to work for me, and the day's work will cost so much, but then the day's work becomes so much shortened that a poor man having done all he can has not enough to live on, what then? I see that the man has no opportunity to work. He is in my power; I can get him for what I want to pay. That is what the rich often do—they spy out occasions to cut down the wages of the poor by half when they have no employment.

The poor offer themselves for any amount they can get to earn their living. A rich man sees this and says, "He is destitute; I can get him for a piece of bread. Since he has to give himself to me to spite his teeth, I will pay him only a half-wage and he will have to be satisfied." When we adopt such cruel measures, even though we have not held back his wage, . . . this subterfuge will not avail before God.[38]

Calvin likewise saw, and denounced, the exploitation inherent in the mercantilism of his day. The passage just cited continues thus:

When a rich man trafficks in goods . . . and a poor man lives by his day's work and there is no money in his [the poor man's] pocket, he will be obliged to sell what he has at a loss. If the purchaser buys thus, knowing the poor man's necessity, it is a manifest oppression; and we ought to quote the familiar proverb, "That is putting one's foot on another's throat." It is a form of brigandage.

Apparently "cut-throat" business deals and "highway robbery" were no uncommon phenomena in Calvin's day! He implies as much in one of his few explicit references to merchants, who, he

[38] Ibid.

says, "are skilled in unnumerable arts of deceiving, and in im-
postures of every kind." [39] Referring to the people of Tyre "whose
merchants are princes," he says that in like manner the merchants
of Venice and of Antwerp think themselves superior to princes and
live in luxury such as the wealthiest of the nobility cannot afford.[40]
In a characterization which aptly puts together his idea of cause
and effect, he remarks:

We may not think that God acted without reason [against Tyre],
for the inhabitants of Tyre were proud, ambitious, lewd and licentious.
These vices follow in the train of wealth and prosperity, and commonly
abound in mercantile cities.[41]

Had Calvin's followers heeded all his words about the unrighteousness of exploitation and the moral dangers of prosperity, Calvinism might have been a deterrent, rather than a promoter, of the
capitalistic spirit. His injunctions to industry, frugality and docility
were heeded; his warnings against avarice were forgotten. The
explanation lies in the almost irresistible power of economic forces
and in the tendencies of human nature. Competition, acquisitiveness, and social conservatism reinforced the one set of teachings,
nullified the other.

7. THE DIVINE RIGHT OF PRIVATE PROPERTY

Calvin believed that the giving or withholding of riches lay not
with any human agency but with God. His injunctions to the poor
to be content with poverty, and to the rich to avoid the corrupting
power of riches, alike grew out of his conviction that God alone
metes out to men their fortunes.

There is, of course, a problem here. How do bad people happen
to have riches? Why exhort people not to plunder their neighbor's
goods, if all wealth is amassed solely by the will of God? Calvin
saw the problem clearly enough to attempt an answer, but not to
surrender his major premise. We are not to think, he says, that
abundance comes from our own merit—it is all in God's hands.

---

[39] *Opera*, xxxvii, 171. Comm. on Is. 47:15.
[40] *Opera*, xxxvi, 390. Comm. on Is. 23:8.
[41] *Opera*, xxxvi, 391. Comm. on Is. 23:9.

God sometimes gives riches to bad people, but this is to bring them to the greater condemnation. They will be punished doubly if they do not profit by the grace vouchsafed to them. Calvin seems to affirm that ethical qualities have nothing whatever to do with the dispensing of riches when he says:

> We must recognize this as a general principle, that riches come not at all to men through their own virtue, nor wisdom, nor toil, but only by the blessing of God.[42]

Nor can fortunes be attributed either to one's own vigilance or a lucky ancestry.

> Though some seem to enrich themselves by vigilance, nevertheless it is God who blesses and cares for them. Though others are rich before they are born, and their fathers have acquired great possessions, nevertheless this is not by accident, but the providence of God rules over it.[43]

It is obvious that this doctrine did not originate with Calvin. It reflects the Hebraic conception of prosperity as a mark of divine favor. The natural inference is that when one acquires riches, he may pride himself with great satisfaction on having found favor in the eyes of God. Many of Calvin's followers drew this inference, and used this divine sanction as a pretext for the amassing of further riches, secure in the thought of being superior persons whom God delights to favor.[44] Such a spirit breeds a smug complacency which has been, and still is, a potent force in the pursuance of profits.

However, Calvin himself was too suspicious of the "inebriation of prosperity" to draw this inference. In repeated warnings he declared that God in bestowing riches on the wealthy has given them, through no merit or fault of theirs, a doubtful blessing. Dangers attend both poor and rich, but the poor are safer. A small boat on a streamlet may strike a tree along the bank, but it is

---

[42] *Opera,* xxvi, 627. Ser. on Deut. 8: 14-20.
[43] *Ibid.*
[44] The author does not intend to suggest here, or elsewhere, that Calvin's followers were the only ones who did this.

safer than a ship on a tempestuous sea.[45] The rich are like those
who skate on ice and are apt to fall, or like those who walk among
thorns and must walk carefully lest they be pricked.[46] Calvin
could not foresee that his followers might use such words to justify
keeping the poor in poverty as a moral service.[47]

•   •   •   •   •   •

Stalwart as was Calvin's opposition to the misuse of riches, he
stood firmly for the right of every man to possess his own. The
savageness of his attacks on the socialism of his day reveals clearly
his conception of the sanctity of private property. Certain com-
munistic tendencies among the Anabaptists and (according to
Calvin) among the Spiritual Libertines inflamed his wrath, and
he berated them as roundly as it is now customary to berate the
Bolshevists. Charges of atheism, free love and anarchy are mixed
up in his attacks, very much as socialists of the present are subjected indiscriminately to this medley of charges. A citation will
reveal his supreme contempt.

We have already seen how these wretches profane marriage, mixing
men with women like brute beasts, as their lust leads them. And how
under the name of spiritual marriage they color up this bestial pol-
lution. . . .
But finally, to leave no order among men, they also make a similar
confusion as to goods: saying that it is the communion of saints for no
one to possess anything of his own but for each to take whatever he
can. At the beginning there were some silly Anabaptists who talked
this way. But now that such an absurdity has been rejected by all as
repugnant to human sense, so that even the original authors are ashamed
of it, these Libertines have taken refuge in it. . . . It is true that on the
surface they have some justification, complaining of the avarice of
those who call themselves Christian.[48]

---

[45] *Opera*, xxxiii, 36. Ser. on Job 2: 2-5.

[46] *Ibid.*, 37.

[47] Weber remarks, in connection with the idea that an unequal distribution of
goods was regarded as a special dispensation of Providence, "Calvin himself had
made the much-quoted statement that only when the people, i.e., the mass of laborers
and craftsmen, were poor did they remain obedient to God." (*Gesammelte Aufsätze*,
p. 199.) He cites no reference, and I have been unable to find any passage in which
Calvin says exactly this. Weber may have in mind such statements as these on the
perils of riches, which, contrary to Calvin's intention, were used to justify the poverty
of the poor.

[48] *Opera*, vii, 214. *Contre la Secte des Libertins.*

At this point Calvin digresses to condemn the avarice of Christians, and the unwillingness of the rich to share with the poor or listen to God's remonstrances. This is followed by an exhortation to contentment and gratitude to God, from whom all things come. Having paid his respects to the shortcomings of the respectable, he gets back to the Libertines.

> This is how we ought to proceed. . . . Since we do not do so, let us recognize it as a just punishment of God that these fanatics come to overthrow all order, wishing to abolish all distinctions of goods, making the world like a forest of brigands where without account or payment everybody takes as his own whatever he can get. However, there are so many witnesses in Scripture to rebuke this villainous confusion, that if we were to recite them all there would be no end.[49]

Whereupon Calvin enters upon a long disquisition to show that the New Testament does not really enjoin community of goods, and he ends with an exhortation to the faithful to adhere to "law and order." One is reminded of the familiar adage that there is nothing new under the sun.

8. CALVIN'S INFLUENCE UPON CAPITALISM

Having traced through three chapters Calvin's views on problems of economic ethics, we must pull together the various threads and summarize his influence.

Calvin's greatest economic contribution was through his advocacy, by precept and example, of what we have termed the middle class virtues. Though reverence and chastity were of economic value in setting standards of respectability, the virtues most directly contributing to economic progress were industry, frugality, honesty and sobriety. Regarding the economic consequences of these virtues among Calvin's followers I agree with Weber, though I believe that he underestimates the degree to which they received religious sanction through non-Calvinistic channels.

Second in importance is Calvin's removal of the prohibition on

[49] *Ibid.*, 216.

usury. We have noted its economic significance in releasing the tradesman's conscience from moral and religious strictures. This release contributed permanently and effectively to the growth of both the form and the spirit of capitalism.

A third influence, in which I am in partial agreement with Weber, is the religious significance which the secular calling assumed in the hands of Calvin and the Calvinists. Both Luther and Calvin passed beyond medieval thought in considering fidelity to one's daily task in the ordinary pursuits of life a duty more divinely imposed than service in a monastery. The double meaning of calling, found only in a subordinate way in Calvin's writings, became explicit and influential among his followers.

A fourth influence is found in Calvin's injunctions to servants to obey their masters without rebellion. Among subsequent Calvinists this tended to produce a docile laboring class, while the doctrine is invoked even to the present to justify the employing classes in their dominance of the economic order. It is no accident that the efforts of labor to organize, and of organized labor to secure redress, are still frowned upon as a moral evil by many of Calvin's spiritual descendants.

A fifth influence grows out of Calvin's doctrine that all material goods are bestowed by God. This was easily used to justify the assumption that prosperity is a special mark of divine favor. This doctrine in conjunction with the idea of the divine right of private property tended to sanction unlimited competition and to put the seal of religious approval on economic power.

Calvin's writings abound in prohibitions of avarice and injunctions to stewardship which, if observed, would have restrained the growth of a system built on competition and the profit motive. Both because of the power of the acquisitive instinct in human nature and the power of economic forces in an increasingly complex civilization, these strictures were largely overlooked, while the elements favoring capitalism came into the ascendancy. Calvinism may justly be considered a potent force in the development of the capitalistic spirit.

CHAPTER XI

GOD AND THE STATE

Two centuries after Calvin's day, Jean Jacques Rousseau wrote of him in his *Social Contract,* "Those who consider Calvin only as a theologian fail to recognize the breadth of his genius. The editing of our wise laws, in which he had a large share, does him as much honor as his *Institutes.* Whatever revolution time may bring in our religion, so long as the love of country and liberty is not extinct among us, the memory of this great man will be held in reverence." [1] This estimate of Calvin's contribution to political liberty is reinforced by the testimony of John Adams upon religious freedom when he says, "Let not Geneva be forgotten or despised. Religious liberty owes it much respect, Servetus notwithstanding." [2]

I. A POLITICAL PARADOX

The variability of judgment with which later observers have estimated Calvin's work is as great with regard to his political influence as his economic doctrine or his theology. A careful student of Calvin, H. D. Foster, holds that Calvin rendered incalculable service to modern liberty by showing how political tyranny could be constitutionally checked, and by cultivating the qualities necessary to revolution and self-government. This verdict is reinforced historically by the fact that the establishment of the Dutch Republic, the revolt of the Scotch against Mary Stuart, the Puritan Revolution in England, and in part the American and the French Revolutions, were pushed through by Calvinists and furthered by the spread of the Calvinistic spirit. Yet other political historians maintain that it was only as Calvinism departed from Calvin himself that it

[1] *Du Contrat Social,* Liv. ii, Ch. 7, n.
[2] *Discourses on Davila,* XIX, *Works,* vi, 313 n.

became the champion of either political or religious liberty. Knox, rather than Calvin, is regarded as the true father of the Puritan doctrine of resistance to tyranny; while many have pointed out that Beza's *Du Droit des Magistrats,* which advocates popular sovereignty and the resistance of tyrannous rulers to the point of deposition, goes so far beyond Calvin as to be virtually a new doctrine.[8]

Those who deny to Calvin any particular contribution to political or religious liberty maintain that both the spirit of resistance and the demand for religious toleration arose after Calvin's time as a spontaneous outcropping of the instinct of self-preservation, after the new religion found itself confronted by hostile political forces. When a religious sect is in favor with the state, it can preach submission to the magistrates and can call upon the sword-bearing arm of the state to exterminate heretics. This was the situation in Geneva in Calvin's day. But when the tables are turned and this same sect becomes a political minority, it must revolt if it is strong enough. If unable to rebel, it must agitate for toleration— toleration, that is, for itself. Often the resistance to tyranny and the demand for religious freedom are combined, as in the Puritan revolution in England; and the victors, having achieved supremacy, then set up a new tyranny and a fresh intolerance.

There is truth in all these estimates of Calvin's influence. Historical circumstances were doubtless more influential than Calvin's own word or example in the rise of the spirit of independence. There was little political liberty in Geneva under Calvin's régime, and still less of religious liberty. His practical influence was on the side of an autocratic state and complete conformity of the individual to the established powers. In his writings also, obedience to magistrates is the dominant political note. The Scriptures plainly state, he says, that rulers get their power from God. To defy a prince

---

[8] Harold Laski discounts the political influence of both Calvin and Beza, and says that Calvin merely recommended submission to the authority of God and the magistrates, prescribing in case of conflict nothing but prayer and exile—a policy which ruined those who accepted it. Introduction to Laski's edition of the *Vindiciæ Contra Tyrannos,* p. 10.

or magistrate is to defy God. The ruler may be oppressive, t.
But this is to try our faith and chasten us for our sins. Calvin
is very sure that rulers govern by divine authority, and as God's
vice-gerents, they must be obeyed.

Yet both practically and theoretically, Calvin left the way open
for political resistance. In his long struggle to establish the Genevan
bibliocracy, we saw him more than once clashing with the civil
powers and contending with all the energy of his being that the
will of God must take precedence over the will of Libertine magistrates. When the issue was made concrete in a case of conflict
between Calvin's will (God's) and that of evil or misguided magistrates (the devil's), Calvin had no doubt as to which will ought to
prevail. By no means did he stand, in practice, for passive obedience. Furthermore, there are passages in his writings which advocate resistance to rulers who demand obedience to what is contrary
to the Law of God. His dominant emphasis is on obedience to the
duly constituted authority even at personal sacrifice, as a form of
divine chastening. But in case of an out-and-out moral conflict,
Calvin is clear in his conviction that one must obey God rather
than men.[4]

This divergent emphasis in Calvin's own attitude is reflected in
the later Calvinists' union of supreme reverence for "law and
order" with the "spirit of '76." This apparent paradox is still a
common phenomenon. It is sometimes pointed out that the Daughters of the American Revolution are inconsistent in opposing those
who venture to criticize the established order, when their own forefathers were the political radicals of their time. They are not
inconsistent; they are merely consistent Calvinists—with less regard
for God's glory than their forefathers had. So too the State of
Massachusetts, a Calvinistic commonwealth which could be the
hot-bed of rebellion and cradle of liberty at one period in its history,
and a century and a half later could sanction the execution of Sacco

---

[4] There is, of course, a difference between disobedience and revolution. Recognition of the legitimacy of the former is a step toward the latter—a step which Calvin
did not take overtly, though he laid the foundations by which his followers took it.

and Vanzetti—perhaps destined like Servetus to go down in history as victims of a judicial murder—in order to uphold the dignity of the established order. It is easy to identify the will of God with the *status quo* when one agrees with the *status quo*, and to insist that God demands resistance when it fails to please us.

2. MAGISTRATES AS GOD'S VICE-GERENTS

Calvin was stating no new idea when he asserted the unqualified duty of obedience to the civil authorities. All the early Reformers proclaimed it, and the Anabaptists, who ventured in a measure to challenge it, paid for their convictions with their lives. Luther carried the non-resistance doctrine to the point of saying, "I will side always with him, however unjust, who endures rebellion and against him who rebels, however justly." [5] The extent to which he carried this doctrine in throwing the force of the Lutheran faith on the side of the nobility against the peasants in the Peasants' War is familiar history. While Luther challenged the temporal power of the Catholic church and abolished the ecclesiastical to leave only the civil magistrates, he virtually transferred to the civil *regnum* the authority formerly vested in the ecclesiastical *sacerdotium*.

Two types of political environment foster a promotion of the doctrine of non-resistance as a religious duty. When a new religion is weak and must rely for its existence on the favor of the established powers, it preaches submission. When it becomes strong and dominates the political situation itself, it again preaches submission. Only in the intermediate stage, when it is strong enough to rebel but not to dominate, is it likely to encourage resistance. Nor is it through any conscious opportunism or compromising of its message that a religious emphasis adjusts itself to political circumstance. It is rather through the subtle psychological processes of rationalization which so often make theory conform to expediency without the possessor's recognizing that he is advocating the expedient.

[5] *An den Christlichen Adel*, 1520. Quoted by Allen, *Political Thought in the Sixteenth Century*, p. 19.

It would be unfair to the memory of Luther and Calvin to assert that either one preached submission to the state against his own convictions, merely for the sake of political support. Both believed firmly that submission to rulers was commanded by God in the Scriptures, and that resistance would not only affront God but disrupt the social fabric. Yet it may be doubted whether they would have seen this side of the case so clearly in a different political situation.

In Luther, there is a change of emphasis after the Peasants' War of 1525. Up till that time he had not hesitated to denounce the sins of the rulers. After that time he laid more stress upon the rights of princes, less upon Christian liberty. He saw that only through the help of the princes could the new faith be established on a solid basis, and this to Luther was the supreme objective. Luther was less of a political philosopher than Calvin, but he saw clearly the need of establishing a reformed and visible church with the aid of the secular magistrates. Also, he was enough of a medieval mystic to set high spiritual value upon the patient endurance of affliction. He believed it to be the religious duty of the Christian to suffer patiently and prayerfully all manner of injustice, if need be, at the hands of a cruel prince. Though he came to recognize the right of a prince to resist the emperor,[6] political expediency joined with mystical passivism to make him advocate, for the citizen, the duty of obedience to the civil powers.

Calvin built on Luther's foundation. He was less influenced by considerations of political expediency, for his struggle for the supremacy of the Reformed faith took place in a much more limited local environment. Geneva was Protestant before he entered it, and there never was a time afterward when it was not prevailingly Protestant. While Calvin was interested in the advancement of the Reformed faith in outside territories, his primary interest lay in performing aright the duties of the Christian ministry in one city. Calvin's fight was not for the existence of Protestantism, nor

[6] Cf. R. H. Bainton, "The Development and Consistency of Luther's Attitude to Religious Liberty," *Harvard Theological Review*, April 1929, p. 133.

to any great extent, for its diffusion. What he was concerned with supremely was the establishment of the Law of God as the law of Geneva. This meant that he was predisposed to enforce obedience to the civil law, so far as it could be conceived to be divinely authorized; also that upon occasion he could preach resistance to such magistrates as had forfeited their divine calling by disobedience to God's will.

Calvin's major emphasis, we noted above, was upon obedience to civil officers as God's representatives. A few citations will make this clear. Civil government, he says, is as necessary to mankind as bread and water, light and air, and far more excellent.[7] Kings are the hands of God.[8] Kings, princes and the highest magistrates are called sons of God because God has chosen to show forth in them especially his majesty.[9] According to the word of God himself, "By me kings reign and princes decree justice." (Prov. 8:15.)[10] "There is no power but of God: the powers that be are ordained of God." (Rom. 13:1.) Even hereditary princes get all their power from God, for by the will and disposal of God they were born as successors of kings, and by his will they are cherished and protected.[11] Kings and magistrates, like prophets and teachers, are called and anointed of God to a special task and are given a special mark of divine election.[12] In fact, Calvin implies, though he never brings himself explicitly to say, that the magistrates are above even the clergy in the sacredness of their office. "Wherefore no doubt ought now to be entertained by any person that civil magistracy is a calling not only holy and legitimate, but far the most sacred and honorable in human life."[13]

Calvin is very clear in his conviction that this divine anointing *ought* to make kings, princes and magistrates appreciate the dignity of their office and rule with wisdom and justice. But he is equally

[7] IV, xx, 3.
[8] *Opera*, xxxv, 152. Ser. on Job 34:10-15.
[9] *Opera*, xxix, 617. Hom. on I Sam. 10.
[10] IV, xx, 4.
[11] *Opera*, xxix, 306. Hom. on I Sam. 2.
[12] *Opera*, xxix, 617. Hom. on I Sam. 10.
[13] IV, xx, 4.

honest in confronting the fact that it does not. Not a little of his eloquence is expended in denouncing the deception, avarice, extravagance and corruption of kings; their vanity and self-adulation; the folly of their alliances; the inordinate ambition which prompts them to burden their subjects with taxation to support unnecessary projects.[14] Princes, he says, are like vast whirlpools that swallow up hard-won money in ridiculous and silly ways. They extort it from their wretched people and then spare neither gold nor silver, but throw it away lavishly in pomp and splendid accoutrements, luxury and lewdness.[15] There is a sting, with homely humor, in Calvin's condemnation both of king and commoner:

We see today princes undertaking such enterprises that if they had things in their own hands, they would like to create eighteen all-new worlds. But the pride which thus displays itself in the great is not absent from the lowest. They act like scorpions that wiggle their tails to throw their venom.[16]

So a dilemma appears. According to the indisputable evidence of Scripture, kings and magistrates rule by God's command, as God's representatives. Manifestly, they should rule in godlike fashion. Manifestly also, they do not so rule. What to do about it?

Calvin's usual answer is characteristically Scriptural. "Whosoever resisteth the power, resisteth the ordinance of God; and they that resist shall receive to themselves damnation." Christians are directed "to be subject to principalities and powers, to obey magistrates." This does not say, "Obey good magistrates." If we obeyed only those who governed well, there would be no merit in our obedience. "If all those in authority ruled like good fathers and we knew that their only care was to govern us well, what would it be to obey them? We would do this out of self-regard. It would not be to *obey God,* but solely for our own profit." [17] Princes are to

14 *Opera,* xxix, 574; xxxvi, 168, 305, 573; xxxix, 4, 230; xli, 7.
15 *Opera,* xxix, 550. Hom. on I Sam. 8: 7-10.
16 *Opera,* xxxv, 76. Ser. on Job 33: 14-17.
17 *Opera,* xxxv, 160. Ser. on Job 34: 16-20.

be obeyed, even if unworthy, out of reverence for God, and by such obedience we show ourselves submissive to God's will.

Calvin insists repeatedly that when the wicked rule, it is because God sends them as a chastisement for our sins. Nobody is apt to deny, he says, that an impious king is a judgment of God's wrath upon the world.[18] Such an event should call us to repentance and move us to prayer, but never to resistance. As the Israelites were commanded to be in subjection to Nebuchadnezzar, so Christians everywhere must submit themselves to such tyrants as God places over them. This duty of non-resistance is set forth so unequivocally that there would be no shadow of justification for political resistance in Calvin if this were his only statement:

Wherefore, if we are cruelly vexed by an inhuman prince, or robbed and plundered by one prodigal and avaricious, or despised and left without protection by one negligent; or even if we are afflicted for the name of God by one sacrilegious and unbelieving, let us first of all remember our own offenses against God which doubtless are chastised by these plagues. Thus humility will curb our impatience. And secondly, let us consider that it is not for us to remedy these evils: for us it remains only to implore the aid of God, in whose hand are the hearts of kings and changes of kingdoms.[19]

God sometimes raises up public avengers, like Moses and Othniel. Being divinely commissioned, such messengers of God's wrath may take up arms against kings. Jeremiah, by a special command of God, could urge the people to violate their oath to the king. But without such divine commission, no man may resist a ruler. The Christian may meditate upon his sins and pray God for deliverance; he may do no more. Such would seem to be the clear teaching of Calvin upon the duty of non-resistance. No Stuart ever proclaimed more vigorously the "divine right" of kings and magistrates to govern.

[18] IV, xx, 25.
[19] IV, xx, 29.

3. THE ABROGATION OF DIVINE RIGHT

There is another side to the story. Even in the *Institutes,* where Calvin speaks most unequivocally for the duty of obedience, there is a little loophole. Toward the end of his chapter on Civil Government, he suggests briefly, in defense of Daniel's disobedience to the king, that if a ruler governs wickedly he forfeits his right to govern. "By lifting up his horns against God, he had virtually abrogated his power." [20] This suggestion is dropped without Calvin's realizing, perhaps, its far-reaching significance.

The angle of the problem upon which he dwells most outspokenly is the duty of passive resistance to an order which contradicts the will of God. One must not obey magistrates if it means disobeying God. "If they command anything against Him, it ought not to have the least attention; nor, in this case, ought we to pay any attention to all that dignity attached to magistrates; to which no injury is done when it is subjected to the unrivalled and supreme power of God." [21] Calvin frankly recognizes that such disobedience brings great danger, for the resister must be willing to take the consequences; but he concludes the *Institutes* by saying that it is better to suffer anything than deviate from piety, remembering the price at which Christ redeemed us.

It should be noted that Calvin here gets only as far as advocating passive, not active, resistance. To obey God rather than men and bear patiently the penalty for such disobedience to human edicts is quite a different matter from attempting to curb the power of the tyrant. Neither is it to be identified with a recognition that the tyrant, through his own misconduct, has lost his divine right to require obedience.

However, in his sermons and commentaries, Calvin goes much further than in the *Institutes* in sanctioning resistance. I believe that those who find in Calvin only a recognition of the duty of passive resistance have attached too little importance to certain

[20] IV, xx, 32.
[21] This was not new. Luther and most of the other early reformers favored passive resistance in such a situation. Cf. Allen, p. 103.

passages which speak squarely for the duty of active resistance against God-defying kings. His clearest statements are again in connection with the sixth chapter of Daniel. In his commentary on Daniel 6:22, he points out that the injunction, "Fear God; honor the king," is based on a rightful sequence, for only God-fearing kings deserve to be honored. Others forfeit their power and must be defied.

Earthly princes lay aside all their power when they rise up against God, and are unworthy to be reckoned in the number of mankind. *We ought rather to spit on their heads than to obey them when they are so restive and wish to rob God of his rights.*[22]

The sermon on Daniel 6:16-21 gives so unequivocally both his primary doctrine and his exception to it that it merits quotation at some length.

God desires that there be civil officers and degrees of honor, and he wants some to rule and others to be subject. As St. Paul shows, power comes only from God. Those who despise this world's superiors make war on God. But when principalities rise up against God, do they not show themselves unworthy of any regard? That is very certain.

The protest Daniel makes is true when he says, I have done thee no hurt.[23] When he disobeys the king to obey God, the king has no occasion to feel angry or aggrieved; for when we are directed to honor the king, it comes after the injunction to fear God. There is no need to put the cart before the ox. This order must be adhered to, that God's pre-eminence be above all, great and small beneath his feet. This is the first thing.

In the second place, we must obey our princes who are set over us. Even though they torture us bodily and use tyranny and cruelty toward us, it is necessary to bear all this, as St. Paul says. *But when they rise against God they must be put down, and held of no more account than worn-out shoes.* And why? The foundation of everything is destroyed. As today, if one looks at the way the world is governed, one finds great excesses of which the princes are guilty. They oppress their subjects; ambition and avarice so transport them that they no longer know who they are; they are so intoxicated and bewitched that they think the world

---

[22] *Opera,* xli, 25 f. Comm. on Dan. 6:22. Italics mine.
[23] Dan. 6:22.

was made for them. In short, they abuse men with no mercy. In all this the subjects must humble themselves and recognize that they are enduring it for their sins, must pray God to give them patience, and do their duty. But when princes forbid the service and worship of God, when they command their subjects to pollute themselves with idolatry and want them to consent to and participate in all the abominations that are contrary to the service of God, *they are not worthy to be regarded as princes or to have any authority attributed to them.*

"And why? Because there is only one foundation of all the power of princes—that God has set them in their places. When they wish to tear God from his throne, can they be respected? . . . God is sovereign and all creatures are beneath him. When we disobey princes to obey him, we do not do wrong; for we ought to have no respect for persons when it is a question of God's honor.[24]

Calvin is as out-spoken here in his defiance of princes that contemn God as he is elsewhere in his injunction to obedience. Nor does he here advocate mere *passive* resistance. Princes that rise against God must be put down, and must be held of no more account than worn-out shoes. The Calvinist took literally the injunction to have no respect for persons when God's honor was at stake. Such doctrine had a sword in it, and was to cost Charles I his head and George III a fair dominion.

4. LAW AND ORDER

Had Calvin faced the issues of his theory to a finish, he would have found himself caught in a jam. One must not resist: the state is sacrosanct. One must resist: God is to be obeyed before men.

It would be easy to charge Calvin with inconsistency. The situation parallels his recurrent insistence both upon man's moral responsibility and his lack of freedom. Inconsistency in affirmations about conflicting loyalties—particularly religious and national loyalties—is not new in the world's history. Whether Calvin is to be called inconsistent depends on whether he is to be commended for sticking to his premises or censured for not detecting the clash in his premises. From the standpoint of implicit reliance on the

[24] *Opera*, xli, 415 f. Italics mine.

authority of a verbally inspired Bible, he could not fail to find
Scriptural justification both for unqualified obedience to rulers and
for active resistance on conscientious grounds.

The legitimacy of armed resistance involves three issues: the
theoretical right to resist, the channel through which resistance is
to be made, and the use of armed force in the process. The first of
these questions centers about the problem of whether resistance, if
any, shall be passive or active. We have seen that Calvin greatly
favored passive resistance, when obedience to God before man
made resistance necessary, but that he also gave a somewhat
reluctant sanction to active resistance. A further look must be
taken at the second problem—the means to be adopted.

Calvin's predilection for having things done decently and in
order is here strongly in evidence. In former times, he says, there
were certain officials whose duty it was to restrain acts of the
chief magistrate. Such were the ephors of Sparta and the tribunes
of Rome, and such "are possibly nowadays in each kingdom the
three estates assembled." [25] So runs a phrase freighted with much
meaning. No private citizen may resist; but the lower magistrates
may resist the higher through legal, constitutional channels.

In the Elizabethan English familiar to English, Scottish and
American readers up to the time of the American Revolution, this
famous passage from the *Institutes* runs as follows:

Though the correcting of unbridled government be the revengement
of the Lord, let us not by and by think that it is committed to us, to
whome there is given no other commaundment but to obey and suffer.
I speake alway of private men. For if there be at this time any magistrates for the behalfe of the people, (such as in olde time were the
Ephori, that were set against the Kinges of Lacedemonia, or the Tribunes of the people, against the Romane Consuls: or the Demarchy,
against the Senate of Athenes: and the same power also which perad-
venture as things are nowe the three estates have in everie realme when
they hold their principall assemblies) I doe so not forbid them according to their office to withstande the outraging licentiousness of kinges:
that I affirme that if they winke at kinges wilfully raging over and

[25] IV, xx, 31.

treading downe the poor communaltie, their dissembling is not without wicked breach of faith, because they deceitfully betray the libertie of the people, whereof they know themselves to bee appointed protectors by the ordinance of God.[26]

This doctrine of constitutional resistance through representative magistrates was influential outside of Geneva in Calvin's day and grew rapidly in its hold on Calvinistic political theory. It was quoted by Knox and the commissioners to Elizabeth in defense of Mary Stuart's deposition. It was cited by the English Puritan, Thomas Cartwright, in 1572 in his *Admonition to Parliament* and by his opponent Archbishop Whitgift. Puritan preachers made much use of it to incite Parliament against Charles I during the Civil War, and it was quoted and widely read by New England Puritans. It was no slight factor in fostering the spirit of independence among Calvin's followers.

Yet clear-cut as his statement is, Calvin himself was not at all eager in a concrete issue to grant the legitimacy of resistance even by the lower magistrates. Charged with having sanctioned the conspiracy of Amboise, he wrote a letter to Coligny [27] in 1561 which indicates much reluctance to sanction rebellion. He had been asked beforehand, he says, whether oppression did not justify active resistance on the part of the children of God, but he had answered that it would be better for the children of God to perish a hundred times than for the Gospel to be dishonored by bloodshed.[28] He had granted, however, that, if the princes of the blood and the Parliament were to take joint action against the sovereign to secure their legal rights, the people would be justified in lending their support. Asked if rebellion by a single prince would justify such support, he had replied in the negative. J. W. Allen interprets this as tantamount to a flat denial of the right of the Huguenots

[26] *Ibid.*, Norton's translation. Quoted in H. D. Foster's *Collected Papers*, p. 77. The doctrine did not originate with Calvin; Luther had already said as much. Calvin's authority, however, greatly promoted its acceptance.

[27] Bonnet, IV, 175 ff.

[28] This seems to me to refute Lord Acton's statement in the *History of Freedom*, p. 178, that Calvin wished to extend religion by the sword.

to take up arms against their oppressors, since the possibility of complete agreement among the princes of the blood and Parliament
was inconceivable.[29]   While I believe that this is to read into
Calvin's words rather more than he intended, it is clear that Calvin
held active resistance, even through the magistrates, to be justifiable only in the rarest of instances.

5. CONSCIENTIOUS OBJECTORS

A further question remains as to the legitimacy of military force.
This is easily answered. It must not be supposed that Calvin's reluctance to justify rebellion by force of arms was due to any
pacifistic scruples. It was regard for the sanctity of civil government, rather than the sanctity of human life, which led him to call
upon his followers to accept persecution as a divine chastening
instead of taking up arms against their oppressors. Calvin decried,
yet justified, war in a fashion quite in keeping with the modern
mood.

It was not an unheard-of thing in Calvin's day to regard war
as unchristian and to believe that it should, and could, be abolished.
Contemporary Anabaptists were calling upon men to abjure it as
savoring of the devil more than of Christ. Erasmus in his *Complaint of Peace* had used the full force of his satirical pen to plead
for the repudiation among Christians of a practice so contrary both
to nature and the law of Christ.[80] The Anabaptists and Erasmus
were Christian pacifists in the modern sense of the term. But
Calvin was a long way from being one.

Calvin was too much of a realist to be captivated by the glamour
of war, and he recognized clearly its evils. He comments upon
"that fierceness which is often found in the military profession,
and which is utterly unbecoming in the servants of Christ."[81]
Urging the elect to greater fidelity in the midst of persecution and
forced migration, he exhorts them to show more courage than

---

[29] *Political Thought in the Sixteenth Century,* p. 59.
[80] Erasmus' *Querela Pacis* is summarized in an article by the author entitled
"Erasmus, Prophet of Peace" in the *Methodist Review,* March-April, 1929.
[81] *Opera,* lii, 283. Comm. on I Tim. 3: 3.

mercenaries who undergo all manner of hardship in war to serve
the devil.[32] He recognized and deplored the unchristian character
of war's accompaniments, "the cruelties, thefts, reprisals, acts of
violence, extortions, and other such unholy deeds which are committed in it." [33] In a measure, he realized its ineffectiveness, for
he remarks that "we are not at all surprised, when a war is finished,
if it begins over again right away." [34] But it seems not to have
crossed his mind that war itself might be contrary to the will of
God.

It is doubtful whether Calvin was acquainted with Erasmus'
pacifism. But he was well aware of the Anabaptists' opposition to
the use of military force, and he had slight patience with it. In
his *Contre les Anabaptistes* he treats of their position with his
usual vigor and virulence. While he begins with an exhortation to
non-resistance and patient endurance as quietistic in tone as any
utterance of Luther's, it apparently did not occur to him that this
might have any real bearing on the rightfulness of war.

Finally they [the Anabaptists] conclude that all use of arms is a
diabolical thing. Now it is true that the use of the sword ought not to
be permitted to any private individual, to make resistance to evil; for
the arms of Christians are prayer and meekness, to possess their lives in
patience and to overcome evil by doing good, according to the doctrine
of the Gospel. The duty then of each of us is to suffer patiently if some
outrage is done us, not to use force and violence.

"But to condemn the public use of the sword, which God has ordained for our protection, is blasphemy against God himself. According to the spirit of God, uttered by St. Paul, the magistrate is a servant
of God in our behalf, to repress and curb the violence of the wicked.
The sword is placed in his hand to punish malefactors. Since God
orders him to do this, who are we to hinder him? . . .

"Furthermore, it is clear that it is the intention of these poor fanatics
to condemn all munitions, fortresses, bearing of arms, and all such
things which make for the defense of the country: and to prevent subjects from obeying their princes and superiors when they want these

[32] *Opera,* viii, 436.
[33] *Opera,* vii, 79.
[34] *Opera,* xxviii, 445.   Ser. on Deut. 28: 46-50.

to be used in time of need. . . . But let us remember that it is to usurp
the authority of God to condemn as bad what our Lord has permitted
to us. He never forbade the use of arms to princes, to maintain their
peace among those who molest them wrongfully: the Scripture does
not say so.[35]

To be sure, Calvin continues, the prophets in speaking of the
reign of Jesus say that swords and spears shall be changed to imple-
ments of labor to till the soil. But, of course, he hastens to explain,
this does not mean it is wrong to fight when necessary. The
Christian prince ought to do all he can to preserve the peace,
even at personal cost, and go to arms only as a last resort. But
when other means fail, "the last refuge is to use the sword which
God has placed in his hand."

Calvin does not attempt to say how one may know when God,
rather than the devil or one's own impulses, has placed the sword
in one's hand. In condemning yet justifying military force, he
merely stated the current Christian concept of his day. Most of
his descendants since have gone on restating it, and scorning the
Anabaptists.

.   .   .   .

We must see in our next chapter how a doctrine which affirmed,
yet denied, the divine right to rule, and which deplored, yet
justified, armed resistance to tyranny, developed into a doctrine
which could form the spiritual foundation of the Puritan Revolution.
In Calvin's thought, the scales, though in uneven balance, were
noticeably tipped in the direction of docile obedience even to
tyrannous rulers. By 1640, the balance had swung so far in the
opposite direction that armed resistance seemed clearly a religious
duty. Apparently forces were at work which Calvin himself
could not foresee.

[35] *Opera,* vii, 77 f.

CHAPTER XII

THE RISE OF POLITICAL LIBERTY

Up till about 1550 the Protestants, Lutherans and Calvinists alike, stood in principle for non-resistance and the patient endurance of oppression, admitting merely the duty of passive resistance to such sovereigns as opposed the will of God. It was a religious duty to support the *status quo* without rebellion. This doctrine served well enough as long as the new faith had the support of the ruling powers. But with changes in fortune came changes in belief. The Puritan doctrine of the right of resistance to tyranny, to the point of revolution and if necessary to tyrannicide, is the product of Calvinism and the logic of events.

We shall attempt in this chapter to show how Calvin's doctrine of the right of constitutional resistance bore fruit in three areas.[1] In Scotland, the rise of political Calvinism was due mainly to the influence of one man, and a radical change in government was actuated more by a personality in action than by a theory. In France, the movement never assumed the proportions of a Calvinistic revolution, but called forth the formulation of a definitely democratic political theory. In England, it bred both theory and action, and became powerful enough to overthrow temporarily the monarchy, behead a king, and set up a Puritan commonwealth. The story of these developments will incidentally throw light on the genesis of two great Calvinistic churches, the Presbyterian and the Congregational.

[1] Calvinistic political theory was, of course, influential in America, and helped to pave the way for the Revolution. I have refrained from trying to trace its course in this country, first, because the democratic tendencies in Calvinism (the thesis of the chapter) came to fruition earliest and most clearly in their Old World setting; second, because the rise of political liberty leading to the American Revolution was only partially of Calvinistic origin.

1. JOHN KNOX AND THE KIRK

It is in John Knox that we find the first unqualified Calvinistic assertion of the duty of armed resistance. To understand his political doctrine we must take a look at his personal history.

Knox was fearless, capable, determined. His was the disposition that got things done, and he was no respecter of persons. He was of yeoman parentage, and his sympathies were always with the common people. His naturally democratic spirit was intensified by studying under the tutelage of John Major, who combined the spirit of the medieval schoolmen with the politically advanced view that all secular authority is derived from the will of the community.[2] Knox entered the priesthood of the Roman church, but withdrew in 1546 when he became a Protestant. After the murder of Cardinal Beaton, he was among the reformers who seized and held the castle of St. Andrews. This being captured by the French, he was condemned to the galleys, where he labored at the oar for a year and a half. In 1549 he was liberated, went to England, and became a licensed preacher.

With the accession of Edward's Catholic sister Mary Tudor, England was no longer a safe abiding-place for this fiery prophet, and he fled to the Continent. At Frankfort and Geneva he labored till 1559, and became one of Calvin's close friends and warm admirers. During this period he absorbed in full Calvin's doctrine and ecclesiastical policy. He made a brief trip to Scotland in 1555, during which he did much to strengthen the Reformed cause by his bold preaching, but he found no welcome from the Catholic queen-regent Mary of Guise. In 1559, at the request of the Protestant leaders of Scotland, he returned to his native country and took up in dead earnest the battle to root out Catholicism and plant Calvinism in its stead.

The effect of his coming was electrical. Storms had been brewing, for not only was there a large Protestant sentiment among the masses, but many of the nobles had embraced Protestantism, not

---

[2] Major was also the tutor of George Buchanan, whose *De Jure Regni apud Scotos* contributed to the cause of popular government in both Scotland and France.

from conviction, but as a means of discomfiting the ruling party. The pent-up enthusiasm of the people was stirred to furious action by a sermon on the idolatry of the Mass and image-worship. A riot ensued; churches were plundered and monasteries destroyed. The "rascal multitude," as Knox called them, broke all bounds and the country was on the verge of a religious war. The assistance of Elizabeth, reluctantly given, and the death of the queen-mother at this juncture, brought matters to a settlement. A truce was proclaimed and a parliament, Protestant in sentiment, was summoned. This parliament met, reorganized the government on a more democratic basis, and in August 1560, swept Catholicism out of official existence in Scotland to substitute the reformed Kirk.

Henceforth, Presbyterianism was to· be the national faith of Scotland. The beautiful Catholic queen, Mary Stuart, destined to come down in history as Mary Queen of Scots, was half-French by birth and wholly French by training, and never understood the blustering democracy or the self-confident Calvinism of her people. Between her and Knox was an impassable gulf. A famous interview, which took place shortly after her arrival in 1561, is thoroughly characteristic of the difference in their points of view.

"Think ye," she asked, "that subjects having power may resist their princes?"

"If princes exceed their bounds, madam, and do against that wherefore they should be obeyed, it is no doubt but they may be resisted, even by power." Knox went on to say that if princes act like lunatics they should be bound and imprisoned, like a father who goes mad and tries to kill his children. "God craves of kings that kings be foster-fathers to his Kirk, and commands queens to be nurses to his people."

"Yea, but ye are not the Kirk that I will nurse. I will defend the Kirk of Rome, for it is, I think, the true Kirk of God."

"Your will, madam, is no reason." (She had not said it was.) Knox then with more arrogance than tact made various remarks about the "Roman harlot" and the way in which the Roman Church had forsaken the purity of the apostolic faith.

"My conscience," the queen answered, "is not so."

"Conscience, madam," said Knox, "requires knowledge; and I fear that right knowledge ye have none."

"But I have both heard and read." The queen then put the crucial question. "Ye interpret the Scripture in one manner and they in another. Whom shall I believe? And who shall be the judge?"

Knox's answer was thoroughly Calvinistic in its dogmatic simplicity. He saw no problem. "Ye shall believe God, that plainly speaketh in his Word. . . . There can remain no doubt but unto such as remain obstinately ignorant."

Then he launched into an irrelevant discourse on the Communion, and Mary went to dinner.[3]

.   .   .   .

This interview is indicative of the trend of Knox's political theory. For its literary expression, we must return to the year 1558 which saw three historic documents emerge from his pen. Staunchly opposed to any woman's sitting on a throne, he wrote his *First Blast of the Trumpet against the Monstrous Regiment of Women*. This was aimed both at the queen-regent Mary of Guise in Scotland and Mary Tudor of England. Its argument is confused, with a jumbled appeal both to the authority of Scripture and the incapacity of woman, "weak, frail, impatient, feeble and foolish," [4] as the ground for asserting that it is against God and nature for a woman to rule. Its chief political importance lies in Knox's declaration that no mere legal succession, if contrary to the law of God, can make a claim valid. On this ground he declared it to be the duty "as well of the Estates as of the people" [5] to depose Mary Tudor.

In his *Appellation*, published later in the same year, Knox goes much further. He was then an exile in Geneva, and not popular in Scottish official circles. In his absence he had been condemned to

---

[3] Abridged, with spelling modernized, from Knox's *History of the Reformation*, IV, p. 290 f.

[4] *Works*, ed. Laing, IV, p. 374.

[5] *Ibid.*, p. 416.

death and burned in effigy. His *Appellation* purports to be an appeal for justice: in reality, it is a call to revolt. Knox's naturally fiery disposition, inflamed by what he regarded as bitterly unjust treatment and given added vehemence by his sense of an affront not only to John Knox but to Almighty God, burst forth in this invective. Its full title suggests its spirit, *The Appellation of John Knox from the cruel and most unjust sentence pronounced against him by the false bishoppes and clergie of Scotland, with his supplication and exhortation to the nobilitie, estates and communaltie of the realme.*

In the *Appellation* Knox flatly asserts that rebellion against idolatrous (i.e., Catholic) sovereigns is the duty of Christian subjects. While his appeal to "the nobilitie, estates and communaltie" approximates Calvin's doctrine of the right of resistance through the lower magistrates, it is announced with none of Calvin's reservations. Knox did not have Calvin's juristic temper. The main thing to him was to get rid of tyrants who oppose the true religion. The means mattered far less to him than the end, and he lumped the duty of deposing idolatrous sovereigns together with the general duty of killing all idolaters.

If Knox be taken at his word, he appears to justify the wholesale assassination of Catholics. After declaring that "no idolatour can be exempted from punishment by Goddes Law," he goes on to assert

> That the punishment of such crimes, as are idolatrie, blasphemie, and others, that tuche the Majestie of God, dothe not appertaine to kinges and chefe rulers only, but also the whole bodie of that people, and to every membre of the same, according to the vocation of everie man, and according to that possibilitie and occasion which God doth minister to revenge the injury done his glorie.[6]

Yet in fairness to Knox, he probably meant that "the whole bodie of that people" must assume responsibility for the purging of the country through judicial channels rather than through mob violence. The duty of the rank and file to participate in rebellion is fur-

6 *Works,* ed. Laing, IV, p. 501.

ther emphasized in a *Letter to the Commonalty of Scotland,* published with the *Appellation,* in which he made it clear that he desired not only the "estates and nobilitie" but the common people to take a hand in rooting Catholicism out of Scotland. He appeals here to "the Communaltie, my Brethren" to "compell your Byshoppes and Clergie to cease their tyrannie and answer by the scriptures of God." [7]

Until his death in 1572 Knox continued to proclaim the right of rebellion. In a famous address before the General Assembly in 1564, quoted by Milton in his *Tenure of Kings,* Knox drove another nail in the coffin of special royal prerogative with the assertion that "subjects might and ought to execute God's judgments upon their kings, . . . who if they offend, have no privilege to be exempted from the punishments of law more than any other subject." In 1567 the General Assembly through his influence passed a resolution requiring kings to defend "the true religioun," and asserting the contract between "the prince and God and his faithful people" to be mutual and reciprocal.[8] In the same year Parliament enacted this resolution into a law, confirmed the deposition of Mary Stuart, and authorized the Confession of Faith, "groundit upon the infallible word of God," as the ultimate criterion not only in matters of belief but of legislative action.[9]

Thus within nine years a reorganization in Church and State, destined to be permanent, was brought about on the basis of the Calvinistic doctrine of constitutional resistance. The Scottish revolution marks the first historical application of this doctrine. It is difficult to say whether the credit belongs more to Calvin, who enunciated the principle but hedged it about with restrictions, or to Knox, who took off the restrictions and plunged ahead toward a bare-fisted rejection of the divine right of tyrannous or idolatrous kings to rule. Due credit being given to both, the explanation lies largely in two other channels—the pressure of opposition and the

7 *Works,* ed. Laing, IV, p. 524.
8 Foster, p. 87.
9 *Acts of the General Assembly,* I, 109; *Acts of the Parliament of Scotland,* III, 11-12, 14, 23-24, 39.

tendency of human nature to burst all bonds when "the true religion," that is, one's own, meets opposition.

2. THE HUGUENOT THEORY OF REBELLION

While these events were taking place in Scotland, a similar development in political theory was being worked out in Huguenot territory. Some of the most important political documents of the sixteenth century appeared in France from the pens of Huguenot writers. They reveal both Calvin's influence and a departure from it.

Calvin's spirit never made the impression upon his mother country that it made in Scotland, England and the Netherlands. This is true in theology and church organization as well as in ethics and politics. Catholicism was too firmly entrenched to permit Calvinism to sweep the country. The Reformation reached France too late, after the Roman church was actively roused to a spirit of hostility.[10] The French government, in the main, was hostile to it; the Renaissance leaders ridiculed it. Yet Calvinism gripped large numbers of the common people, and not a few of the nobility embraced it with the hope of using it to assert their power against the king.

The Huguenots had a theory of rebellion, more carefully thought out than that of Knox, but less drastic in its scope. The French Calvinists had no desire to see themselves governed by presbyteries and consistories, and what they contended for mainly was not the overthrow of the monarchy but the right to worship undisturbed. They were restrained from carrying rebellion to the proportions which it assumed in Scotland, not only by a deeply imbedded respect for the French monarchy, but by the fact that there was too little cohesion among the various Huguenot groups for united action and too little chance of success if a revolution were to be attempted. But to be a Protestant in France meant to face persecution, and the ever-present necessity of contending for the right

[10] Preserved Smith, *The Age of the Reformation*, p. 230 ff.

to worship in the Reformed way had no little influence in giving religious sanction to a theory of political liberty.

The tendency of events to modify doctrine is nowhere better illustrated than in the change which came over Huguenot literature after the massacre of St. Bartholomew's Eve in 1572. Until this time, in spite of the machinations of the queen mother, Catharine de' Medici, the Huguenot writers went on reiterating the orthodox political theory of the duty of obedience even to tyrannous rulers. Between 1559 and 1572 a good many pamphlets appeared, the most famous being Hotman's *Epître au Tigre de la France* after the failure of the conspiracy of Amboise. Most of these contain violent attacks upon the Guises, and are of slight importance as political documents. But throughout all of them runs a note of professed loyalty to Charles IX and an insistence that the Huguenots, though they were fighting in defense of ancient laws and liberties, were not rebels against king or state.

This professed submission is clearly in evidence also in the Gallic Confession, adopted at La Rochelle in 1559. The last two of its forty articles deal directly with the political duty of Christians. After dwelling on the divine origin of the civil magistracy and the right of rulers to use the sword to suppress offenses against the first two commandments (i.e. heresy and idolatry) it concludes—

> We hold, therefore, that it is necessary to obey their laws and statutes; to pay the tributes, imposts and other duties; and to bear the yoke of subjection with a good and free will, even though they be unfaithful, in order that the sovereign empire of God may dwell in its entirety.

However, with the massacre of 1572, a new note appears. In this bloody plot, more than two thousand Huguenots, including their gallant leader Coligny, lost their lives. To escape further persecution, many fled to Holland, Switzerland and England, and some to America. Those who remained could feel less confident of the duty of passive obedience. The Crown seemed bent on a policy of extermination. The issue was now clear-cut, apparently with the choice of submission, or exile, or death. The psychology

of the situation drove large numbers of the Huguenots to feel that
rebellion was justified as the only means of self-preservation, since
to recant was unthinkable. The next step was to justify rebellion as
a religious duty. With no shade of conscious insincerity, the Huguenot writers began to announce that rebellion against tyrannous and
idolatrous kings was not only permitted but demanded by the
Word of God.

Among the earliest and most interesting of the documents appearing after the massacre of 1572 was Francois Hotman's *Franco-
Gallia*, published at Geneva in 1573. Hotman attempts here to
prove by an appeal to history the right of a national representative
body—the Estates-General or an earlier equivalent—to curtail the
power of the king. His polemic is hidden behind a sketch of
the constitutional history of France, but the object of the book is
clearly to show that bad kings may be deposed, that local autonomy
is the root of political freedom, and that no woman has a right to
rule—the last a hit at the regency of Catharine. Similar views are
expressed in the anonymous *Reveille Matin*, which appeared in
1574. Its main point is that the community as a whole confers
power and that the king holds it conditionally. Sovereignty is conferred on magistrates as well as kings, and it is their duty to resist
the tyranny of monarchs. Both the *Franco-Gallia* and the *Reveille
Matin* accord with Calvin's theory of the right of the lower powers
to restrain the higher; but though Calvinistic in political sentiment
they differ radically from Calvin in making only incidental reference to the authority of *la parole de Dieu*.

A more famous treatise is Beza's *Du Droit des Magistrats*, which
was written about the same time as Hotman's *Franco-Gallia* in
1573 and was probably shown to him before its publication. It
was apparently first printed in 1574, and it appeared again in a collection of *Memoires de l'Etat de France sous Charles IX* brought
out by Simon Goulart in 1576. This document, published anony-
mously, goes so far beyond Calvin in sanctioning resistance that
it was long doubted whether it could have been written by Calvin's

disciple and successor, though Beza's authorship is now generally conceded.[11]

Beza starts from the Calvinistic premises of the duty to obey princes who do not violate the law of God, and the right of redress through magistrates when rulers prove unfaithful to their trust. However, his major contribution, which does not appear in Calvin, is a doctrine of popular sovereignty and the duty of all to coöperate in securing "the common lawful assembly." The power to grant authority to kings and to deprive them of it, according to Beza, lies with "God and the Estates." Though the only absolute sovereignty resides in God, the Estates are above kings. On the basis of the sovereignty and law of God, Beza develops these concepts: (1) the sovereignty of the people, represented by their estates and elective magistrates, (2) the responsibility of these representatives to God and the people, (3) the mutual compact of king and representatives; (4) the subjection of both to fundamental law; and (5) the consequent obligation of constitutional resistance to tyranny.[12]

Like Calvin and most of the Huguenot writers, Beza has much to say about "the magistrates," but is not very clear as to who these magistrates are. "There exists a mutual obligation between a king and the officers of the realm"; and if the king manifestly violates the conditions on which he has been accepted, "these protectors of the rights of sovereignty" have the power to depose him.[13] The term approximates some concreteness in the assertion that such power resides in "the Estates or others ordained to serve as bridle to sovereigns."[14] But at best, in spite of a clear-cut assertion that the people have a right to rid themselves of kings, Beza leaves much uncertainty about the channels through which such action may be taken.

Beza's influence was very great. His advice was much sought

---

11 Beza's authorship has been established from the archives by Cartier in *Bulletin de la Société d'Histoire et d'Archéologie de Genève* (1900), II, pp. 187-206.

12 Foster, in *Collected Papers*, p. 93.

13 Beza in *Memoires de l'État de France sous Charles IX*, II, pp. 493, 496.

14 *Ibid.*, p. 496 margin.

after, and his writings were read and quoted by Huguenot, Dutch, Scotch, English and American Calvinists. According to Professor Foster's estimate, on an average one edition of his Latin Testament, teaching political Calvinism through its annotations, appeared annually, and some one of his works in English semi-annually, for a half-century.[15] Though a lesser light than Calvin, his authority could scarcely fail to carry weight.

One more Huguenot treatise must be mentioned, the *Vindiciæ Contra Tyrannos* of 1579. Its authorship is still in dispute, but it was probably the work of Duplessis Mornay, adviser to Henry of Navarre. Like Beza and Hotman, its author makes much of popular sovereignty and the right of the people through representative government to restrain tyrannous kings. A good deal is said also of the *fœdus* or *pactum* between prince and people—apparently not a civil compact but a reciprocal obligation arising from the will of God and the nature of things. A prince violating his part of the covenant is declared thereby to forfeit his right to demand obedience.

A case in point at the time the *Vindiciæ* appeared was the attempt of William the Silent and the Dutch Calvinists to throw off the tyranny of Philip II, who through his agent the Duke of Alva had been slaughtering thousands of Dutch Protestants. The Netherland provinces were cited as furnishing examples of express agreements, the violation of which justified revolt. The *Vindiciæ* exerted much influence among Dutch and English Calvinists well into the seventeenth century; in fact, it was more widely read in Holland and England than in France.

In all these documents there is evident a growing assertion of the principles of democracy. The divine right to resist, beginning as a right, assumed under pressure the compulsion of a duty. As Harold Laski has epitomized the process, "Religions which began by protesting that they were entirely innocuous to the existing civil order, continued by insisting that it was the duty of the state to suit its character to the new spiritual dispensation, and they

[15] *Collected Papers*, p. 93 f.

ended by denying the legitimacy of any government which did not admit the merit of toleration." [16]

3. POLITICAL PURITANISM

The term "Puritan" is of very broad and slippery meaning. It may be used, with accuracy but not with explicitness, to refer (1) to a broad religious movement, essentially Calvinistic, (2) to an attitude toward life, religious in its foundation but not necessarily in its manifestations, (3) to a sectarian movement of protest within the English church—a usage which may, in turn, either include or exclude the Separatists,[17] (4) to a political party based upon this movement. We have used the term in all these senses as occasion required, but must now look at the processes which gave it its political connotation.

The earliest use of the term Puritan seems to have been about 1566. In the following year a certain London congregation was referred to as "Puritans or Unspottyd Lambs of the Lord." This body, which met secretly in Plumbers Hall, called their sect "the pure or stainless religion."[18] What they meant, and what later Puritans maintained, was that they had cast out of their religion all human invention, to follow the "pure" word of God.

However, there were Calvinists in England before these "Unspottyd Lambs" gave their sect the name. In Edward's reign, 1547-1553, Calvinism began to creep into English thought. The Forty-two Articles compiled by Cranmer, the antecedents of the famous Thirty-nine, show marks of Calvin's influence. A considerable number, both of leaders and laity, by the end of Edward's reign had accepted the Reformed faith, but there was not yet a sharp differentiation between the Anglican and Calvinistic strains in the English Reformation.

---

[16] Introduction to his edition of *Vindiciæ Contra Tyrannos*, p. 4.

[17] It used to be thought necessary, in the interests of scholarly accuracy, to distinguish sharply between the *Pilgrims* of Plymouth who were Separatists, and the *Puritans* of the Massachusetts Bay Colony, who kept their connection with the Established Church till it was severed by circumstances. However, common usage now permits the term Puritan to apply to both.

[18] C. Burrage, *The Early English Dissenters in the Light of Recent Research, 1550-1641*, I, pp. 84, 85.

With the accession of Edward's sister, the Catholic Mary Tudor, the fires of persecution blazed. Of the clergy who would not disavow their Protestantism, some like Cranmer, Ridley and Latimer went to the stake, and scores of others were beheaded. But many fled to the Continent to find refuge in Germany and Switzerland. It was these Marian exiles who, like Knox, came in direct contact with Calvin and drank in his ideas, that were the most potent factors in the transplantation of Calvinism to England. The Calvinism which came from Switzerland with the return of the exiles under Elizabeth mingled also with that which came by way of Holland and the Dutch refugees from Alva's fury. These two strains, enhanced further by influences that trickled down from Scotch Calvinism in the north, were to grow in power until, a century afterward, Puritanism was able to overthrow the Stuarts and set up the Commonwealth.

After Elizabeth came to the throne, most of the refugees, returning to England, took the Oath of Supremacy which she imposed. Those who favored breaking with the Established Church were much in the minority. The vestiarian controversy arose over the surplice, the more radical Puritans maintaining that to force ministers to wear it was an infringement on Christian liberty and its use an idolatrous practice savoring of Romanism. But given a choice of wearing the surplice or being deprived of one's living, most of the clergy chose to wear the surplice. It was possible to satisfy both conscience and congregation by saying it was better to wear it and preach the Word than to give up both surplice and God's service.

At first the Puritans were not interested in politics. They did not see very clearly—probably not so clearly as the queen—the connection between the royal supremacy and the use of the ritual and ceremonies of the State Church. But the episcopacy brought the question into the political arena. About 1570 a group arose, led by Thomas Cartwright, who desired the displacement of the bishops and the transformation of the Church of England into something essentially like that of Scotland. In 1572 they presented to the

House of Commons an *Aamonition to the Parliament* which listed the grievances of the Puritans and called for the abolition of the episcopacy, the election of ministers by congregations, and a reform of ritual. The leaven of democracy inherent in Calvinism was working. It became evident that to place the government of the church in the hands of a representative body like the General Assembly might do more than curtail the power of the bishops—it might lead to a denial of the place of the monarch as head of the church. This intimation became concrete in a second *Admonition,* written by Cartwright, which stated that instead of being governed by bishops and king, the church ought to obey only assemblies of ministers and elders chosen by the parish. This was no mere heresy; it was sedition! Archbishop Whitgift was chosen by the bishops to reply to Cartwright. The controversy which followed sharpened the issue for both parties, and drove Cartwright to Geneva to be the more thoroughly indoctrinated with Calvinism.

From this time forth, it was not doctrine and ritual which formed the crucial point of contention. Doctrinal disagreements figured comparatively little. The Thirty-nine Articles, the work of Anglican clergy with Calvinistic leanings, were on the whole more pleasing to the Calvinists than to Elizabeth. Ritual continued to be a source of friction, and formed a line of demarcation between the High Church and Low Church Anglicans. But the issue which brought matters to a cleavage lay in church government and its bearing on the royal supremacy. The practice of the Apostolic Church, interpreted by Calvin, seemed to the Puritans to sanction a representative or democratic form of control rather than an episcopate. Furthermore, to recognize the monarch as the Supreme Head of the church was to give to a mere man the honor due to Christ alone. Such creature-worship was intolerable.

The Puritans felt it their religious duty to protest, and this protest made Puritanism a political movement. It spread rapidly, and gripped the masses. Meetings were held in many sections. Political discussion was mixed with religious exhortation. Banned by the government, these Puritan meetings continued to be held secretly. A ferment was brewing which could not be suppressed.

. . . .

English Puritanism was not all of one piece. Low Church Anglicans, Presbyterians and Congregationalists were embraced under the term. Between the first two, there was not the sharp demarcation that their present differences suggest. They agreed in wanting a less Romish ritual than the High Church, and disagreed on the episcopacy; but since many of the English Presbyterians remained in the Church of England, it is impossible to draw the line sharply. Between this group and the Congregationalists the distinction is clearer, for the latter—called also Independents, Brownists or Separatists—"separated" from the Established Church.

The Presbyterian group looked hopefully for the establishment in England of something like the Scottish Kirk. A representative system of consistories and presbyteries culminating in a General Assembly with supreme authority would have been very pleasing to English Puritans of the Cartwright stamp. They were the descendants of Knox as well as Calvin. The Independents, on the other hand, declared for the separation of Church and State, and for complete democracy in ecclesiastical organization. The latter group were the more clear-cut in their position, and since they withdrew outright from the Established Church they had to suffer more for their convictions.

Both Presbyterians and Independents were Calvinists in doctrine. They differed mainly in that Presbyterianism stood for a *representative,* Congregationalism for a *democratic,* form of organization. Borgeaud thus summarizes the difference: "Presbyterianism is Calvinism tempered by the aristocratic tendencies of Calvin. Independency or, as it was first called, Congregationalism, is Calvinism without Calvin." [19] It is, however, hardly fair to say this of Congregationalism. It is rather a Calvinism in which the pressure of opposition had brought into the forefront the democracy latent

[19] *The Rise of Modern Democracy in Old and New England* (London, 1894), p. 31.

in Calvin's theory of the equality of the elect in the eyes of God—equality, that is, except in so far as God pleases to bestow more of his grace on one than on another. Calvin's energetic refusal ever to let State dominate Church in matters of religion is the predecessor of Robert Browne's forthright rejection of the royal supremacy and the political power of the episcopate.

While Browne was not the originator of the Separatist principle, he was the most vigorous exponent of early Congregationalism and to him the group owes much of its corporate identity. He was the pastor of an English church which migrated to Holland in 1581, though he subsequently returned and lived in relative peace in spite of the radical nature of his doctrine. A pupil of Cartwright, he went beyond him in declaring that the State had no right whatever to interfere with the internal affairs of the Church. In his famous *Treatise of Reformation without Tarrying for Anie* published in 1582, he declared that the State had no authority "to compel religion, to plant churches by power, and to force a submission to ecclesiastical government." [20] He would have each congregation a voluntary body of true believers, looking to no head but God.

. . . .

By the end of the sixteenth century, Puritanism had become fairly well differentiated into the Presbyterian and Congregationalist strains. In spite of differences in policy and aim, both were moving toward a break with the established order. In fact, indefinite as is the term Puritan, it seems to have connoted, as a common element, some measure of resistance to authority. "All those who came to be called Puritans objected to a number of rites, ceremonies, observances and arrangements established by law." [21] Underneath divergence, there was a common Calvinistic body of doctrine, and a common Calvinistic aversion to anything which savored of Romanism in ritual or government.

When Elizabeth died in 1603 and James I moved over from

[20] *Op. cit.*, pp. 12, 13.
[21] Allen, p. 214.

Scotland to the English throne, the hopes of the Puritans were high. He was nominally a Presbyterian and had been reared by his Scotch tutors in the atmosphere of the Kirk. But these hopes were short-lived. James was more interested in his own supremacy as God's representative than in any particular religious sect. He had little love for the Presbyterians who had condemned and deposed his Catholic mother, and his Presbyterianism was mainly that of diplomacy while in Scottish hands.

James was no great statesman, though in 1598 he had written a political treatise entitled *The Trew Law of Free Monarchies* which set forth the simple and somewhat startling doctrine that a free monarchy is one in which the monarch is free, and above all law. When he ascended the English throne, his sympathies, already predisposed toward the Anglicans, were fed both by the flattery of the bishops and by his own awareness that his crown was safer with the support of the Established Church than it could be without it. The Puritans, he said, were aiming at a Scotch presbytery "which agrees with monarchy as well as God with the devil; then Jack and Will and Dick shall meet, and at their pleasure censure me and my Council." There is an ominous note in his words at the Hampton Court meeting soon after his accession, "I will make them conform themselves or else I will harrie them out of the land, or else do worse." [22]

He did make them conform, in a measure; he harried some of them out of the land, to go to Holland or America. But James had the type of mind that took pleasure in making the Puritans uncomfortable by petty annoyances rather than drastic persecution. There is an example of this in his *Book of Sports,* a program of amusements for Sunday afternoon, which he issued in 1618. Its ostensible purpose was "to encourage recreations and sports on the Lord's day;" its real purpose to annoy the Puritans. It was ordered to be read publicly in all the parish churches of England. This would be comparable, in psychological effect, to asking Catholics to read an order forbidding Mass, or Jews an edict com-

[22] Neal, *History of the Puritans* (London, 1733), p. 19.

manding the eating of pork. Had the order been insisted upon, many Puritan clergy would have lost their livings. Through the influence of Archbishop Abbot the crisis was averted, and the order allowed to lapse. Fifteen years later, Charles I, at the instigation of Archbishop Laud, revived the edict, and ordered it read and obeyed. This time there was no protector at court, and many of the Puritan clergy, rather than read it, gave up their livings and were turned out into the world penniless.

Charles I held to his father's conviction of the divine right of kings and the inviolability of the royal supremacy, but he carried out these principles with greater consistency and rigor. Unable to bend Parliament to his will, he dissolved it, to rule without one for eleven years. The Nonconformists were made to conform or get out. Archbishop Laud stimulated the king to systematic persecution. Geneva Bibles were prohibited, the ritual made more Catholic, and Puritan ministers deprived of their benefices. All this fanned the rising fires of Puritan protest. When the Long Parliament came into power in 1640, it was mainly Presbyterian in sentiment.

Charles and the Parliament were arrayed against each other, and in 1642 civil war broke out. The Cavaliers and the Roundheads took shape from a medley of social, political and religious factors. On the side of Charles were the aristocrats, Catholics and anti-Puritans; with Parliament were arrayed the various strains of Puritanism and those who stood for social and political democracy. The Independents rose rapidly in numbers and power. When Cromwell took command of the army, he appealed to the religious enthusiasm of this group, and the army became the stronghold of Independency. A mixture of sectarian with political factors now complicated the situation, for Parliament was largely Presbyterian, the army Independent. Charles was shrewd enough to see the possibilities in such division, and his subsequent overtures to the Scots grew out of a hope of playing the Presbyterians against the Independents.

However, after the defeat of the royal army in the battles of

Marston Moor and Naseby, Charles' chances of success were slight. The ensuing events—the outbreak of a second civil war, Charles' negotiations for Scottish aid, Cromwell's defeat of the Scotch army which invaded England, Pride's Purge and the formation of the Rump Parliament—are familiar history. On January 30, 1649, Charles was beheaded in front of his palace of Whitehall, and Cromwell and the Puritans were masters of England. So they were to remain until Cromwell's death a decade later broke the power of the Protectorate.

. . . .

The overthrow of the monarchy was the result of an intermingling of political and religious factors. Cromwell had on his side a group of plain-living, vigorous religious enthusiasts who had been trained in the school of John Calvin and Robert Browne. For a century, opposition to the Established Church and the royal supremacy had been paving the way for opposition to the monarchy. Cromwell was not slow to capitalize the religious devotion of the Puritans and turn it to political ends. He was able to seize and hold the reins, not only by his personal power and executive skill, but by appearing to them—doubtless also to himself—as a divinely appointed leader called of God to deliver his chosen ones from bondage. Borgeaud remarks that in his speeches and conversations Cromwell "marches before the people of England as Gideon did before Israel." [23] The Puritan revolt was a political movement, but it was a political movement of which the inception and chief dynamic lay in the arena of religion.

It is impossible to estimate with precision how far the Puritan revolt is to be attributed to Presbyterian and how far to Separatist influence. It was the latter group which brought it to fruition. In addition to Cromwell and his Independent army, no little influence was exerted in England in the decade from 1640 to 1650 by Congregationalist settlers returning from New England. John Cotton's *Way of the Churches of Christ in New England* was published in London in 1645, and was widely read. In fact, Independency came

---

[23] *The Rise of Modern Democracy in Old and New England,* p. 97.

to be spoken of as "the New England Way." The influence of Browne and subsequent Congregationalists in rejecting outright the royal supremacy and the right of the State to control the Church must not be minimized in estimating the factors which fostered political democracy and overthrew the Stuarts. Yet the Puritan revolt grew up on a Presbyterian foundation. The example of the organization of the Scotch church was ever before the English Puritans. John Knox contributed not a little to Cromwell's power. Up till the decade of its victory, Presbyterianism was the dominant factor in the rising current of protest. Borgeaud summarizes compactly, though perhaps too simply, the contribution of each group when he says, "Episcopacy was abolished by the Presbyterians; monarchy by the Independents." [24]

Back of both the Presbyterian and the Independent wings of Puritanism lay Calvin and Calvinism. Calvinistic doctrine, Calvinistic plainness of living, Calvinistic devotion to duty, Calvinistic simplicity of worship, Calvinistic loyalty to the Bible, Calvinistic reliance upon God, Calvinistic love of liberty,—all these were common to the various strains we group together and call Puritan. Without Calvin, there might have been a revolt from political autocracy. But without Calvin, there would have been no Puritanism.

It must be evident, even from a hasty survey of events, that inherent in the Puritan revolt were both the Calvinistic conscience and the pressure of circumstance. When Elizabeth imposed the Oath of Supremacy, it called forth protest against the royal supremacy, and awoke the Puritans to an awareness of the political implications of their position. When James "harried" the Puritans, he harried some of them out of the land to spread the gospel of Calvinism; and he harried many more, not into conformity, but into a repudiation of conformity. When Charles tried to rule with an autocracy which flouted Puritan sentiment, he fanned it into white heat. As elsewhere, the Calvinists, beginning their political fortunes with a prevailing belief in the duty of obedience of the

[24] *Ibid.*, p. 28.

Crown, found themselves developing under persecution the religious duty of resistance. Both obedience and resistance were thoroughly Scriptural and thoroughly Calvinistic. The demand of the Calvinistic conscience for political liberty was the result of the interpenetration of Calvinistic logic with the logic of events, and the outcome was predestined.

CHAPTER XIII

CONCLUSION

The sixteenth was a great century. It was the century of Raphael and Michelangelo, of Spenser and Shakespeare, of Erasmus and Rabelais, of Copernicus and Galileo, of Luther and Calvin. Of all the figures that gave greatness to this century, none left a more lasting heritage than Calvin. It would be inaccurate to call him the greatest man of his times, for greatness has no common denominator. Yet one who takes the trouble to acquaint himself with the life and thought of this half-forgotten reformer can scarcely doubt either the power of his personality or the sweep of his influence.

Some of the men who helped to make history in the sixteenth century adorned their age with a lasting gift of grace and beauty. Not so Calvin. His function was not to adorn. Rather, it was to lay a granite foundation. In Geneva he put together in solid fashion the foundation stones on which a sturdy moral structure could be reared. He did his work so well that the structure still stands, altered but undestroyed. The structure is not faultless. It has rough edges and jagged points, and some of these not even the wear and jostle of four centuries have brought to smoothness. But it is an enduring structure, and one not wholly lacking in a stern sort of beauty.

There is no need to bore the reader with a long conclusion. There is so much in Calvin's ethical theory and practice which finds a parallel in modern life that it would be easy to point morals —to end the book with "This story teaches—" This temptation I shall resist, confident that the reader who wants such morals will draw them for himself.

The book does not need to end with a Q.E.D., for it was not

written to prove anything. It aims simply to tell the truth about Calvin. Its author has tried to present without prejudice the story of this man of great faults and great virtues, and to give an accurate account of his moral theory and practice. As Calvin said of himself, "I have not to my knowledge corrupted or twisted a single passage . . . and when I could have drawn out a far-fetched meaning, if I had studied subtlety, I have put that temptation under foot." [1] The author is not a Calvinist, either by church affiliation or conviction, and holds no brief for Calvin or for Calvinism. But with the study of this rugged figure has come a growing sense of comradeship—almost of personal friendship—and it may be that these chapters have endeavored, beyond their writer's original intent, to lift from Calvin's shoulders some of the opprobrium which has settled there through the centuries.

The story is told, but not finished. Much has been omitted which would have added interest and value to a longer book, and there are problems in the field of Calvin's influence which have been scarcely touched. The investigator who wishes to probe further into the Calvinistic moral philosophy will find plenty of fresh territory. In the words of Calvin's disciple, Cotton Mather, "The author hath done as well and as much as he could, that whatever was worthy of a mention might have it; . . . and now he hath done, he hath not pull'd up the Ladder after him; others may go on as they please with a compleater Composure." [2]

[1] *Opera*, ix, 893.
[2] Preface to *Decennium Luctuosum*, in *Original Narratives of Early American History*, XIV, p. 182.

INDEX